BREWER STATE JR. COLLEGE
LIBRARY
TUSCALOOSA CENT

W9-BZM-367

HB
161
.T69
1821a

Torrens,
An essay on the production
of wealth. 1821.

DISCARDED

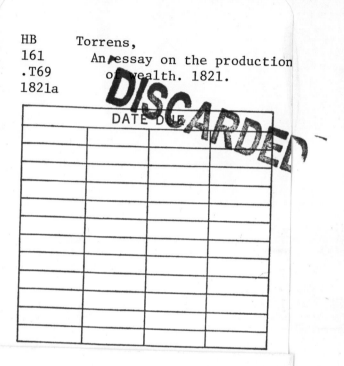

DATE DUE

BREWER STATE JR. COLLEGE
LIBRARY
TUSCALOOSA CENTER

REPRINTS OF ECONOMIC CLASSICS

AN ESSAY ON THE PRODUCTION OF WEALTH

BREWER STATE JR. COLLEGE
LIBRARY
TUSCALOOSA CENTER

An

ESSAY

On The

PRODUCTION

Of

WEALTH

By

ROBERT TORRENS

[1821]

With an Introductory Essay
"*Robert Torrens and American
Economic Thought*"
By *JOSEPH DORFMAN*

REPRINTS OF ECONOMIC CLASSICS

AUGUSTUS M. KELLEY • PUBLISHER
NEW YORK • 1965

LIBRARY OF CONGRESS CATALOGUE CARD NUMBER
64-7670

PRINTED IN THE UNITED STATES OF AMERICA
by SENTRY PRESS, NEW YORK, N. Y. 10019

ROBERT TORRENS AND AMERICAN ECONOMIC THOUGHT

By now Colonel Robert Torrens (1780-1864) has acquired quite a standing as one of the architects of the system of classical economics which, if broadly conceived, is the ancestor of all the systems which have since influenced the development of economic thought and policy. Beginning in the 1950's a considerable literature has grown up on the life and thought of this British economist who flourished in the Ricardian age.[1] As might be expected, the reprinting of his works has already begun. The first, *Letters on Commercial Policy* (1833) with an introduction by Lionel (now Baron) Robbins was reprinted in 1958. The second which is reprinted below, *An Essay on the Production of Wealth; with an Appendix in Which the Principles of Political Economy are Applied to the Actual Circumstances of the Country* (1821), has been well described as "the one ostensibly general work in Political Economy published

---

[1] The current revival began with S. A. Meenai, "Robert Torrens —1780-1864," *Economica*, February 1956, pp. 49-61. Meenai has published extensively on Torrens as an economist. An interesting, detailed account of Torrens' career as an officer of the Marines and its effect on his economics is given by F. W. Fetter, "Robert Torrens: Colonel of Marines, and Political Economist," *Economica*, May 1962, pp. 152-165.

5

by Torrens."[2] More reprints may be expected in the near future because of the relevance of his insights on current policy, especially in the areas of money and banking, colonization, and commercial policy.

One aspect that has hitherto received very little attention is the interest that American economists had taken in Torrens' work. The first significant reference of this kind was an outgrowth of the publication in 1825 of the American edition of the essay, "Political Economy" in the *Encyclopaedia Britannica* by J. R. McCulloch who, through his popularization, powerfully helped make the system of David Ricardo the dominant one. The Reverend John McVickar who taught political economy at Columbia College (now Columbia University) had taken the article, added copious notes and a summary, and published it under the title, *Outlines of Political Economy* (1825).[3] He sent a copy to his Columbia colleague, the great jurist, James Kent.[4] Among the passages

---

[2] Lionel Robbins, *Robert Torrens and the Evolution of Classical Economics* (London: Macmillan, 1958) p. 283.

[3] On McVickar, see Josph Dorfman and Rexford Guy Tugwell, "The Reverend John McVickar: Christian Teacher and Economist," in their *Early American Policy: Six Columbia Contributors* (New York: Columbia University Press, 1960) pp. 99-154.

[4] On Kent as an economist, see Joseph Dorfman, "Chancellor James Kent and the Developing American Economy," *Columbia Law Review*, November 1961, pp. 1290-1327. Kent, like McVickar, was a free trade Federalist; that is, he supported Alexander Hamilton's views on political philosophy and organization but was a staunch believer in the free trade economics of Adam Smith's *The Wealth of Nations* which he read at least twice.

6

that Kent marked in the book was the one in which
McCulloch stated that Torrens' *An Essay on the
Production of Wealth* is a "valuable work" and then
added that Torrens' theory of value that "the relative, or exchangeable value is . . . determined by the
quantities of capital expended on their production,"
did not substantially differ from his own more
strictly Ricardian view that the exchange value of
commodities depended on the "total quantities of
labor required to bring them to market." At the same
time Kent saw that McVickar had omitted Torrens'
treatise from the list he made in a note of "some
of the principal works since the time of Adam Smith,
and which partake more or less of the principles he
has so conclusively settled." So at the bottom of the
page of the note, Kent wrote, "See also Colonel
Torrens, *Essay on the Production of Wealth*" and
called attention to McCulloch's discussion of it.[5]

A year later there appeared more evidence that

---

[5] McVickar, *Outlines of Political Economy; Republication of
the Article upon that Subject Contained in the Edinburgh Sup-
plement to the Encyclopaedia Britannica* (New York: Wilder &
Campbell, 1825) pp. 43, 141.

Kent's copy with the markings and annotations is in Special
Collections, Columbia University Libraries. The extensive com-
ments in his copy amply bear out his statement to McVickar that
he had "made himself master of the text & of the notes." [Kent
to McVickar, October 19, 1825, in J. B. Langstaff, *The Enter-
prising Life: John McVickar, 1787-1868* (New York: St. Martin's,
1961) p. 75.]

Torrens' work had attracted the attention of influential Americans, such as Gulian C. Verplanck and William Beach Lawrence. Verplanck was prominent in national and state politics, in the world of letters and theology, and was active in some large business ventures. Lawrence took up law, served in the London embassy in 1826-28 where he became an intimate of Jeremy Bentham, the philosophic fountainhead of the classical school[6]; was active in the promotion of the Erie Railroad, served in later years as lieutenant governor of Rhode Island and achieved an international reputation as an authority on international law. Both Verplanck and Lawrence were members of the conservative wing of Jefferson's Democratic party, great admirers of Ricardo, and staunch supporters of free trade.

It appears that Verplanck, while in the federal House of Representatives, got Lawrence to read Torrens' works. In January 1826, Lawrence wrote Verplanck, thanking him for "pointing out Torrens'

---

[6] Lawrence shortly after resigning his post of chargé d'affaires, wrote an anonymous article for the first Benthamite organ, "Government in the United States," *The Westminster Review,* January 1829, pp. 51-71. Those who have been engaged in identifying the authors of the unsigned articles in *The Westminster Review* have had to report a blank on Lawrence's article, doubtless because they have not suspected that he might be an American. On Lawrence's authorship, see Joseph Dorfman and Rexford Guy Tugwell, "William Beach Lawrence: American Benthamite," in *Early American Policy: Six Columbia Contributors,* p. 218.

works, though I have not been able to purchase them in this city" [New York]. Three months later, he informed Verplanck that Torrens "has made a great addition to our economical learning."[7] In 1831 in public lectures on political economy, after saluting Torrens as "an eminent disciple of the Ricardian School," he quoted from *An Essay on the Production of Wealth*, as to the proper method in economics. "The science of Political Economy is analogous to the mixed mathematics. The data upon which it proceeds are formulated by observation and experience; while the conclusions to which it leads are attained by a process of ratiocination, self-evident in all its steps."[8] Later in the lectures, he added that the foremost disciples of Ricardo, James "Mill and McCulloch, have elucidated the doctrines of Ricardo while some of the expositions of Torrens lay just claim to originality."[9]

Even leading American protectionists showed respect for Torrens' publications, especially *An Essay on the Production of Wealth*. Thus, Stephen Colwell,

---

[7] Lawrence to Verplanck, January 29, April 13, 1826, in Verplanck papers, New York Historical Society.

[8] Below, p. x. Quoted in Lawrence, *Two Lectures on Political Economy, delivered at Clinton Hall before the Mercantile Library Association of the City of New York, on the 23rd and 30th of December, 1831* (New York: C. and C. and H. Carvill, 1832) p. 1. The first lecture was devoted to "The History of Political Economy," and the second to "The Ricardian Theory."
The Mercantile Library Association was an embryonic school of business.

[9] *Two Lectures on Political Economy*, p. 28.

the Pennsylvania ironmaster, outstanding leader in the Presbyterian Church, and the ablest student of the monetary and banking field in the pre-Civil War period,[10] declared in 1856 that "Torrens' works have always commanded attention and respect."[11]

In the post-Civil War era very little attention was given to Torrens in the United States as well as in his native land. Certainly in orthodox circles the *Essay* was either ignored or deprecated generally. McCulloch in England had long ceased describing *An Essay on the Production of Wealth* as a valuable work. In his widely used *The Literature of Political Economy* (1845) he said of it that it was "generally sound; but this, like the greater number of the author's works, has rather too many illustrative examples which are not always very happily chosen or easy to follow." But such of Torrens' topical writings that expressed without substantial qualifications the tenets of Ricardo, McCulloch praised. Thus, *The Economists*

---

[10] *"Colwell's Ways and Means of Payment,* (1859), the most impressive single work on banking produced in America before 1860, stamps him as a writer of the first rank." [Harry E. Miller, *Banking Theories in the United States Before 1860* (Cambridge, Mass.: Harvard University Press, 1927) p. 66.]

[11] Colwell, "Preliminary Essay," to Friedrich List, *National System of Political Economy,* translated from the German by G. A. Matile (Philadelphia: Lippincott, 1856) p. li.

Colwell was unique in questioning Torrens' prediction, in *An Essay on the Production of Wealth,* that "twenty years hence there will scarcely exist a doubt respecting any of . . . [the] fundamental principles [of Political Economy]." (See below, p. xiii).

Refuted (1808) which attempted to answer those who questioned that commerce is not a source of national wealth, was described by McCulloch as follows: "This is among the earliest contributions to political economy of the gallant and learned author, who has since continued to be one of its most assiduous cultivators."[12]

Only in heterodox circles was there much sympathy for Torrens. Prophetic of the modern view of Torrens, was the opinion expressed by a leader of the British wing of the historical school of economics, J. K. Ingram in his *A History of Political Economy,* (1888).[13] He wrote that Torrens, "was a prolific writer, partly on economic theory, but principally on its applications to financial and commercial policy. Almost the whole of the programme which was carried out in legislation by Sir Robert Peel had been laid down in principle in the writings of Torrens. He gave substantially the same theory of foreign trade

---

[12] *The Literature of Political Economy,* (London: Longman, et. al., 1845) pp. 18, 56. In describing *An Essay on the External Corn Trade,* (1815), which attacked the restrictive effect of a protective tariff on the import of foodstuffs (the famous corn laws) McCulloch simply presented Ricardo's glowing commendation. Other works of Torrens were listed without comment.

[13] Ingram's *History* was actually an expansion of the article, "Political Economy" in the ninth edition (1885) of the *Encyclopaedia Britannica.* It was first published in book form in the United States with an introduction by E. J. James, a leader of the American wing of the historical school, then at the University of Pennsylvania, and later president first of Northwestern University and subsequently of the University of Illinois.

11

which was afterwards advocated by J. S. Mill in one of his *Essays on Some Unsettled Questions of Political Economy,* (1844). He was an early and earnest advocate of the repeal of the corn laws, but was not in favor of a general system of absolute free trade, maintaining that it is expedient to impose retaliatory duties to countervail similar duties imposed by foreign countries, and that a lowering of import duties on the productions of countries retaining their hostile tariffs would occasion an abstraction of the precious metals and a decline in prices, profits and wages."[14]

Edwin Cannan, in his influential *A History of the Theories of Production and Distribution in English Political Economy from 1776 to 1848* (1893) has some respectful references to Torrens but the reader was hardly encouraged to pursue Torrens. Cannan characteristically prefaced his references with such phrases as the "magniloquent Torrens," or "Torrens, with his usual turgidity."

As far as American economists were concerned, dominant opinion ran along the lines of the British view. In 1891 a widely used reading guide edited by two old fashioned believers in extreme laissez faire, included *An Essay on the Production of Wealth* and

---

[14] *A History of Political Economy,* (New York: Macmillan, 1888) p. 140. In a footnote on the same page, Ingram added that "Mill, however, tells us in his Preface to those essays that his own views on . . . [foreign trade] had been entertained and committed to writing before the publication of similar opinions."

The Principles and Practical Operation of Sir Robert Peel's Bill of 1844, Explained and Defended, 2nd ed., 1857, but simply by title without comment.[15] Frank W. Taussig of Harvard, who, like Cannan, had some sympathies for the historical school, in his historical survey in *Wages and Capital: An Examination of the Wages Fund Doctrine* (1896) spoke of the "soldier-scholar" as "an able hand" but Taussig's emphasis on Torrens' defects obscured his references to Torrens' positive contributions.

At the close of the century, in 1899 to be more precise, the fate of Torrens seemed sealed when the first edition of that epitome of economic doctrine, at least for the Anglo-American world, Palgrave's *Dictionary of Political Economy,* gave its verdict. It devoted six lines to his economic studies, closing with the statement that his works, "as a rule are devoid of permanent merit. He was a great supporter of the so-called Reciprocity . . . system."[16]

But in 1903, the tide turned. In a remarkable paper in *The Economic Journal* that year, Professor Edwin R. A. Seligman of Columbia University, strikingly pointed out that a goodly number of British economists of the Ricardian age who had modern

---

15 The *Reader's Guide in Economic, Social and Political Science,* edited by R. R. Bowker and George Iles (New York: The Society for Political Education, 1891) pp. 17, 42.

16 *Dictionary of Political Economy,* ed. by R. H. Inglis Palgrave, 3 vols. (London: Macmillan, 1894-1899) III, p. 550.

insights, had been unduly neglected. This article, "Some Neglected British Economists," "first drew attention to the significance of Torrens' contribution and the need for its comprehensive study."[17] Seligman claimed for Torrens' four basic pivots and improvements of the Ricardian system, the first three of which were drawn from *An Essay on the External Corn Trade* and the last one from *An Essay on the Production of Wealth*. Firstly, Seligman asserted that Torrens should be "credited with at least a simultaneous and independent discovery" in 1815 of "the law of rent" based upon the principle of diminishing returns in agriculture. Secondly, he advanced the view that wages were influenced by the standard of life, a wage theory that was adopted by Ricardo. Thirdly, he claimed that Torrens, not Ricardo, should be credited with the law of comparative cost which in the Ricardian system was used to explain the values of goods in international trade, while absolute costs of production explained the value of goods in the domestic trade. Finally, Torrens formulated "a theory of profits which differed from that of Ricardo, and which is considerably nearer the truth." Where Ricardo held that profits varied inversely as wages, Torrens maintained that profits were a surplus over costs, and as a consequence in periods of

---

[17] Meenai, "Robert Torrens—1780-1864," *Economica*, February 1956, p. 49.

technological advance, profits might increase without entailing a reduction in wages.[18]

Seligman's contentions were generally accepted and in the appendix of the second edition of *Palgrave's Dictionary of Political Economy* (1926) there were twenty-five lines on Torrens, almost all a quotation from Seligman's article on his contributions to economic theory. On one point,—the matter of priority as regards the law of comparative cost in international exchange,—a controversy broke out in 1911 between Seligman and Jacob H. Hollander of Johns Hopkins University. Hollander who as Seligman asserted in 1928, "knew more about Ricardo than anybody else," held out for Ricardo,[19] but Seligman stuck by his guns, and the verdict is now that among other things, Torrens is to be remembered chiefly in that "he formulated clearly the famous theory of comparative costs in international trade—

---

[18] "On Some Neglected British Economists," 1903; reprinted in his *Essays in Economics* (New York: Macmillan, 1925) p. 71.

[19] "Lectures Notes on the History of Economics by Professor Edwin R. A. Seligman (1927-1928)" mimeographed notes taken down by F. S. Allen, p. 127.

Hollander first questioned Seligman's verdict on priority in his *David Ricardo: A Centenary Estimate* (1910); the following year Seligman and Hollander continued the discussion in "Ricardo and Torrens," in *The Economic Journal*, September 1911, pp. 448-468. Seligman, it should be noted, agreed that Ricardo was a more powerful mind than Torrens.

15

this independently of Ricardo, and before him in time."[20]

Torrens' current vogue is, in good part, due to the interest in certain areas which were hardly mentioned by Seligman. He is now credited as noted above, with important contributions to the fields of money and banking, colonization and international economics. The systematic foundation for all this still remains *An Essay on the Production of Wealth*. His analysis "of the effect which a fall and a rise in the value of currency are respectively calculated to produce," has in some respects a more modern ring, than his later studies in money and banking for which he has been highly commended. But in addition, the *Essay* contains certain insights which have not yet been sufficiently stressed. The section on Money and Paper Currency makes an impressive case for the contention that the ill effects of deflation far outweigh those of inflation; and suggests that in any event devaluation is generally preferable to deflation as a remedy for inflation under the gold standard. Torrens by no means ignored the disturbances of inflation. As the late Professor Wesley C. Mitchell early put it, in his lecture notes, Torrens' treatise contains "an acute analysis of the effects produced by

---

[20] Robbins, "Introduction," in reprint of Torrens' *Letters on Commercial Policy*, (London: Longman, 1833; reprint, London: London School of Economics and Political Science, 1958) p. vi.

a fall and by a rise in the value of money upon wages, profit, rent, and the interests of debtors, creditors and salaried people."[21]

Perhaps the most novel feature of *An Essay in the Production of Wealth* was its portrayal of the advantages of large cities in achieving a nation's industrialization and economic growth, a problem which now attracts so much attention.

Broadly speaking, Torrens was a leading architect of what became known as the "Ricardian" or orthodox system of economics, but his views were, at certain points, sufficiently independent that a full hearing for them had to wait until an age when his one-time heresies were commended by such a large number of influential economists as to constitute if not a rival orthodoxy, at least acceptable qualifications of the older faith.

Joseph Dorfman

Columbia University
July 15, 1965

---

[21] Undated note, Mitchell papers, Special Collections in Columbia University Libraries. The note was written around 1914-1916.

AN ESSAY

ON

THE PRODUCTION OF WEALTH;

WITH

AN APPENDIX,

IN WHICH THE PRINCIPLES

OF

Political Economy

ARE

APPLIED TO THE ACTUAL CIRCUMSTANCES OF
THIS COUNTRY.

———

By R. TORRENS, Esq. F.R.S.

———

LONDON:

PRINTED FOR
LONGMAN, HURST, REES, ORME, AND BROWN,
PATERNOSTER ROW.

1821.

PREFACE.

---◆---

IN offering the following volume to the public, the Author has had two objects in view. He has sought, in the first place, to present a systematic and comprehensive treatise upon that division of Political Economy which relates to the production of wealth; and he has attempted, in the second place, to apply the general principles of the science to the actual circumstances of this country. The importance of these subjects it is unnecessary to enforce. The Author has only to apprehend, that he has ventured upon a task, to the execution of which he is unequal.

Many persons will probably imagine, that after the elaborate treatises with which Mr. Ricardo and Mr. Malthus have recently enriched the science of Political Economy, the work now offered to the public must be superfluous. The Author is of a different opinion. He conceives, that the writings of these celebrated economists, instead of rendering the present attempt unnecessary, have created a demand for a systematic treatise on the general principles of Political Economy. Neither Mr. Ricardo nor Mr. Malthus has aimed at presenting the science as a consentaneous whole; while both have fallen into a faulty mode of investigation, which occasionally leads them into error, and at all times retards the reception of the very original and valuable lights which they have thrown upon this department of knowledge.

Though Mr. Ricardo has done more for the science of Political Economy than any other writer, with the single exception perhaps of Dr. Adam Smith, yet he sometimes falls into a species of error to which men of great original genius seem peculiarly exposed, and, in the ardour of discovery, generalises too hastily, and fails to establish his principles on a sufficiently extensive induction. In the inventive faculty, and in the power of pure and continuous ratiocination, he has seldom been surpassed; but in the capacity for accurate observation, his pre-eminence is less apparent.

Mr. Malthus, whose Essays on Population, and on the origin and nature of Rent, have contributed so much to the progress of economical science, exhibits throughout his writings, an intellectual character, altogether opposite to that which has been here described. He possesses in a very eminent degree the faculty of observing particular phenomena, but is somewhat deficient in that power of analysis which distinguishes between coincidence and necessary connexion, and enables us to trace the sequence of causes and effects. If Mr. Ricardo generalises too much, Mr. Malthus generalises too little. If the former occasionally erects his principles without waiting to base them upon a sufficiently extensive induction from particulars, the latter is so occupied with particulars, that he neglects

that inductive process which extends individual experience throughout the infinitude of things, and imparts
to human knowledge the character of science. As
presented by Mr. Ricardo, Political Economy possess
a regularity and simplicity beyond what exists in
nature; as exhibited by Mr. Malthus, it is a chaos of
original but unconnected elements.

Should the criticisms now hazarded be correct, it
will follow, that a general treatise upon Political
Economy, combining with the principles of Adam
Smith, so much of the more recent doctrines as may be
conformable to truth, and embodying the whole into
one consentaneous system, remains to the present day a
desideratum in our literature. This desideratum, as
far as relates to the Production of Wealth, the Author
has attempted to supply in the present volume; and on
some future occasion, perhaps he may venture to complete the task by remodelling and extending the disquisitions respecting the distribution of wealth, which he
has already laid before the public*. Yet, while his
ambition is awakened by his conviction, that however
abundantly the great mart of literature is supplied,
there still remains an opening for a systematic and
comprehensive treatise on economical science, his hopes
are destroyed by a perception of the qualifications
requisite to the performance of the task. In order to
produce a complete and accurate system of Political
Econony, and to establish its principles by a process of
induction sufficiently extensive to set controversy at rest,

---

* Essay on the Corn Trade, Second Edition, Part IV.

it is necessary that Mr. Ricardo's habits of generalization should be combined with that faculty for observing particular phenomena which characterises Mr. Malthus. The Author of the present Essay ventures to submit his work to the public, because in an undertaking, the successful execution of which requires such a rare combination of opposite powers, failure cannot be discreditable.

In the following work, the Author has not confined his attempt to presenting, under the form of a consentaneous system, the principles respecting the production of wealth established by preceding writers. Many of the disquisitions are, he conceives, original. On the theory of exchangeable value,—on the manner in which trade and commerce contribute to the increase of wealth,—and on the principles of demand and supply,—it is imagined that the doctrines unfolded in the present volume, are now submitted to the public for the first time.

With respect to the theory of value, Adam Smith has observed, that in that early period of society which precedes the accumulation of stock, and the appropriation of land, the labour expended on production is the only circumstance which causes a given quantity of one commodity to be exchanged for a given quantity of another; and Mr. Ricardo has pushed this principle still further, and contended, that in all periods of society, whether before or after the accumulation of capital and appropriation of land, the labour expended upon production is the sole regulator of value. Neither of these celebrated economists, however, has given a

sufficiently accurate explanation of what is meant by
" the labour expended on production." In the rudest
as well as in the most advanced periods of society, two
different kinds of labour are required in bringing commodities to market; namely, the immediate labour of the
persons employed, and the previous labour accumulated on the several articles with which and upon which
they work. Are we then to understand by the expression, " the labour expended on production," immediate
labour, or accumulated labour, or both? and in which
of these senses is it true, that the labour expended
on production determines exchangeable value? The
Author conceives, that in his chapter upon Value, he has
given, for the first time, the correct solution of these
fundamental questions, and has shewn, that it is neither
the immediate labour, nor the sum of the immediate and
accumulated labour, but solely the accumulated labour
expended on production, which determines the quantity
of one article which shall be exchanged against a given
quantity of another.

The principle that the accumulated labour, or, in
other words, the capital expended on production, determines the exchangeable value of commodities, while it
is derived from an extensive induction from particular
cases, affords a satisfactory solution of some of the most
important phenomena connected with the distribution
of wealth. Without this correction or limitation of
Mr. Ricardo's theory of value, it is impossible to give a
clear and unexceptionable demonstration of that gentle-
man's very original and valuable doctrine respecting
the profits of stock.

Many disquisitions contained in the chapter on Mercantile Industry, were published by the Author several years ago, in a little treatise entitled, " The Economists " Refuted." The manner in which trade and commerce aid the production of wealth, the Author does not remember to have seen adequately explained by any preceding writer. When Adam Smith says, that the capital of the merchant replaces the capitals of the farmer and the manufacturer, he seems to be unacquainted with the fact, that trade and commerce, except when they transport articles from places where they have no utility, to places where they have, are not directly productive of wealth, and can contribute to the replacement of capital, only by aiding, through the medium of the divisons of employment, the effective powers of those directly productive branches of industry, which raise or fabricate the articles of which capital is composed. And when M. Say tells us that mercantile industry promotes the wealth of a country by increasing the value of the commodities which it transports and vends, he falls into errors still more serious, evincing not only that he has failed to distinguish between the direct and indirect sources of wealth, but that he has formed no adequate conception of that in which wealth consists. The defects of these celebrated economists, the Author hopes he may have in some measure supplied in his chapter upon Mercantile Industry. He believes also, that some of the other doctrines in this chapter will be found to be original; and particularly that respecting the injury which, in certain extraordinary cases, may be sustained in consequence of exporting the necessaries of life in exchange for superfluities.

Were it permitted to the Author to express an opinion on the subject, he would say, that the most original and, in the present stage of economical science, the most important division of this work, is that in which he discusses the principles of demand and supply. To M. Say and Mr. Mill belong the merit of having been the first to bring forward the very important doctrine, that as commodities are purchased with commodities, one half will furnish a market for the other half, and increased production will be the occasion of increased demand. But this doctrine, though it embraces the very key-stone of economical science, is not correct in the general and unqualified sense in which these distinguished writers have stated it. Though one half of our commodities should be of the same value as the other half, and though the two halves should freely exchange against each other, it is yet possible that there may be an effectual demand for neither. It is quite obvious that there can exist no reciprocal effectual demand, unless the interchange of two different sets of commodities replaces, with a surplus, the expenditure incurred in the production of both. Now, what is that specific relation or proportion between commodities, which occasions the exchange of one half of them against the other half, to replace, with a surplus, the cost of producing both? The Author has not been able to discover the solution of this fundamental question in the writings either of M. Say or of Mr. Mill. He has therefore attempted to supply the deficiency, and thus to rectify and extend the new principles of demand and supply which originated with these able economists.

Having given this account of the nature of the doctrines contained in the present volume, it may be proper to say a few words respecting the manner in which they are discussed. It has been suggested to the Author by a friend, for whose authority on such matters he entertains the highest possible respect, that the illustrative cases and analytical processes to which he resorts for the purpose of explaining and demonstrating his propositions, may fatigue the attention of the reader, and render the work tedious and unattractive. He conceives that the following considerations are sufficient to obviate this objection.

The science of Political Economy is analogous to the mixed mathematics. The data upon which it proceeds are furnished by observation and experience; while the conclusions to which it leads, are attained by a process of ratiocination self-evident in all its steps. To give this science, therefore, the exactness and certainty of which it is susceptible, it must be presented under the analytical and demonstrative form. Now, it is to be remembered, that though analytical and demonstrative processes may be fatiguing and unattractive, yet in mastering a single volume in which these processes are successfully carried on, we make ourselves masters of the science; while we may wade through a thousand volumes of general terms and abstract reasonings, without acquiring a precise idea or arriving at a satisfactory conclusion on one abstruse or controverted question.

Had the analytical method of induction from particular cases been more frequently resorted to by Mr.

Ricardo, that most original and profound economist
would not by his recent deviations* from his original

---

* In the third edition of his work upon Political Economy and
Taxation, Mr. Ricardo has given an additional chapter upon the
effects of machinery, in which he has fallen into some fundamental
and dangerous errors. He contends, that the introduction of machinery occasions a permanent diminution in the demand for labour.
This doctrine is altogether incorrect. Let us suppose, that a capitalist, carrying on the double business of a farmer and manufacturer of
necessaries, advances two hundred quarters of corn and two hundred
suits of clothing to two hundred labourers, who reproduce two hundred
and twenty quarters and two hundred and twenty suits, and then the
rate of profit will be ten per cent. and the surplus of twenty quarters of corn and twenty suits of clothing which remains over and above
the replacement of the capitalist's advances, may be exchanged for
superfluiteis, or may be employed in putting twenty additional
labourers in motion. Now, let us suppose, that instead of exchanging
his surplus of twenty quarters of corn and twenty suits of clothing
for luxuries, our capitalist exchanges them for implements and machines, which enable his two hundred labourers to raise and fabricate
two hundred and fifty-three quarters and two hundred and fifty-
three suits; and then the surplus will be fifteen per cent., the gross
revenue will be increased as well as the net revenue, and the implements and machines, instead of diminishing the demand for labour,
will enable the capitalist to employ fifty-three additional labourers
instead of twenty.

But Mr. Ricardo supposes, that the capitalist, instead of purchasing
machinery out of his surplus or profit, employs a part of the labourers
who formerly produced corn and clothing, in making it; and that as
less corn and clothing must in this case be raised and fabricated, he
will have a smaller quantity of subsistence in the ensuing year to advance to his labourers. The case supposed never yet occurred. The
production of corn and of clothing is not diminished in order to construct machinery. But even if the fact were so, it could not subserve
the argument. Supposing that our capitalist, instead of advancing
two hundred quarters of corn and two hundred suits of clothing to two
hundred labourers who raise and fabricate two hundred and twenty

xii

doctrines, have retarded the progress of the science for which he has achieved so much; and had this method been adopted by Mr. Malthus, he would not have appeared as the ingenious opponent of the new theory of profit, which may be traced by a process of reasoning, self-evident in all its steps, from those dis-

---

quarters and two hundred and twenty suits, advances one hundred quarters and one hundred suits to one hundred labourers, who raise and fabricate one hundred and ten quarters and one hundred and ten suits, and that he advances one hundred quarters and one hundred suits to another one hundred labourers who construct machinery, which being equal in productive cost, is also equal in exchangeable value to one hundred and ten quarters of corn and one hundred and ten suits of clothing, and then in the ensuing season he will be able to advance only subsistence for one hundred and ten labourers instead of for two hundred and twenty. In this case the demand for labour will be reduced one half. But in the nature of things this calamitous effect can only be temporary. The capitalist could have had no motive for constructing his machine unless it enabled him to realise a higher rate of profit than before. But as profits rose capital would accumulate more rapidly, and this more rapid accumulation of capital would speedily restore the original demand for labour. Nay, as every machine which facilitates the production of the necessaries of life must (wages not rising) increase the rate of profit, and thus throw to a greater distance the limits beyond which cultivation can neither be heightened nor extended, improved machinery enables us to extract from the soil a greater quantity of raw produce, and furnishes the means of supporting a more numerous manufacturing population. Even when we concede to Mr. Ricardo that which never yet occurred in practice, namely, that the construction of machinery suspends the production of necessaries, still it remains strictly demonstrable, that the introduction of machinery, after occasioning a temporary diminution, leads to a permanent increase in the demand for labour. The reader will see this subject further unfolded in an admirable article on the Effects of Machinery and Accumulation, in No. LXIX. of the Edinburgh Review.

coveries respecting the nature and origin of rent which he himself has made.

The controversies which at present exist amongst the most celebrated masters of Political Economy have been brought forward by a lively and ingenious author as an objection against the study of the science. A similar objection might have been urged, in a certain stage of its progress, against every branch of human knowledge. A few years ago, when the brilliant discoveries in chymistry began to supersede the ancient doctrine of phlogiston, controversies, analogous to those which now exist amongst Political Economists, divided the professors of natural knowledge; and Dr. Priestley, like Mr. Malthus, appeared as the pertinacious champion of the theories which the facts established by himself had so largely contributed to overthrow. In the progress of the human mind a period of controversy amongst the cultivators of any branch of science must necessarily precede the period of their unanimity. But this, instead of furnishing a reason for abandoning the pursuits of science while its first principles remain in uncertainty, should stimulate us to prosecute our studies with more ardour and perseverance, until upon every question within the compass of the human faculties, doubt is removed and certainty attained. With respect to Political Economy the period of controversy is passing away, and that of unanimity rapidly approaching. Twenty years hence there will scarcely exist a doubt respecting any of its fundamental principles.

LONDON, June 30, 1821.

CONTENTS.

CHAP. I.

WEALTH—VALUE—PRICE. . . . . . . page 1

CHAP. II.

ON THE INSTRUMENTS OF PRODUCTION, AND
THE DIFFERENT KINDS OF INDUSTRY. 66

CHAP. III.

APPROPRIATIVE INDUSTRY. 75

CHAP. IV.

MANUFACTURING INDUSTRY. 83

CHAP. V.

AGRICULTURAL INDUSTRY. 103

CHAP. VI.

MERCANTILE INDUSTRY.

SECTION. I. *Origin and Effects of Barter or Trade*.............................. page 147

.... II. *On the Home Trade*..................... 195

.... III. *On the Colonial Trade*...... 228

.... IV. *On Foreign Trade, or Commerce*.... 248

.... V. *On Money and Paper Currency*..... 290

.... VI. *On the Principles of Demand and Supply* 339

ON

THE SOURCES OF WEALTH.

———◆———

CHAP. I.

WEALTH—VALUE—PRICE.

W EALTH, considered as the object of economical science, consists of those material articles
which are useful or desirable to man, and which
it requires some portion of voluntary exertion
to procure or to preserve. Thus, two things are
essential to wealth:—the possession of utility,—
and the requiring of some portion of voluntary
exertion or labour. That which has no utility,
which serves neither to supply our wants, nor
to gratify our desires, is as the dust beneath our
feet, or as the sand upon the shore, and obviously
forms no portion of our wealth: while, on the

other hand, things which possess the highest utility, and which are even necessary to our existence, come not under the denomination of wealth, unless, to the possession of utility be superadded the circumstance of having been procured by some voluntary exertion. Though the air which we breathe, and the sun-beams by which we are warmed, are in the highest degree useful and necessary, it would be a departure from the precision of language, to denominate them articles of wealth. But the bread which appeases the cravings of hunger, and the clothing which protects us from the rigour of the season, though not more indispensably requisite than the former, are with propriety classed under the term, wealth; because, to the possession of utility, they add the circumstance of having been procured by labour.

In order to give a clear and precise idea of wealth, it may be expedient to shew, not only what it is, but what it is not. A term of extensive signification, and comprising under one general denomination a number of particulars, is peculiarly liable to ambiguity; and in popular discourse is almost always employed in a sense vague and indeterminate. By a common figure of speech, we put a part for the whole; we substitute the species for the genus; a quality for its subject; and limit the meaning of our general term to some leading particular which it comprises. On the ordinary topics of discourse, where no great precision is required, this loose and figurative language may not be productive of much inconvenience: but, in economical science, it has frequently led the inquirer into irreconcileable inconsistencies, and inveterate error; and, if we would arrive at clear conceptions, or just conclusions, must be scrupulously avoided.

In common discourse the term, wealth, has two different significations. When we say, a man of wealth, the term implies quantity, and signifies an abundance of the comforts and luxuries of life. But when we say, agriculture is a source of wealth, the accessory idea of quantity is not implied, and the term comprises the products of agriculture, whether they be raised from one acre, or from a million; whether they are capable of subsisting an individual, or a nation. It is obvious that the latter is the correct and philosophic import of the term. The chemist would become the object of ridicule, who should define water to consist in an abundance of the fluid formed by the union of oxygen and hydrogen. The political economist, who defines wealth to consist in an abundance of commodities, is in no way entitled to more courteous treatment.

Wealth has sometimes been confounded with capital; but there is a distinction between them which it is important to keep in view. Capital consists in those things on which some portion of labour is bestowed, and which are destined, not for the immediate supply of our wants, but for the purpose of aiding us in obtaining other articles of utility. It would be extending the signification of the term beyond the scope of political economy, were we to give the denomination of capital to those natural agents over which human industry exerts no control. The rain and the sunshine which mature our harvests, though they are powerful and indispensable instruments of production, yet constitute no portion of our capital; while reservoirs for irrigating our fields, and stoves for forcing the fruits of the earth, very frequently do. It would be rather a vague and indefinite use of the language of economical science, to call unreclaimed and unappropriated land, however great its natural fertility, by the name of capital; though a most important portion of capital will consist in the enclosures, drains, and improvements, by which the productive powers of land are increased.

Now, as capital consists in articles which are useful to man, and on which some portion of his labour has been expended, it is evident that it comes under the denomination of wealth, as that term has been here defined. Capital, indeed, is but a particular species of wealth; and the only peculiar and distinguishing circumstance belonging to it is that of being destined, not to the immediate supplying of our wants, but to the obtaining of other articles of utility. Whenever an article of wealth is used to aid the human arm in executing the work of production, then the article so employed becomes a portion of capital. But though capital must always be wealth, yet wealth may not always be capital. Wealth is the generic, capital the specific term; and it would be inaccurate to use the one as the synonyme of the other.

The term, money, has been frequently employed, both in discourse and writing, as synonimous with that of wealth. Money, indeed, possessing utility, and receiving its form from labour, is unquestionably an article of wealth. But then, food and clothing also possess utility, and are acquired by voluntary exertion, and therefore participate in an equal degree with money in all that is essential to wealth. The error of confounding the signification of the terms, wealth, and money, is even more considerable than that of confounding the meaning of the terms, wealth, and capital; for, as we shall see hereafter, money is only a part, and comparatively an inconsiderable part, of capital. But capital is itself only a species of wealth; and therefore, money, instead of constituting wealth, is no more than a variety of a species, of which wealth is the genus. The substituting of money for wealth, seems to have led to the principal misconceptions and false conclusions of the mercantile system. This source of error, however, is now sufficiently detected and exploded: and it is pretty generally acknowledged by those who have given any attention to the principles of economical science, that wealth does not consist in the precious metals.

Even in the present day, however, political philosophers fall into the error of confounding wealth with value. Our great economist, Adam Smith, is chargeable with this misconception and confusion. M. Say, also, in his justly celebrated Treatise on Political Economy, tells us, that wealth consists in value, and that the quantity of wealth is determined by the sum of values of which it is composed. This is a fundamental error, which leads its author to false conclusions, and involves him in direct contradictions. It becomes necessary, therefore, that we should demonstrate, that wealth does not consist in value; and that we should point out the distinction between them, and the relation which each bears to the other.

There are two kinds of value:—value in

use,—and value in exchange. Now, value in use is the same thing as utility; and we have already shewn that utility does not of itself constitute wealth. Political economy is a branch of the great science of human nature: its investigations and its reasonings are confined to that class of phenomena which human industry presents; and therefore, in the language which it employs, the signification of the term, wealth, is restricted to those useful things on which some portion of voluntary human effort has been bestowed. The utility existing in those things of which nature furnishes an unlimited and spontaneous supply, and which are neither appropriated, nor produced, nor distributed, nor in any visible degree consumed by human agency, though it may be regarded as natural opulence, yet comes not within the scope and compass of economical science; and consequently wealth, regarded as the object of that science, cannot consist of value in use.

A little consideration will also satisfy us, that wealth cannot consist of value in exchange. If two independent savages were to return from

the chase, each bringing with him as many dead
animals as he could consume while they continued fit for food, and as many branches and
boughs as were sufficient to replace the bows
and arrows he had expended, they could have
no wish to barter with each other; and the
useful articles which they had toiled to acquire,
would possess no value in exchange. But let
one of these savages bring home more game
than he could consume before it became unfit
for food, without having found any branches
adapted to replace the bows and arrows expended in the chase; while the other returned
with his hunger unappeased, but with the materials for more bows and arrows than he could
use; and their respective wants would immediately inspire them with a desire of trafficking
with each other, and would consequently bestow
on their commodities the property of exchangeable value. The superfluous food of the one
would be given for the superfluous implements
of the other; and, in this manner, the irregularity in the distribution of their possessions
would be corrected, and each would be supplied

with that which he required. Now, if exchangeable value constituted wealth, then, when each
of these savages had been so fortunate as to
supply himself abundantly with all the articles
he required, there would be no wealth; while,
if each had been in his own person partially
unsuccessful, and could obtain the articles necessary to his present and future support, only by
the circuitous mode of barter and exchange,
then wealth would appear. This is evidently
absurd. If food, and implements for procuring
food, have not the character of wealth while
distributed in such regular proportions that each
individual has the quantity which he wants, it
is impossible that they should acquire this character from the circumstance of their being so
irregularly distributed, that each person, having
too much of one article, and too little of another,
wishes to exchange his superfluity with that of
his neighbour. Nothing but a vague and inaccurate use of language could have led to the
notion, that exchangeable value constitutes
wealth. When we say that any article of utility
possesses exchangeable value, the expression is

figurative, and, in its precise and real import, does not predicate any quality, or attribute, as inhering in this article; but merely implies, that there are persons able and willing to give other articles of utility instead of it. The phrase, exchangeable value, has a reference to the power and the inclinations of those persons who possess articles of utility, and not to any thing actually belonging and essential to these articles themselves. Exchangeable value, therefore, depending on the will and the ability to give one thing for another, is an accident, a casual circumstance, which sometimes is, and sometimes is not, found to exist in connexion with those articles which supply our wants, and gratify our desires. Defining wealth to consist in exchangeable value, is the same thing as defining it to consist, not in any qualities or forms belonging to material subjects, but in the motives and volitions of moral agents. When we define it to consist in articles possessing exchangeable value, or, to speak more correctly, in those articles which men are able and willing to exchange, we avoid this absurdity: but then we involve ourselves in the inconsistency of representing the same things, while possessing the same properties, and applied to the same use, as sometimes constituting, and sometimes not constituting, wealth. If wealth consist in articles which possess exchangeable value, then (to refer to our former illustration) the food and implements which are articles of wealth to day, if either of our huntsmen should lose the inclination or power to barter with the other, may not be articles of wealth to-morrow.

As the misconception which confounds wealth with value, has greatly retarded the progress of economical science; and hitherto it has been very general; I trust I may not appear unnecessarily minute or tedious, if I produce a few farther illustrations for the purpose of correcting it.

Let us suppose that a single family, shut out from all intercourse with the rest of mankind, cultivates the ground, and prepares its produce for use. Now, it is evident, that if this family lived upon a fertile soil, and directed its labour with any moderate degree of skill and perseverance, it might supply itself with all the necessaries, and with many of the comforts of life; but it is equally evident, that these products of its industry, however useful in quality, and abundant in quantity, would be destitute of value in exchange, and could purchase nothing. If, therefore, wealth consist in exchangeable value, this family, though the fruits of its labour were sufficient to enable it to live in plenty, and even in luxury, would not be in possession of a single article of wealth.

Again; in a country, however extensive, and however populous it might be, in which the divisions of labour were unestablished, and in which each man combined in his own person a variety of employments, and procured and prepared for his family whatever articles they consumed, it is plain that, as in the former case, barter and sale, and consequently value in exchange, would be unknown. Each individual might exert a considerable portion of industry, and be supplied not only with the natural opulence bestowed gratuitously upon man, but also with those use-

ful articles which are obtained by voluntary
exertion; but nothing would be brought to market,—there would be neither buyers nor sellers,
neither exchanges nor value in exchange. If,
therefore, wealth consists in exchangeable value,
this nation, like the isolated family of the former
illustration, would not, with whatever success it
might apply its industry, and however abundantly it might supply itself with useful commodities, be in possession of a single article of
wealth.

Once more. A society having an internal
community of goods, and no external trade,
might avail itself of all the advantages of the
home divisions of labour, and supply itself in
great abundance with the necessaries, comforts,
and luxuries of life; though it is plain, that the
useful commodities which it procured and accumulated could possess no value in exchange.
Under the supposition, no exchanges would be
made, and no equivalents required. Each individual would exert that portion of industry
which the regulations of the society prescribed,
and would receive from the common stock

whatever he consumed. Industry might be applied with great perseverance and success; the society (as is said to be the case in a small community which has been established in the territory of Pennsylvania, under the name of Harmony,) might procure by their labour a more abundant supply of the necessaries of life, than any equal number of individuals in the most wealthy European country; and yet, if wealth consists in exchangeable value, not one article of wealth would exist in the society.

These illustrations have, I trust, been sufficient to shew the distinction, as well as the relation, between wealth and value. Wealth consists of articles which possess utility, and which are procured by some portion of voluntary effort. When the divisions of labour, and private property, are established, then each individual lives by giving the surplus produce of his own, for the surplus produce of his neighbour's industry, and the articles of wealth are exchanged one against another; or, to employ the usual mode of expression, acquire the property of exchangeable value. But exchangeable value, even taken in the common acceptation of the term, is not an essential quality of wealth; but an accident, belonging to it only under those particular circumstances in which the divisions of labour and private property exist. Abolish the divisions of labour, or establish a community of goods, and in either case exchangeable value will be lost. It is to be remembered, moreover, that the term, exchangeable value, does not, even under the particular circumstances in which one commodity is given for another, stand for any property or quality actually inhering in, or belonging to the articles of wealth. The expression merely implies, that there exists a desire and the power of giving one article of wealth for another: and perhaps, if it were not too great a departure from established usage, it might not be improper to dismiss it from the nomenclature of economical science, and to substitute in its stead a phraseology less liable to ambiguity.

But although, in those early periods of society when each person prepares for himself whatever he consumes, and in those small associations where all things are in common, exchanges and

equivalents will be unknown; yet, as improvement advances, and population increases, the
division of labour, and the acquisition of private
property, will inevitably take place: and consequently almost every article of utility on which
any portion of labour has been employed, will
find a purchaser in the market; and (to employ
the current phraseology) wealth, in addition to
its other properties, will possess that of value in
exchange. Hence, value in exchange, though
not absolutely an essential attribute of wealth,
is an accident which very generally pertains to
it, and which exerts an important influence both
over its formation and its distribution. To give
an exact analysis of the nature of value, or, in
other words, to trace out the circumstances
which cause any given quantity of one article to
be offered for any given quantity of another,
becomes the indispensable business of the political economist.

In that early period of society which precedes
any permanent establishment of the divisions of
employment, if two savage hunters were to
return from the chase, the one with more game

than he could consume, but with all his bows
and arrows expended; the other with his hunger unappeased, but with his supply of arrows
still entire, they would be mutually seized with
the desire of bartering their respective superfluities: but there could exist no principle to determine the terms of the exchange, except what
might arise out of the degree of inclination
which each might feel to possess the commodity
of the other. The desire of the unsuccessful
hunter to obtain food, would be immediate and
urgent; that of his neighbour to obtain implements for future excursions, would be more
remote and less strongly felt; and, therefore, in
adjusting the terms of the exchange, the more
fortunate adventurer might obtain from the
necessities of the other a large supply of arrows
for a small supply of game. If two or three
unsuccessful hunters sought to obtain the wild
animals of the more fortunate adventurer, the
terms of the exchange would be rendered still
more unequal; and implements, which it had
cost several days' labour to prepare, might be
offered for a supply of subsistence which half a

day's ordinary exertion would procure. In this rude and early state, therefore, there would be no fixed criterion to regulate or determine exchangeable value; and the terms of the barter which occasionally took place, would, in each successive instance, be regulated by the immediate wants and desires of the contracting parties.

The case would be different as soon as the frequency of exchanges began to lead to permanent divisions of employment. In this state of society, the individual who devotes himself to a particular occupation, must be able to obtain, in exchange for the surplus produce of his labour, such a portion of the things produced by the labour of others, as will place him in a situation at least as good as that in which he found himself when he combined in his own person a variety of employments. If two savage hunters, without any division of employment, could each supply himself with implements, and kill a deer a day; and if, when one prepared implements, and the other went to the chase, they could kill three deer a day; then it is evident that the person who prepares the bows and arrows, cannot be prevailed upon to accept in exchange for a day's work, less than a whole deer : because, if his comrade attempted to drive a hard and unequal bargain, it would be his interest to discontinue the division of employment, and to hunt down wild animals for himself. Nay, under the case supposed, the preparer of bows and arrows would get in exchange for a day's labour, not only a whole deer, but a deer and a half; because, if the hunter should at any time obtain a more than equal share of the advantages arising from the division of employment, his anxiety to continue it would be stronger than that of the manufacturer of implements, and consequently, when any discussion arose respecting the terms of the exchange, his motive to make concessions would be stronger also, and he would necessarily yield to the demands of the manufacturer, until the division of employment conferred upon each an equal benefit.

Thus we see, that as soon as men begin to devote themselves to particular employments, the competition to participate in the advantages resulting from the division of employment, de-

termines the exchangeable value of their respective commodities. Before the community divides
itself into a class of capitalists and a class of
labourers, this competition turns entirely on the
total quantity of labour employed; and the produce of a day's work in one occupation will be
exchanged for the produce of a day's exertion
in another. If, in a tribe which lived by appropriating the spontaneous gifts of nature, it
usually required twice as much labour to procure
animal, as it required to procure vegetable food;
then a day's subsistence consisting of the former,
would naturally exchange for, or be worth, two
days' subsistence consisting of the latter. Nor,
while the same individual continues to be both
labourer and capitalist, can we conceive any
principle capable of permanently altering this
rate of equivalency. If, while the same quantity of labour which procured one day's supply
of animal, was sufficient to procure two days'
supply of vegetable food, the class of hunters
combined to obtain three days' supply of the
latter, for one of the former; then it is evident
that the class which collected fruits, in consent-

ing to such terms, would obtain a less quantity of animal food than if they engaged personally in the chase. It would, therefore, become the interest of the collectors of vegetable food to discontinue the divisions of employment: but as the class of hunters would have a strong interest in continuing them, the moment the former evinced an intention of abandoning their peculiar occupation, the latter would relax from their unreasonable demands, until the divisions of employment again became mutually and equally beneficial.

Before the labourer and capitalist become distinct persons, the produce of a day's labour in one occupation will, *cæteris paribus,* be always equivalent to the produce of a day's labour in another occupation, whether the whole labour is employed immediately and directly in obtaining articles for consumption, or whether a portion of it is previously employed in acquiring the capital necessary to the production of such articles. If, previous to the separation of society into labourers and capitalists, vegetable productions were gathered without the aid of capital;

while, in appropriating animal productions, it required that for every day's labour employed in the field, another day's labour should be employed in preparing implements for the chase; or, in other words, the hunter's capital; then it is evident that the produce of one day's direct labour in the chase, would be equivalent to the produce of two days' labour employed in gathering fruits. In adjusting the terms of the exchange, the labour which prepared the capital would be taken into account, no less than the labour which actually applied it. If, on their returning in the evening from their respective occupations, the collector of vegetable productions should offer the fruits which he had gathered in the course of the day, in exchange for the animals which the hunter had killed during the same period, the latter would naturally reply,—" The arrows expended during the " chase cost me a day's labour; the animals " which I have killed are in reality the produce " of two days' labour; and therefore, you must " give me the quantity of fruits collected by two " days' labour in exchange for them." To this demand the collector of fruits would be under the necessity of acceding, in order to prevent the hunter from abandoning the divisions of employment, and collecting vegetable productions for himself. It would be impossible to induce the hunter to give, for any length of time, more than the produce of a day's labour for a quantity of fruit which a day's labour might at any time procure for him. If, under any particular circumstances, the produce of a day's labour employed in gathering fruits should exchange for more than the produce of a day's labour employed in the chase, then the occupation of gathering fruits would be more beneficial than that of hunting; and individuals desirous of obtaining a supply of animal food, would renounce the latter, and betake themselves to the former, until the level were restored, and the produce of a day's labour in the one, exchanged for the produce of a day's labour in the other.

Thus then it clearly appears, that before the class of labourers becomes distinct from that of capitalists, and while the labourer prepares for himself whatever capital he employs, the whole quantity of labour, including that accumulated in capital, as well as that directly applied, which is expended in production, determines the quantity of one article which shall be offered in exchange for a given quantity of another. In this early stage of society, things upon which equal portions of labour have been bestowed will be equivalent to each other.

We must now proceed to more advanced and complicated stages of society, and inquire what it is which determines the quantity of one commodity that shall be given in exchange for another, when capitalists and labourers have been separated into distinct classes.

Let there be two identical capitals, each consisting of a hundred quarters of corn, and a thousand pounds of wool; and let the proprietor of one of these capitals employ it in manufacturing broad cloth, while the proprietor of the other capital employs it in preparing carpeting. Now, it must be evident, that the cloth and carpeting on which equal capitals were expended, would be of equal value. If either of these manufacturers offered a *part* of his productions in exchange for the whole of the productions of the other, the other would immediately reply,— " For the articles which I have had fabricated " from a hundred quarters of corn, and a thou- " sand pounds of wool, you must give me the " whole of the articles which you have had pre- " pared from a like capital. My capital is of " equal power with yours; and if you will not " barter upon equal terms, I can at any time " employ as many labourers as will produce to " me that which you refuse." To this no reasonable objection could be urged. Hence we see, that *when the capitalists become a class distinct from the labourers, the results obtained by the employment of identical capitals, or identical quantities of accumulated labour, will be equal in exchangeable value.*

Again: let there be two equivalent capitals, the one consisting of subsistence for one hundred labourers, with a thousand pounds of wool, equal in value to this subsistence; and the other of subsistence for one hundred, with a thousand pounds of cotton, also equal in value to this subsistence; and let the proprietor of the former employ one hundred labourers in making woollens, and the proprietor of the latter one hundred in making cottons. Now, it is evident, that the woollen and cotton goods thus produced, would be of equal exchangeable value. For, if the quantity of woollens, on the production of which subsistence for one hundred, with material equal to it in value, had been expended, exchanged at any time for a quantity of cotton goods greater than that on which subsistence for one hundred, with material equal to it in value, had been expended, then the manufacturing of wool would become more beneficial than the manufacturing of cotton. But capital ever seeks its most beneficial employment; and in this case it would be withdrawn from the cotton to the woollen manufacture, until the equilibrium were restored. Thus, from the perpetually operating law of competition, from self-interest ever seeking to throw capital into the most beneficial channel, it inevitably follows, that *after the community divides itself into a class of capitalists and a class of labourers, the results obtained by the employment of equivalent capitals or equal quantities of accumulated labour, will be equal in exchangeable value.*

Equivalent capitals may possess very different degrees of durability; but this circumstance, when it occurs, does not form any exception to our general principle, that the results obtained by the employment of equal capitals will be of equal exchangeable value. If a woollen and a silk manufacturer were each to employ a capital of 2000*l.*; and if the former were to employ 1500*l.* in durable machines, and 500*l.* in wages and materials; while the latter employed only 500*l.* in durable machines, and 1500*l.* in wages and materials; then the results of these equal capitals would, from the law of competition, be of equal exchangeable value; that is, the woollens, with the residue of the fixed capitals employed in preparing them, would be worth the same sum as the silks, with the residue of the fixed capital employed in their manufacture. Supposing that a tenth of these fixed capitals is annually consumed, and that the rate of profit is ten per cent., then, as the results of the woollen manufacturer's capital of 2000*l.*, must, to give him this profit, be 2200*l.*, and as the value of his fixed capital has been reduced by the process of production from 1500*l.* to 1350*l.*, the goods produced must sell for 850*l.* And, in like manner, as the fixed capital of the silk manufacturer is by the process of production reduced one-tenth, or from 500*l.* to 450*l.*, the silks produced must, in order to yield him the customary rate of profit upon his whole capital of 2000*l.*, sell for 1750*l.* When the capitals employed are of equal value, and of equal degrees of durability, the goods produced by them will bear equal prices in the market. But when capitals equal in amount, but of different degrees of durability, are employed, the articles produced, together with the residue of capital, in one occupation, will be equal in exchangeable value to the things produced, and the residue of capital, in another occupation.

Equal capitals, or, in other words, equal quantities of accumulated labour, will often put in motion different quantities of immediate labour; but neither does this furnish any exception to our general principle, that, after the society has been divided into a class of labourers and a class of capitalists, the results obtained by the employment of equal capitals will be of equal value in exchange. Let there be two capitals, each containing fifty days' accumulated labour, and consisting of wages for ninety common labourers, with a piece of metal equivalent to wages for ten; and let the proprietor of the one capital employ it in setting nailors at work, while the proprietor of the other employs it in setting engravers at work. Now, in this case, the nails and the engraved plates, being the results, not only of equivalent, but of identical capitals, must be of equal exchangeable value. But though, from the law of competition, their values must be equal, it by no means follows, that the entire quantities of labour bestowed upon their production, must have been equal also. The engravers, in consequence of the taste and genius which are required in their elegant art, and which are scarcely ever proportional to the previous labour devoted to their acquisition, might be able to demand quadruple wages, while the nailors obtained but a bare subsistence. The portion of capital, therefore, consisting of wages, would employ ninety nailors, while it employed only twenty-two engravers. As each of these equivalent and identical capitals had been produced by fifty days' labour, then the whole labour, accumulated and immediate, expended in obtaining the nails will be one hundred and forty days, while the whole labour, accumulated and immediate, expended upon the engraved plates, will be only seventy-two. Yet the plates must be of equal value with the nails, otherwise an equal capital would not be laid out in procuring them.

Again: even though there should be no difference in the rate of wages, yet capitals containing equal quantities of accumulated labour, and equal both in amount and in durability, will put in motion unequal quantities of immediate labour. If a woollen manufacturer, with a capital of 2000*l.*, or two thousand days' accumulated labour, invested 500*l.* in machinery, 500*l.* in materials, and paid 1000*l.* in wages, he would employ just twice as many labourers as a silk manufacturer, who, with a capital of

2000*l.*, invested 500*l.* in machinery, 1000*l.* in materials, and paid 500*l.* in wages. But though these two capitals put in motion such different quantities of immediate labour, the products would be equivalent; and the woollens obtained by the employment of a capital of two thousand days' accumulated labour, would exchange for neither more nor less than the silks obtained by the employment of a capital of like amount. For, if at any time the woollen manufacturer should obtain in exchange for the products of his capital either more or less than the products of capitals equal in amount, his business would be more or less profitable than others, until, other capitalists entering into it in the former case, and deserting it in the latter, the level would be restored, and the products of equivalent capitals rendered of equal exchangeable value.

Once more. Capitals containing equal quantities of accumulated labour, and equal in amount and in durability, may put unequal quantities of immediate labour in motion, even though the proportion of raw materials should be the same in each. The woollen manufacturer, with his capital of 2000*l*., might invest 500*l*. in machinery, 500*l*. in material, and pay 1000*l*. in wages to the labourers by whom his machinery was wrought; while the silk manufacturer also investing 500*l*. in machinery, and 500*l*. in raw material, might partly work his machinery by the force of steam, and lay out 500*l*. in fuel, and only 500*l*. in wages. Here again (wages being supposed the same in both occupations) the first capital puts in motion twice as much immediate labour as the second; and yet the law of competition equalizing the rate of profit, would necessarily render the woollens and wrought silks, upon which equal sums had been expended, of equal exchangeable value.

It is hoped that these illustrations have been sufficient to establish the following principles:—

I. In that early period of society which precedes the separation of the community into a class of capitalists and a class of labourers, and in which the individual who undertakes any branch of industry, performs his own work, the total quantity of labour, accumulated and immediate, expended on production, is that on which comparison and competition turn, and which, in the transactions of barter or sale, ultimately determines the quantity of one commodity which shall be received for a given quantity of another.

II. When stock has accumulated, when capitalists become a class distinct from labourers, and when the person who undertakes any branch of industry, does not perform his own work, but advances subsistence and materials to others, then it is the amount of capital, or the quantity of accumulated labour expended in production, on which comparison and competition turn, and which determines the exchangeable power of commodities.

The reason why, in these different stages of society, exchangeable value should be determined upon different principles, is sufficiently obvious. Every person seeks to obtain the objects of his desire at the smallest possible sacrifice. When all labour for themselves, no one will for any length of time give more than the result of a day's labour for that which a day's labour can procure for him; and, in like manner, when the capitalist hires others to work for him, he will not consent to part with more than the product of a given capital (say a hundred days' subsistence) in exchange for that which, by the expenditure of a hundred days' subsistence, he can cause to be prepared for himself. For example; while each individual laboured for himself, if a woollen manufacturer were to employ ten days' labour in procuring raw material and ninety days in working it up; and a silk manufacturer employed forty-five days in obtaining raw material, and five days in fabricating it; the woollen cloths would be of twice the value of the wrought silks; and if the silk manufacturer objected to barter upon these terms, the other would naturally reply,—" The " labour which it has cost me to produce half " my goods, would have procured for me a " quantity of silks equal to that which I demand; " and if you refuse to give this quantity for " half my woollens, it will be my interest to " change the direction of my labour, and to " manufacture silks for myself." To this no reasonable objection could be urged; and the

silk manufacturer would find himself compelled
to barter the article on which he had employed
fifty days of accumulated and immediate labour,
for half that on which his neighbour had employed a hundred days of accumulated and
immediate labour.   On the contrary, when there
is a class of capitalists and a class of labourers,
if a woollen manufacturer were to advance
wages to ninety labourers, with material equivalent to wages for ten; and if a silk manufacturer were to advance wages to twenty, with
material equivalent to wages for eighty; the
woollens and the wrought silk, notwithstanding
that such unequal portions of labour had been
employed in their fabrication, would be of equal
exchangeable value.   It would be in vain for
the woollen manufacturer to urge, that in working up his commodity, he had given employment to ninety, while the other had given employment to no more than twenty, labourers.
Nay, it would be even useless for him to go a
step farther back, and to say,—" My capital,
" consisting of wages for ninety, with material
" equivalent to wages for ten, cost me fifty

" days' labour: your capital, consisting of wages
" for twenty, with material equivalent to wages
" for eighty, was also produced by fifty days'
" labour; and therefore, it is equitable, that my
" article, obtained by ninety days' labour, with a
" capital which cost fifty days' labour, should be
" twice as valuable as your's, which was obtained
" by twenty days, with a capital which also cost
" fifty. The whole quantity of labour required
" to procure mine is double the whole quantity
" required to procure yours, and should natu-
" rally bestow on it a double power in ex-
" change." To this the silk manufacturer
would reply,—" The question does not turn
" upon the quantities of labour required to pro-
" cure our respective articles. Our capitals are
" each worth a hundred days' wages: they are
" equivalent and convertible; and, if you refuse
" to exchange their respective products upon
" equal terms, I can, at the same cost which
" fabricates my silk, obtain wages for ninety,
" with wool equivalent to wages for ten, and
" thus have wrought up for me the same quan-
" tity of woollens which I require of you. You

" cannot expect that I should accept in exchange
" for the product of my capital, a less quantity
" of any article, than that capital might at any
" time procure for me, if I chose to manufacture
" it for myself." To this no farther objection
could reasonably be urged. After capitalists
become a class distinct from labourers, competition turns, not upon the quantity of labour, but
upon the amount of capital expended in production; and the results obtained after the employment of equal capitals, will always tend to an
equality of value in the market.

After the division of the industrious members
of a community into a class of capitalists and a
class of labourers, there is only one case, and
that of extremely rare occurrence, in which the
exchangeable value of commodities will be in
proportion to the total quantity of labour, both
accumulated and immediate, employed in their
production. This case is, when equal capitals
or quantities of accumulated labour, happen to
give employment to equal quantities of immediate labour. If the capitals of a silk and of a
woollen manufacturer were each worth 1000*l*.

and put each a hundred labourers in motion,
then the wrought silk and the woollen cloths
fabricated by these capitals would, at one and the
same time, be the products of equal quantities
of labour, and possess equal exchangeable value.
But it must be evident on the slightest examination, that this is no more than a merely accidental coincidence. As long as these two capitals
continue equal, the law of competition, always
tending to equalize the profits of stock, will
keep their products of equal exchangeable value,
however we may vary the quantity of immediate
labour which they put in motion, or which their
products may require. While, on the contrary,
if we render these capitals unequal in amount,
the same law must render their products of unequal value, though the total quantity of labour
expended upon each, should be precisely equal.
This is a clear and complete demonstration that,
after the separation of capitalists and labourers,
it is always the amount of capital, or quantity
of accumulated labour, and not as before this separation, the sum of accumulated and immediate
labour, expended on production, which determines

the exchangeable value of commodities. When capitals equal in amount happen to put equal quantities of immediate labour in motion, then the value of things will be in proportion to the total quantity of labour bestowed upon them; but to conclude from this, that it is the total quantity of labour, and not the accumulated labour or capital, which determines the degree of exchangeable value, is to mistake an accidental coincidence for a necessary connexion.

It may be necessary to remark that, in all the foregoing illustrations, we have taken it for granted, that the return upon capital is equally quick. If two equal capitals are employed, the one in fabricating silks, and the other in manufacturing woollens; and if the former could not be brought to market under six months, while the latter could be brought there in three, then, from the principle of competition, the silks produced would be more valuable than the woollens. The same result would take place if manufacturing the one was attended with more risk or more discredit than fabricating the other.

The principle, that the exchangeable value of

commodities is determined by the amount of capital expended in their production, is liable to some other exceptions and limitations which it is necessary to notice. It is the law of competition which determines universally the quantity of any one article that shall be offered and accepted for a given quantity of another; but under different circumstances this law will operate in a different manner, and give different results. In any given state of the market, it turns upon demand and supply; and consequently the exchangeable value of every commodity will, in any given state of the market, be determined exclusively by the proportion which exists between the supply of it and the demand for it. Hence, in the debate between buyers and sellers, it will frequently occur, that the product of a given capital will exchange for much more or much less than the product of another and equal capital. But it is to be considered, that that state of the market upon which competition turns to-day, a previous competition must have produced, and a future competition will either continue or destroy. When

the product of a given capital sells for more or
less than the products of other and equal capitals, it will be the interest of individuals to
betake themselves to the more, or to desert the
less, advantageous occupation; and consequently,
wherever competition is allowed to operate, it
will so regulate the state of the market, or, in
other words, so determine the proportions in
which commodities shall be produced, and offered
in exchange for each other, that, notwithstanding occasional fluctuations, the results obtained
by the employment of equal capitals will on the
average and in the long run be of equal exchangeable value.

The principle, that the results obtained from
the employment of equal capitals will be of equal
exchangeable value, is liable to exception in all
cases of monopoly, whether natural or artificial.
A monopoly may be defined to be, a suspension
of the law of competition, with respect to the
production of commodities, and the equalization
of profits. Wherever this suspension takes place,
the advantages obtained from the employment
of capital in one occupation, may greatly ex-

ceed those which can be gained by employing it in others; and the exchangeable value of commodities will be determined, not by the amount of capital expended on their production, but by the number and the wealth of those who may be desirous of obtaining them. In such cases, the products of equal capitals may, for any length of time, be of unequal exchangeable value in the market. When, for example, nature has limited the quantity of soil necessary to the production of a peculiar sort of wine, the value of this wine will not be determined by the quantity either of labour or of capital which may be employed in preparing it, but solely by the quantity of the other products of industry which may be offered in exchange for it. If the persons desirous of consuming wine, possess few of the products of industry beyond what is necessary for their subsistence, the exchangeable value of this luxury will be low. While, on the contrary, if those desirous of procuring it are numerous, and possessed of incomes much beyond what their necessities require, the exchangeable value of the peculiar sort of wine may, for any length of time, exceed, in almost any degree, that of other articles on which equal portions of labour or of capital are bestowed. Supposing that while it required a hundred days' labour, or a capital of a hundred days' subsistence, to raise the peculiar sort of wine, those desirous of consuming it possessed the products of a thousand days' labour, or of a capital consisting of a thousand days' subsistence, beyond what was requisite to supply them with necessaries; then this peculiar wine, the product of a hundred days' labour, or of a hundred days' subsistence, might exchange against, or, in other words, be of equal value with, the products of a thousand days' labour, or of a capital of a thousand days' subsistence. This would, no doubt, render those who had the disposal of labour or of capital, eager to produce the wine; but by the supposition, the soil necessary to its production is of limited extent; the operation of the law of competition is suspended; and, therefore, it is possible that our peculiar sort of wine may continue of ten times more value, than the other things on which equal portions of labour or of capital are bestowed.

When a monopoly, whether natural or artificial, affects articles of luxury, there is no limit to their possible rise in exchangeable value, except that which may be set by the amount of the wealth, and the degree of the desire, possessed by their consumers. Gems, statues, and pictures, when, from the barrenness of mines, or the dearth of genius, they exist in scarcity, may possess an exchangeable value greater by a thousand, or a hundred thousand fold, than the cost of their production. The case is different with respect to the necessaries of life. A monopoly affecting these, can never, for any permanency, raise their value so high, that the product of a day's labour, or of a capital sufficient to put a day's labour in motion, shall not be exchangeable for a day's subsistence. The reason is obvious. If the produce of a day's labour were exchangeable for less than a day's subsistence, the labourer would starve; and if the product of a capital sufficient to put a day's labour in motion should become of less value than a day's subsistence; then, as subsistence must always be a part of the things advanced by the capitalist, his capital would not be returned to him. In every case of a monopoly, whether artificial or natural, population must be cut off, and production suspended, before the necessaries of life can be so raised in value, that the product of a day's labour, or of a capital sufficient to put a day's labour in motion, will exchange for less than a day's subsistence.

It is true, indeed, that a monopoly, or any other cause which diminishes the usual supply of any particular class of commodities, has a much greater effect for a short period in enhancing the value of necessaries, than it could have in enhancing that of superfluities. If an unfavourable vintage were to raise the price of wine, the public having an option to diminish their consumption in some article or other, many would diminish it in wine; and thus the reduction in the supply would be accompanied by some reduction in the demand. But, if a bad harvest raised the price of corn, the people would be eager to part with superfluities and comforts rather than give up their usual quantity of this great necessary of life: the reduction in the supply would not be accompanied by any diminution in the competition, or demand; and consequently, the rise in the exchangeable value of corn would be much greater than that which a proportional falling off in the supply, could effect in that of wine. It is, however, abundantly evident, that no deficiency in the harvest could, for any length of time, so raise the price of corn, as to render a day's subsistence more valuable than the produce of a day's labour, or of a capital sufficient to put a day's labour in motion; because, as soon as this took place, the labourers, after parting with the superfluities they might have accumulated, must perish of want, and by consequence the demand for corn be diminished, until the value of a day's subsistence sunk below the value of a day's labour. Though, during a short period, monopolies may raise the value of necessaries more than they raise the value of superfluities, yet for a permanency it will be found that they can sustain the price of superfluities at an elevation far beyond that to which they can keep up the price of necessaries.

Having thus traced the principles which in

different circumstances determine exchangeable value, and noticed the chief exceptions to which these principles are liable, it will now be necessary to point out the distinction, as well as the relation, between exchangeable value and price.

The term, exchangeable value, expresses the power of purchasing with respect to commodities in general:—the term, price, denotes the same power with respect to some particular commodity, the quantity of which is given. Thus, when I speak of the exchangeable value of cotton as rising or falling, I imply, that it will purchase a greater or a less quantity of corn, and wine, and labour, and other marketable commodities: but when I talk of the price of cotton as rising or falling, I mean, that it will purchase a greater or less quantity of some one particular commodity, such as corn, or wine, or labour, or money, which is either expressed or understood. Exchangeable value may rise while price falls, or fall while price rises. For example, if cotton were, from any cause, to acquire twice its former power of purchasing with respect to commodities in general, while gold, the particular commodity in which the price of cotton is expressed, rose in a still higher ratio, and acquired four times its former power in the market; —then, though the exchangeable value of cotton would be doubled, its price would fall one half. Again; if cotton would purchase only half the former quantity of commodities in general, while it purchased twice the quantity of some particular commodity, such as corn, or wine, or labour, or money,—then its exchangeable value would have sunk one half, while its price, as expressed in corn, or wine, or labour, or money, became double. And again;—if cotton, and the particular commodity in which its price is expressed, should rise or fall in the same proportion with each other, then the exchangeable value of cotton, or its general power of purchasing, would fluctuate, while its price remained stationary.

Price, then, is the quantity of that particular thing or commodity which is given in order to procure another commodity. As the precious metals are the things which general consent has rendered the immediate instruments of effecting exchanges, the term, price, when employed singly and without qualification, is understood to imply the sum in the metals, or in the representatives of the metals, which must be given for the article we require. The qualified terms, corn price, labour price, &c. signify, of course, the quantity of corn or of labour which must be parted with, in order to obtain any given quantity of the commodity we want.

The price of things being that which is given in order to procure them, it follows, that there must be two kinds of price; namely, market price, and natural price. Market price, as the term sufficiently denotes, is that which we give in order to obtain any commodity by way of exchange in the market :—natural price, on the contrary, is that which we must give in order to obtain the article we want from the great warehouse of nature, and is the same thing as the cost of production.

Economists have contended, that natural and market price, notwithstanding occasional and temporary fluctuations, always tend to a common level, and are upon the average equivalent and equal. This is an error. Market price must always include the customary rate of profit for the time being, otherwise industry would be suspended; but natural price, consisting of the cost of production, or, in other words, of the capital expended in raising or fabricating commodities, cannot include the rate of profit. Hence, market, instead of equalizing itself with natural price, will exceed it by the customary rate of profit.

Those writers, indeed, who contend for the general equality of market and natural price, include the customary rate of profit under the term, natural price, or cost of production. But this classification is highly unphilosophical and incorrect. The profits of stock never make any part of the expense of production; they are, on the contrary, a new creation, brought into existence in consequence of this expense. The farmer, we will suppose, expends one hundred quarters of corn in cultivating his fields, and obtains in return one hundred and twenty quarters. In this case, twenty quarters, being the excess of produce above expenditure, constitute the farmer's profit; but it would be absurd to call this excess, or profit, a part of the expenditure. The expenditure, or cost of production, was one hundred quarters. It has been now repaid, with a surplus of twenty quarters; and unless the surplus which remains after expenditure is replaced, be a part of the expenditure; unless, in fact, one hundred and twenty quarters be equal to one hundred, it is impossible that market price should be equivalent to natural. Supposing that corn is 3*l.* per quarter, then, in the case we have stated, the natural price of the farmer's produce, or the hundred quarters expended upon production, will be equivalent to 300*l.*, while the produce of one hundred and twenty quarters obtained in return, will be equivalent to 360*l.* Thus, estimated in money, the natural price of the farmer's produce is equal to 300*l.*, while its market price is 360*l.* The excess of market above natural price, or cost of production, is profit; and to contend that this profit is included in the cost of production, is the same thing as contending that the hundred quarters, or 300*l.* laid out in cultivation, are equal to the one hundred and twenty quarters, or 360*l*. thereby obtained.

In manufacturing, as well as in agricultural industry, the profit of stock is distinct from the cost of production. The master manufacturer expends a certain quantity of raw material, of tools and implements of trade, and of subsistence for labour, and obtains in return a quantity of finished work. This finished work must possess a higher exchangeable value than the materials, tools, and subsistence, by the advance of which it was obtained; otherwise the master could have no inducement to continue his business. Manufacturing industry would cease, if the value produced did not exceed the value expended. But it is the excess of value which the finished work possesses above the value of the material, implements, and subsistence expended, that constitutes the master's profit; and therefore, we cannot assert that the profit of his stock is included in the cost of production, without affirming the gross absurdity, that the excess of value above the expenditure, constitutes a part of expenditure. Supposing that the materials, tools, and subsistence, cost 300*l.* and that the finished work is worth 360*l.*, then the difference will be the master's profit; and we cannot maintain that the amount of profit is included in the amount of expenditure, or cost of production, without urging the contradiction, that 300*l.* are equal to 360*l.*

The profit of stock, so far from forming any part of the cost of production, is a surplus remaining after this cost has been completely replaced. In carrying on their business, the farmer and manufacturer do not expend their profit;—they create it. It forms no part of their first advances; on the contrary, it constitutes a portion of their subsequent returns. It could not have been employed in carrying on the work of production, because, until this work was completed, it had no existence. It is essentially a surplus—a new creation—over and above all that is necessary to replace the cost of production, or, in other words, the capital advanced. It is hoped that enough has been said, to convince the reader of the nature of the error into which those economists fall, who maintain that the profit of stock is included in the expense of production, and that natural and market price tend to an equality. Market price is that which we give in order to obtain a commodity by exchange in the market; natural price is that which we give to effect a purchase at the great warehouse of nature: it consists of the several articles of capital employed in production, and cannot by possibility include the surplus or profit created during the process of production.

Things equal in natural price will also, upon the average, be equal in market price. After capitalists and labourers become distinct classes, the natural price of things, or the cost of production, consists of the capital employed in raising or fabricating them; and we have already seen that articles on which equal capitals have been expended, are of equal exchangeable value. But when articles are of equal exchangeable value, or have the same power of purchasing with respect to commodities in general, they will have the same power of purchasing with respect to any particular commodity; or will be of equal market price.

From what has been said respecting the nature and foundation of exchangeable value, and price, it follows, that they cannot admit of any accurate standard. A standard, by a reference to which we may ascertain the fluctuations in the exchangeable power of other things, must itself possess an exchangeable value fixed and unalterable. But there is nothing in existence which possesses such a quality. In the first place, exchangeable value is determined by the cost of production; and there is no commodity the cost of producing which is not liable to perpetual fluctuation. In the second place, even if a commodity could be found which always required the same expenditure for its production, it would not therefore be of invariable exchangeable value, so as to serve as a standard for measuring the value of other things. Exchangeable value is determined, not by the absolute, but by the relative cost of production. If the cost of producing gold remained the same, while the cost of producing all other things should be doubled, then would gold have a less power of purchasing all other things than before; or, in other words, its exchangeable value would fall one half; and this diminution in its exchangeable value would be precisely the same in effect, as if the cost of producing all other things remained unaltered, while that of producing gold had been reduced one half. In the very term, exchangeable value, a relative, and not an absolute quantity is implied. If gold should have a greater or a less power of purchasing all other things, then all other things would have a greater or a less power of purchasing gold. It is impossible to increase the exchangeable value of one set of commodities, without at the same time diminishing the exchangeable power of the other set of commodities with which the first is compared. If one half of the commodities of a country consisted of raw produce, and the other half of wrought goods; and if the one was equal in value to, and annually exchanged against the other ; then, if we were to double the exchangeable value of the raw produce, one half of it would acquire the power of purchasing the whole of the wrought goods : but this rise in the exchangeable value of the former would necessarily be accompanied by a corresponding fall in the exchangeable value of the latter; and it would require the whole of the wrought goods to purchase the half of the raw produce. To bestow upon any article an invariable exchangeable value, and thus qualify it to be a standard for measuring the exchangeable value of other things, it would be necessary that the cost of its production should not only remain the same, but that it should at all times bear the same proportion to the cost of. producing commodities in general.

Finding that no one of the products of labour possessed an invariable exchangeable value, economists have imagined that in labour itself they have discovered the standard which they sought. They have not, indeed, been very accurate in explaining whether their standard consists in the quantity of labour employed in producing commodities, or in the quantity of it which commodities will purchase in the market; but the ambiguity of their language is of little importance, since neither the one nor the other possesses the qualities of a criterion of value. We have already seen that the total quantity of labour expended on production is not the foundation of value in exchange; and that commodities obtained by equal quantities of labour, will seldom or ever be equivalent in the market. But even if the labour expended on production were the foundation of exchangeable value, it by no means follows, that it could be a standard for measuring exchangeable value. Nothing can be an accurate measure of value, except that which itself possesses an invariable value. But the exchangeable value of the labour expended on production is so far from being invariable, that it fluctuates with every change of time and place; and is liable to inequalities even at the same time and place. This also holds good with respect to the quantity of labour which commodities will purchase in the market; and it is quite in vain to urge, as Adam Smith has done, that when a given quantity of labour will purchase a greater or a less quantity of commodities than usual, it is the commodities, and not the labour, in which the variation in exchangeable value takes place. By Smith's own shewing, exchangeable value is nothing more than the power of purchasing; and therefore, as labour purchases a greater or less quantity of commodities in general, its exchangeable value is increased or diminished, and it becomes incapable of serving as a standard for measuring the value of other things.

Convinced that nothing actually in existence can serve as a standard of exchangeable value, economists have sometimes endeavoured to substitute an abstract or ideal one. In any given state of the market, the several commodities exposed for sale will bear a definite relation to each other in exchangeable value; as, for example, an ox may be worth four sheep, a sheep two lambs, and a lamb worth two fowls. Unit, therefore, may be taken as representing indifferently the whole value of a fowl, half the value of a lamb, a sixth of the value of a sheep, or the twenty-fourth of the value of an ox; and thus, not standing for the value contained in any particular article, but expressing the relation between the values of things in general, may serve as a standard for determining the variations in the worth of all. For example; if an ox were brought to market, of such superior size and fatness, that it exchanged for eight sheep, twenty-four lambs, and forty-eight fowls, then its value would be expressed by forty-eight units, instead of twenty-four. And if a supply of fowls were to be brought in, so inferior, that it required four to purchase a lamb, twelve to purchase a sheep, and forty-eight to purchase an ox; then the value of each fowl would be expressed by one half of the standard unit. Thus the variations in the value of the particular commodity from which the denomination might have been originally derived, would not be communicated to it; but, on the contrary, the denomination standing for determinate portions of the value of all the commodities usually brought to market, would continue to be the general representative of these, and therefore serve to mark the fluctuations even in that particular article from which it might have been originally borrowed. This very subtle and ingenious theory I may perhaps consider more fully on some future occasion. It is stated in this place, for the purpose of shewing that no abstract denomination, or standard unit, as it is called, can possibly serve as an invariable measure for ascertaining the fluctuations in exchangeable value. An abstract denomination, or ideal unit, cannot by possibility possess in itself any power of purchasing, or value in exchange; and therefore, when it is employed to measure value, it must be taken either as a particular sign representing the value contained in some one commodity, as in a given weight of silver; or, as a general sign representing indifferently portions of value, existing in the mass of commodities, as half the value of a lamb, or a sixth of the value of a sheep, or a twenty-fourth of the value of an ox. But if the denomination, or unit, represent the value of any individual commodity, its value will necessarily fluctuate with that of the individual commodity, and it will be unfit for a standard; and therefore the only question to be considered is, whether it can acquire the character of an invariable standard by representing some component part of the values contained in commodities in general.

Supposing, as before, that an ox is usually

worth four sheep, or twelve lambs, or twenty-four fowls; and that one unit represents the value of a fowl, two that of a lamb, six that of a sheep, and twenty-four that of an ox; and then, if the usual value of an ox were to be reduced one half, the unit, retaining its former relation to commodities in general, that is, continuing to represent the value of one fowl, or half that of a lamb, or a sixth of that of a sheep, would now represent a twelfth instead of a twenty-fourth of the value of an ox; and would thus shew correctly the degree in which the ox's exchangeable value, or power of purchasing commodities in general, had been diminished. But supposing that both oxen and sheep lost half their usual power of purchasing, as compared with lambs and fowls; and then the result would be materially different. For if the unit or denomination continued to represent the value of one fowl, or of half a lamb, it would acquire twice its former power of purchasing with respect to sheep and oxen; and if it continued to represent one-sixth of the value of a sheep, or one twenty-fourth of that of an ox, it would lose half its former power of purchasing with respect to fowls and lambs. The exchangeable value of commodities is in a perpetual state of fluctuation; and when one portion of the commodities in any market rises or falls with respect to the other, then the unit, or denomination, which represented, not the value of any one thing in particular, but certain portions of the values of things in general, must retain its former relation either to the class of commodities which has risen, or to the class which has fallen in value. But if it retains its former relation to the commodities which have a greater power of purchasing than before, its value rises; and if it retains this relation to the commodities which have lost a portion of their power in exchange, its value falls; and in either case it is deprived of the character of an uniform measure or standard.

Thus we find, not only that there is no actual and real standard, but that exchangeable value being always relative, and an increase or diminution in the power of purchasing possessed by one set of commodities, necessarily implying a corresponding diminution of the same power in some other quarter, we cannot, without involving ourselves in contradiction and absurdity, conceive the possibility of an abstract or ideal standard. As every marketable commodity which exists, or which can be supposed to exist, is perpetually varying in its power of effecting purchases, it is as impossible to discover a measure or standard of exchangeable value, as it would be to obtain a measure of length, or of weight, if every thing in nature were undergoing incessant changes in its dimensions and specific gravity. Lord Lauderdale has justly observed, in his work on Public Wealth, that the search of economists after a measure of exchangeable value, is just as irrational and as hopeless as was that of the alchemists in quest of the philosopher's stone. All we can do is to ascertain the circumstances which cause a given quantity of one thing to be offered and received for a given quantity of another.

CHAP. II.

ON THE INSTRUMENTS OF PRODUCTION, AND THE DIFFERENT KINDS OF INDUSTRY.

IN the language of political economy, the original acquisition of wealth is called production; and those things by means of which this acquisition is made, are termed instruments of production. Thus the land which supplies the primary materials of wealth, the labour by which these materials are appropriated, prepared, augmented, or transferred, and the capital that aids these several operations, are all instruments of production. I shall briefly explain the peculiar manner in which each contributes to the formation of wealth.

When we contemplate the world which we inhabit, we not only observe order and regularity in the succession of events, but discover a system of adaptation and harmony, and see one part of nature corresponding with, and answering to, another. The earth supplies, spontaneously, productions calculated to supply the wants and gratify the desires of the sensitive beings which dwell upon her surface. The surrounding atmosphere, the depths of the waters, the bowels of the earth, and, above all, the exterior soil, abound with materials adapted to our use. Hence, the air, the waters, and the earth, and even the physical laws which determine their combinations, may be considered as the primary instruments in the formation of wealth. To avoid unnecessary circumlocution, however, the natural agents which constitute the primary instruments of production are usually included under the term, land; because land is the most important of the class, and because the possession of it generally gives the command of all the others*. Throughout the subsequent dis-

---

* The proprietors of the soil are also the proprietors of the mines beneath its surface, and the right of fishing, even upon banks situated in the open seas, is generally admitted to belong to the possessors of the adjacent shores.

quisitions, therefore, the term, land, will be used in this extensive sense, as denoting all the natural sources from which the materials of wealth are originally derived; and when the territorial surface is alluded to as an instrument of production, and is to be distinguished from mines and fisheries, the term, soil, will be employed.

That land must always be a main instrument in the formation of wealth, will appear abundantly evident from the consideration that man, incapable of creating any thing, can do no more than appropriate, or in some way modify, the materials which nature has presented to his hand. Wealth is matter, under a particular form. The form we may give, but the creation of the matter is not only beyond our power, but above our comprehension; and without the natural agents, without land, or the things supplied by land, it would be impossible to advance a single step towards the acquisition of wealth. Land, therefore, including under the term, mines and fisheries, must always be regarded as the primary instrument of production.

The next great instrument of production is
labour. We have already shewn that wealth
consists in those useful things which it requires
some portion of voluntary exertion to obtain;
and that such productions of nature as air, heat,
and light, even though we should regard them
as constituting natural opulence, yet, as they
come not within the scope of that science which
has for its objects the laws and principles according to which men acquire and distribute the
things which supply their wants and gratify
their desires, cannot be denominated wealth in
the sense in which that term is employed by the
political economist. With the economist, riches
are always more or less an artificial acquisition,
requiring for their formation that some portion
of human exertion should second the agency of
nature. From the essential character of wealth,
therefore, as defined in the preceding chapter, it
necessarily follows, that labour must always be
one of the instruments by which it is produced.

Capital, which has been already shewn to consist of those parts of wealth which are destined
not for the immediate supplying of our wants,

but for aiding in the acquisition of other articles of utility, is always a powerful, and in most cases an indispensable instrument of production. The employing of capital seems peculiar to the human species. Nature has furnished the several tribes of inferior animals with instruments by means of which they procure food, and perform whatever labour may be necessary to their well-being: man she sends into the world naked and unarmed; but has compensated those deficiencies by the gift of that reason, or that instinct, which, even in his rudest state, suggests the use of implements of toil, and weapons of offence. It is a mistake to suppose that the employment of capital is confined to advanced and cultivated periods of society. The most uninstructed savage avails himself of some rude instrument to abridge his labour, or to perform that which the unaided human arm would be incapable of performing. In the first stone which he flings at the wild animal he pursues, in the first stick that he seizes to strike down the fruit which hangs above his reach, we see the appropriation of one article for the purpose of aiding in the acquisition of another, and thus discover the origin of capital. As society advances, the employment of this instrument of production, the origin of which may be traced to the earliest and rudest periods, is pushed to an astonishing extent, and improvements are perpetually taking place in all kinds of implements and machinery, until, in the application of wind, water, and steam, in our mechanical operations, we press the powers of nature into our service, and, in the literal sense of the terms, " arm us with the force of all the " elements."

The employment of the several instruments of production, or of land, labour, and capital, for the procuring of wealth, is denominated industry. In the strictness of economical language, therefore, there is a distinction between the import of the terms, production, and industry: the former signifying the formation of wealth; and the latter the means employed in order to effect such formation. It would be contradictory and absurd to say, unproductive production; but no impropriety is involved in the expression unproductive industry. When a farmer does not obtain from his fields so great a quantity of produce as he expended on their cultivation; his industry is obviously unproductive; that is, the means he employed to effect the formation of wealth or production have failed, and the projected increase in the quantity of useful articles has not taken place.

As land, labour, and capital, may be employed in a great variety of ways, industry, or the application of these instruments of production to the formation of wealth, must be of many different kinds. All the different kinds of industry may, however, be classed under four general heads; namely, appropriative industry, or that which is applied to the mere collecting or appropriation of the things which nature spontaneously supplies; manufacturing industry, or that which is exerted for the purpose of adapting the productions of nature to our use; agricultural industry, or that which is directed to second the operations of nature, so as to increase the quantity of her useful productions; and commercial industry, or that which is employed to transport and to exchange the articles of wealth acquired by the three former means.

Some political economists class all the different kinds of industry under three general heads only; comprising under the term, agriculture, every application of the instruments of production which has for its object the attaining of raw material, whether it be the spontaneous gift of nature, or the result of cultivation. This classification seems evidently erroneous. In the first place, it appears to be a very violent, as well as a very unnecessary departure from established usage, to give the name of agriculture to the occupations carried on by the huntsman in the North American forests, and by the fisherman upon the banks of Newfoundland. In the next place, appropriating the productions of the earth is the first, and augmenting their quantity the last, attainment of human industry; and, it is evident that the order of nature, when there is no good reason for departing from it, should be conformed to in our arrangements.

But, in the present case, no good reason can be assigned. Applying the instruments of production to appropriate the spontaneous gifts of nature, is a species of industry generically different from that which augments their quantity by cultivating the soil; and, as will subsequently appear, there are several facts of the highest importance in economical science which may be predicated of the former, but which cannot be predicated of the latter.

From these considerations I have been induced to arrange the several kinds of industry under four general heads, which I shall now proceed to consider in the order in which they have been enumerated.

CHAP. III.

APPROPRIATIVE INDUSTRY.

THE spontaneous productions of nature distribute themselves into two great classes—the one consisting of things, such as air and daylight, which it requires no voluntary effort to obtain; the other comprising articles, such as the flesh of wild animals, which cannot be procured without some portion of exertion. Now, from the simple classification of these different kinds of natural productions, it is self-evident, that the latter are the only objects to the appropriation of which the instruments of production can be applied. If a man were thrown naked and destitute upon an uninhabited shore, as his eye opened, the light would enter; as his chest expanded, the air would rush in: but these involuntary movements could not be considered as exertions of industry. When, however, he approached a tree and gathered its fruits, or removed the earth in quest of nutricious roots, the application of his labour to appropriate these things would be an act of industry; and the things themselves would be the products of industry, and would consequently acquire the character of wealth.

The appropriation of spontaneous productions must obviously have been the first species of industry exercised by man. It is the origin and foundation of all the others. Nothing can be prepared for consumption, or applied in any way to minister to our wants, until it has been previously drawn from the original warehouse of nature. Manufactures, agriculture, and commerce, never could have existed, if we had not previously appropriated the materials and implements by which they are respectively carried on.

In appropriating the spontaneous productions of nature, the labour of man could not, for some little time at least, have received any aid from the employment of capital. To refer to our former illustration, a person cast naked upon an uninhabited coast, must appropriate the articles which may serve as capital before he can use them. Whatever his previously acquired skill in the application of capital might be, his first efforts, upon being thrown into this new situation, must necessarily be performed by the labour of his unaided arm. Now, if this must be the case even with a person previously acquainted with the use of capital, it must be still more emphatically so with respect to uninstructed savages at the origin of society. Appetite and instinct would in the first instance prompt them to employ the immediate and most direct means of supplying their wants; and they would seize the fruit within their reach, and spring upon inferior prey, before they provided implements with which to draw down the loftier branches, or overcome the larger animals.

But though the labour of the naked hand must necessarily have preceded the employment of capital, yet the latter could not fail to have been very early suggested. Even in the most savage countries, man has never yet been found in a state of such perfect ignorance as to be unacquainted with the use of capital. The wretched native of New Holland has his spear, his fish-gig, and his canoe, for the purpose of abridging his labour,—of performing operations of which he would be otherwise incapable, and appropriating productions of nature, which, but for the aid of those rude implements, would for ever have remained beyond his reach.

The application of the instruments of production for the purpose of appropriating the spontaneous gifts of nature, constitutes the principal, and, with a few exceptions to be hereafter mentioned, the only species of industry exercised in the rude and early period of society which is denominated the hunting or savage state. This species of industry, however, continues to be carried on throughout all the subsequent stages of improvement and civilization, though in advanced periods it furnishes a comparatively trifling proportion of our wealth. The chase, instead of being, as in the savage state, a principal source of subsistence, is almost exclusively resorted to as a means of amusement and recrea-

tion; and the application of labour and capital
to the appropriation of nature's spontaneous
gifts (the branch of industry by which man was
originally supplied with the whole of his possessions) is principally directed to the occupations
of fishing and of mining. These are, no doubt,
of considerable importance. The former enlarges
the means of subsistence; and the latter, in supplying us with the metals, and particularly with
iron, furnishes the most powerful instruments
for future production.

The productiveness of appropriative industry,
or, in other words, the quantity of the spontaneous gifts of nature which in any community
can be rendered serviceable to man, will be determined by three several circumstances; namely,
the fertility of the land (including under the
term mines and fisheries), the quantity of labour
employed, and the degree in which this labour
is aided by capital. Of these three circumstances, the fertility of the land, or abundance
of spontaneous gifts, may frequently be found
the least important. The productions of nature
possess no utility for man until he has rendered

them his own. The ungathered fruits of the earth, and the beasts of the chase roaming at large in the forest, constitute no portion of wealth. The circumstance of nature's having abundantly bestowed the materials for supplying our wants would have been of no consequence whatever, unless we had possessed the skill to apply our labour to the appropriation of her gifts. Nor, in appropriating spontaneous productions, is the quantity of labour so important, as the degree in which it is aided by capital. Without this instrument of production our supply of spontaneous produce would be miserably deficient; and however lavishly nature might spread abroad her gifts, and with whatever energy and perseverance we might labour to appropriate them, the fruits of the forest, with a few of the more helpless animals which inhabit it, would constitute our only wealth. It is by the employment of capital alone that man is enabled to subdue the earth. Ten men, abundantly supplied with capital, and skilful in the use of it, would be able to appropriate a greater quantity of fish, and of useful mineral productions, than could be appropriated by ten thousand whose only instrument of production was the labour of their hands. Indeed, without the aid of capital, the tenants of the deep, and the treasures of the mine, would remain for ever inaccessible to man. But, on the contrary, when capital accumulates, and improvements are effected in the various implements and machines in which it mainly consists, the effective powers of appropriative industry may go on perpetually increasing until the bounty of nature fails, and forests, fisheries, and mines, begin to be exhausted.

In stating the effect which improvements in implements and machines have in heightening the powers of appropriative industry, we necessarily imply that the instruments of production have been previously directed, not only to appropriate the materials of which such machines and implements are composed, but also to form and construct them. This naturally conducts us to the consideration of manufacturing industry, while it shews us how invariably one branch of industry is connected with, and runs into another. It seems strange that a fact so obvious and so important should not have been more attended to by the economists, and have guarded them against the vain and subtle paradoxes by which they attempted to shew, that one application of labour and capital is productive, while other applications of them are unproductive of wealth. In the great work of production, the exertion of each branch of industry heightens the powers of all. This important principle will be developed more at large hereafter. At present we must proceed to that application of the instruments of production which prepares raw material for our use.

CHAP. IV.

MANUFACTURING INDUSTRY.

SOME of the spontaneous productions of nature, such as fruits and the flesh of certain animals, may be used the instant they are appropriated; while others, such as flax and iron, require considerable preparation before they can supply our wants or gratify our desires. Now, the industry which fits this latter class of productions for consumption, is evidently a source of wealth. Out of materials which would otherwise possess no utility, it forms articles useful and desirable to man; and the definition of wealth is, that it consists of such articles so obtained.

The industry which prepares, is necessarily in the order of time secondary to that which appropriates the gifts of nature. But though man must originally have lived by merely availing himself of nature's spontaneous gifts; yet the very first, or at most, the very second step towards knowledge and improvement must have led him to the attempt of superadding to these gifts some rude species of preparation. As no society of men has ever been discovered in so low a state of barbarism as to be unable in some degree to aid their labour by the employment of capital, so none has ever been found in which the spontaneous gifts of nature did not receive some species of preparation. After the savage had become accustomed to seize sticks and stones to aid him in the chase, it could not fail to suggest itself to him, that the sharp edge of his stone might serve to remove the skin from his prey, or to point the stick with which he armed himself. Thus capital would be employed not only to appropriate, but also to prepare the productions of nature; and thus we see that the origin of manufacturing industry, though not exactly contemporary with, must yet have been immediately subsequent to, appropriative industry.

Though manufacturing industry is secondary to appropriative, with respect to the order of

time, yet it is by no means so with respect to
its importance as a source of wealth. Almost
the whole of the productions of nature are presented to us in a raw or rude state; and if it
were not for the application of labour and capital to the preparing and forming of them, would
be absolutely without utility. Without manufacturing or adaptive industry, therefore, our
wealth would be necessarily limited to that
scanty supply of necessaries which nature presents in a state fit for immediate consumption.
Man would be reduced to a more destitute and
helpless state than that in which he has ever
yet been found, even in the most barbarous and
savage countries. He would possess no species
of clothing whatever; his only shelter from the
rigours of the climate would be the hollows of
trees, and the caverns of the earth; and his only
food would be fruits, roots, and the flesh of such
of the smaller animals as he might, in his naked
and helpless state, be able to outrun and overcome. Indeed, with respect to the supply of
his wants, he would be placed far below the
condition of the inferior animals; for these are

clothed by the hand of nature, and are furnished with implements of admirable construction for the performance of every function necessary for their well being.

Another consideration calculated to impress us with the great importance of manufacturing industry is, that without its co-operation, no other branch of industry can be effectually carried on. To fell the forest, to pierce the mine, and to traverse the waters, we must have the aid of appropriate implements and machines; and these can be supplied only by manufacturing industry. This application of the instruments of production not only gives utility to articles which could not otherwise possess it, but also furnishes us with the power of appropriating useful materials which, without its co-operation, would be for ever inaccessible. If we would form a just estimate of the importance of manufacturing industry, we must not confine our view to its direct and simple operation of preparing rude produce for immediate consumption, but must also take into consideration its complex and secondary operation in supplying the implements of trade to all the other branches of industry. We have already seen that the manufacturer not only prepares, but also co-operates in appropriating, the spontaneous productions of nature; and in the two subsequent chapters we shall perceive in what manner he assists in cultivating the earth, and navigating the waters.

In the preceding chapter, we saw that the operation of appropriating spontaneous productions might, in some imperfect manner, and to a very limited extent, be carried on without the aid of capital. This could not be the case with respect to manufactures. The idea of manufacturing industry implies that there is material to be wrought upon. Now, this material, without which it is impossible that manufacturing industry can operate, is capital, or wealth destined, not for the immediate supply of our wants, but for the reproduction of wealth under another form.

Thus the very subject on which manufacturing industry operates, is one of the component parts of manufacturing capital. Farther, as it is necessary that a man should have food to support him while at work, the subsistence which enables the manufacturer to prepare the raw material may be considered as destined for the reproduction of other wealth, and therefore, as constituting another portion of manufacturing capital. Nor can this be deemed in any way a forced and unwarrantable extension of the meaning of the term, capital, when we consider that in the great majority of cases the capitalist is a distinct person from the labourer, and advances him his subsistence, no less than the raw material, for the express purpose of obtaining a reproductive return; or, in other words, of having it reproduced to him under another form. All the tools and machinery which the workman employs in preparing rude produce, are obviously portions of capital, whether advanced by the capitalist or not. Indeed, the workman, if these things are his own property, is, in strictness of language, to that extent a capitalist. Manufacturing capital, therefore, consists of three distinct portions; material, subsistence, and implements; including under the term all kinds of tools and machinery employed in working up materials.

The effective powers of manufacturing industry depend much more upon the skilful use of capital, than on the quantity of direct labour which may be employed. The hand of man is not armed with any efficient natural instrument, such as the beak of the bird, or the claw of the quadruped, for operating directly upon the materials presented to him; but it is admirably adapted for seizing and applying artificial implements, and for employing the powers of one substance to produce the desired changes in another. Hence almost all the grand results of manufacturing industry are brought about by means of capital. Throughout the world there are no very striking inequalities in the muscular force by which direct labour is performed; and it is mainly owing to the differences in the quantity of capital, and in the skill with which it is applied, that in one country man is found naked and destitute, and that in another all the rude productions of the earth, and all the forces of nature, are made to contribute to his comfort, and to augment his power.

During the progress of improvement, and

while capital continues to accumulate, and the number of labourers to increase, no limits can be assigned to the powers of manufacturing industry. The quantity of wrought goods which it required a hundred men to prepare in a rude, may be wrought by ten men in an advanced period of society. This arises from a two-fold cause. In the first place, as men acquire experience and knowledge they are perpetually inventing improved machinery for the abridgment of labour; and, in the second place, as capital accumulates, the work to be done is divided and subdivided, until each individual acquires in his peculiar branch of the business a dexterity and skill unattainable in those small establishments where several operations must be performed by the same hand. The first cause which we have assigned for the progressive increase in the powers of manufacturing industry is sufficiently obvious, and requires no farther illustration :— the latter will come again under discussion when we treat of mercantile industry, and of the divisions of employment to which it gives occasion.

After the view of the subject which has been

here presented, it must excite considerable surprise that manufacturing industry should ever
have been represented as barren and unproductive, and incapable of effecting any addition to
wealth. Yet this was one of the leading doctrines of the sect of philosophers in France,
commonly known by the name of "the Econo-
" mists." Their pretended demonstrations were
founded on the supposition that manufacturers
consume while at work a quantity of subsistence
equal in value to the value which they add to
the raw material. But this supposition, even if
it had been conformable to fact, could not have
established the doctrines of the Economists.
Value is not wealth. Though it should be
granted that the manufacturer consumed while
at work, a value equal to that which he added
to his material, yet it would by no means follow,
that he made no addition to the mass of useful
commodities. Though the exchangeable value
of a plough should not exceed that of the materials and subsistence consumed in its fabrication,
yet the industry which gave existence to this
powerful instrument of reproduction would be a

most important source of wealth. But the effect of manufactures in heightening the powers of agricultural industry falls more naturally within the scope of the succeeding chapter. At present we shall confine ourselves to the examination of the hypothesis, that the manufacturer does no more than add to the raw material the value of the subsistence which he consumes while at work.

The manner, and according to the different stages of improvement, the degree, in which manufacturing industry adds to the value of the material supplied by the other branches of industry, have not, as far as I recollect, been attended to by any preceding writer. This deficiency we shall now endeavour to supply; and the topics to be discussed will be found both novel and important. A right understanding of the principle which determines the difference between the value of produce when in a raw, and when in a manufactured state, is useful not only as a means of overthrowing the pretended demonstrations of the French Economists, but as furnishing the only satisfactory solution to some very nice and momentous questions with respect both' to the production and the distribution of wealth.

From the perpetually operating law of competition, the results obtained by the employment of equal capitals will be of equal exchangeable value. Let us suppose, for the sake of illustration, that no rent being as yet paid for the use of land, a farmer's capital consists of food for three hundred labourers, together with seed and other things necessary to cultivation, equal in value to food for three hundred more ; and that his produce is food for six hundred, with six thousand pounds of flax, which, being raised at the same expense, is equal in value to subsistence for six hundred; and let us suppose farther, that a manufacturer's capital consists of food for three hundred, with three thousand pounds of flax, equal in value to food for three hundred more, and that his product is this quantity of flax converted into linen cloth. In this case, the farmer and manufacturer will have expended equal capitals, and therefore their respective products will be of equal exchangeable value;

that is, three thousand pounds of manufactured flax, the product of the manufacturer's capital, will be equivalent to food for six hundred, with six thousand pounds of raw flax, the product of the farmer's equal capital. But the linen cloth which is thus of equal value with a quantity of agricultural produce, consisting of six thousand pounds of unwrought flax, with food for six hundred labourers, was produced from three thousand pounds of flax, with food for three hundred; and consequently, while the power of production continues at this high rate, manufacturing industry will double the value of raw produce, including food, and the material upon which it is employed.

Let us now vary our supposition.—Let us assume that the productive powers of agriculture are so far reduced, that the farmer's capital, consisting, as before, of food for three hundred labourers, with other things necessary to cultivation, equal in value to food for three hundred, is capable of raising no more than food for four hundred and fifty, with four thousand five hundred pounds of flax, equal in value to food for four hundred and fifty; while, in consequence of the powers of manufacturing industry remaining unaltered, food for three hundred labourers continues to be sufficient for the working up of three thousand pounds of flax. In this case, the wrought goods, as compared with agricultural produce, would fall in exchangeable power, and manufacturing industry, instead of doubling, would add only one half, or fifty per cent. to the value of the food and the material on which it was employed. The linen cloth produced by a capital consisting of food for three hundred, with three thousand pounds of flax, would be equivalent to the agricultural produce raised by a similar capital. But a similar capital employed in agriculture raises, by our supposition, food for four hundred and fifty, with four thousand five hundred pounds of raw flax; and consequently the linen cloth manufactured from three thousand pounds of flax, with food for three hundred, would be equivalent to four thousand five hundred pounds of flax, together with food for four hundred and fifty.

In proportion as it requires a greater quantity

of capital to raise the same quantity of agricultural produce, the exchangeable value of this produce will rise; or, in other words, the exchangeable value of wrought goods, as compared with produce, will fall. And even if the effective powers of appropriative and agricultural industry were to sustain no diminution, still, in the progress of wealth and population, the exchangeable value of wrought goods, as compared with raw produce, would gradually fall. As capital accumulates, and as labourers multiply, improvements take place in the application of machinery, and in the divisions of employment, and enable a smaller number of hands to work up the same quantity of material. Supposing that in the progress of wealth one hundred and fifty labourers can work up the three thousand pounds of flax, originally wrought up by three hundred; then, though the expense of raising agricultural produce had in no way increased, the exchangeable value of the manufactured article would fall in relation to the material form in which it was prepared. We have just seen, that when an expenditure of

food for three hundred, with other things equivalent thereto, raised food for six hundred, with
six thousand pounds of flax, equal in value to
food for six hundred; then the expending in
manufacturing industry three thousand pounds
of flax (equivalent, by the supposition, to food
for three hundred), with food for three hundred
persons, employed in working up this material,
would give a quantity of linen equivalent to six
thousand pounds of flax, with food for six
hundred. But as food for six hundred is, by
the supposition, worth six thousand pounds of
raw flax, the wrought article, which is worth
food for six hundred, with six thousand pounds
of raw flax, will be equivalent to twelve thousand pounds of raw flax. When, however, this
three thousand pounds of flax can be wrought
up by one hundred and fifty, the linen obtained
from it can be no longer worth so great a quantity of material. In working up the three
thousand pounds of flax, food for one hundred
and fifty, instead of for three hundred, is expended; and as food constituted a moiety of
the capital employed, diminishing it one half,

reduces the whole capital one fourth; and consequently the value of the linen cloth will fall one
fourth, with respect to every article of which
the cost of production remains unabated. But,
by the supposition, the cost of obtaining raw
material remains as before, and therefore three
thousand pounds of flax, in a manufactured
state, which formerly was worth twelve thousand
pounds of raw flax, will now be worth no more
than nine hundred pounds.

Though every improvement in manufacturing
industry, which enables material to be wrought
up with the expenditure of a less quantity of
subsistence, must, in this manner, reduce the
exchangeable value of manufactured goods, as
compared with the fruits of the soil; yet we
must not conclude that the additional exchangeable value which material acquires in the hands
of the manufacturer, arises solely from the
amount of subsistence which he consumes while
at work. Supposing that machinery could be
obtained for nothing, and were of such extreme
excellence, that without labour, or expenditure
for the maintenance of labour, it wrought up

raw material in a period just equal to that in which such material could be grown; yet still, even in this last conceivable degree of manufacturing improvement, the manufactured article would acquire a higher exchangeable value than that possessed by the material from which it had been prepared. The results of equal capitals are equivalent. If an agricultural capital worth three hundred pounds of flax, could, in any given time, raise six hundred pounds, then three hundred pounds of flax, wrought up in the same space of time, by a machine which required no labour, and which cost nothing, would be worth six hundred pounds of raw flax. But if no such machine could be obtained, and if the material could not be prepared without the expenditure of a quantity of subsistence equivalent to itself; then the three hundred pounds of flax, in a wrought state, being the product of a double manufacturing capital, would be equal in value to the product of a double agricultural capital; that is, supposing the powers of agricultural industry to remain as before, would be worth one thousand two hundred pounds, instead of six hundred pounds of flax in a raw state.

These illustrations, it is hoped, are sufficient to shew in what manner, and, under different circumstances, in what degree, wrought goods acquire a higher value than the material from which they were obtained. The exchangeable value of commodities is in proportion to the quantity of capital requisite to bring them to market. Manufacturing capital consists in material, machinery, and subsistence; and any improvement in manufacturing skill which reduces the cost of machinery, or diminishes the number of workmen to whom subsistence must be advanced, lowers the difference between the amount of the capitals which raise, and which fabricate materials; and consequently brings the exchangeable value of wrought goods nearer to that of the materials from which they were made. But material must always enter into manufacturing capital, and must likewise always exceed in exchangeable value the agricultural capital which raised it; otherwise cultivation would cease. If, however, material always exceed in exchangeable value, the agricultural capital which produced it, the manufacturing capital into which the material enters must also exceed this agricultural capital in exchangeable value; and thus the wrought article, being the product of the larger capital, must, even could the expense of workmen be reduced to nothing, possess a larger exchangeable value than that which it possessed under the form of raw material.

The improvements in manufacturing industry which, by enabling a smaller number of hands to perform the same quantity of work, cause a less expenditure of subsistence, in fabricating the raw material, will lower the exchangeable value of the several kinds of wrought goods in very different proportions. Supposing that improvements in manufacturing skill enable fifty hands to do the work formerly effected by one hundred; then, in those branches of business in which the subsistence paid to labourers had constituted half the capital employed, wrought goods would fall one fourth;—in those branches in which subsistence may form two thirds of the whole capital, they would fall one third;—and in those in which it formed one third, they would fall one sixth, as compared with raw produce. These proportions would, indeed, be liable to some modifications, if, while the improvements took place in manufactures, any alteration took place in the amount of capital necessary to bring raw produce to market; and, in fact, it is always found, that increasing wealth and population, while they diminish the expense of working up material, have a tendency to augment the cost of raising it; so that in the progress of society, the value of wrought goods, as compared with agricultural produce, is diminished by a two-fold cause. But to explain the effect which increasing wealth and populations have on the cost of raising agricultural produce, belongs to the succeeding chapter.

CHAP. V.

AGRICULTURAL INDUSTRY.

W E give the term, agriculture, or agricultural industry, to those applications of the instruments of production, the object of which is to augment or to improve the useful products of the soil. The denomination includes pasturage, as well as tillage;—embraces the operations which multiply the articles of utility derived from the animal, no less than those which multiply the articles of utility derived from the vegetable kingdom.

One of the earliest observations which could have forced itself upon the mind of the uninstructed savage, must have been, that the flesh of the animals he hunted down became in a little time unfit for use. The knowledge of this fact, when he chanced to overtake a young or wounded animal, which was not required for his immediate sustenance, would naturally suggest the expediency of preserving it alive, in order to render it subservient to the supplying of his future wants. The animals thus preserved, particularly if they were of the less ferocious tribes, would gradually become reconciled to the hand which fed them, and be domesticated with man; while, protected from beasts of prey, and, as their food began to fail in one part of the forest, conducted to regions which afforded a fresh supply, their numbers would increase more rapidly than if they had continued wild and unsubjugated. Thus, in consequence of the transition from the occupations of the hunter to those of the shepherd, and of raising domestic animals instead of pursuing wild ones, the supply of subsistence would be rendered more abundant, and less precarious, and an important accession of wealth would be obtained.

Again;—man could not have looked with any considerable degree of attention upon the events which were taking place around him, without observing, that when shed upon the soil, the seeds of the vegetable tribes do not perish there, but spring up in their season, and yield a perennial supply of food, either for himself or for some of the inferior animals. Now, when this observation had become familiar, and when the peculiar situations in which the most useful plants were seen to flourish, had been distinguished, some savage, more intelligent than the rest of his tribe, would be led by a short and obvious train of thought, to imitate the process which he saw nature perpetually performing, and to deposit her seeds in the earth, for the purpose of obtaining a future increase. Here, then, we discover the origin of tillage. Man, in the course of that progressive improvement, the capacity for which seems to form the most remarkable feature of his character, first begins to domesticate and breed up the inferior animals for his use; and then to multiply those vegetable productions which are in any way calculated to supply his wants or gratify his desires.

Upon the vast importance of agriculture as a source of wealth, it is unnecessary to enlarge.

Indeed, when we compare the quantity of food and of useful materials which is obtained from a given surface in England or in France, with that which is procured from the same extent of surface in those naturally fertile districts of America which continue to be inhabited by nations of hunters, the effective powers of agricultural industry appear almost miraculous; and our surprise will somewhat abate that, in the infancy of economical science, philosophers should have been arrested in their inquiries by the striking phenomena which it exhibits, and should have concluded that the only productive labour is that which is employed upon the soil.

Though it is hoped that, in the preceding chapter, where we treated of appropriative and manufacturing industry, sufficient may have been said to overthrow the agricultural theory of the French Economists, and to shew that their principal conclusion rests on a narrow and partial induction from the phenomena attending the formation of wealth; yet, as their opinions still find occasional supporters, and have been asserted by the French translator of the Wealth of Nations, to be demonstratively true, it may be proper to trace the precise limits of agricultural industry, and to shew in what circumstances wealth may be created without its aid.

It is obvious that long before we learn the art of applying our labour so as to augment the productions of nature, the industry which appropriates and prepares her spontaneous gifts may furnish us with articles adapted to supply our wants. Let us suppose the existence of a country circumstanced in some respects like the islands in the Pacific Ocean, and in which the forests should consist of the bread fruit, the waters should abound with fish, and the flax plant grow wild as in New Zealand. Now, is it not evident that in this country the industry employed to appropriate and prepare the materials presented by nature, might supply all our wants, and gratify many of our desires? Food, clothing, habitation, furniture, nay, many of the embellishments and luxuries of life, might exist in very considerable abundance, though both pasturage and tillage were wholly unknown.

Nor would the doctrine of the French Economists be tenable, though the term, agriculture, should, after the example of M. Say and others, be made to denote not only pasturage and tillage, but every application of labour by which food and material can be obtained. Even when we employ the term in this extended, and, as I conceive, erroneous sense, it is not true that agriculture is the only source of wealth. For, in the first place, were it not for manufacturing industry, almost the whole of the raw material which the other applications of labour procure, would be without utility, and consequently could not constitute any portion of our wealth. The greater part of the productions of nature, whether spontaneous or otherwise, are, in the first instance, presented in a state unfit for consumption. It is not agricultural industry, even in the most extended application of that term, which bestows the form and character of wealth on such things as timber, flax, and the several metallic ores. Without the industry which fits these articles for use, the industry which originally draws them from the great warehouse of nature would be totally barren and unproductive.

It is true, that there can be no wealth without the industry which appropriates food and materials; but it is also true, that without the industry which adapts materials to our use, there can be no wealth beyond that scanty supply of fruits, herbs, and animals, which nature presents in a state fit for immediate consumption.

In the second place, even though we should admit that raw produce exclusively constitutes wealth, yet it would by no means follow that agricultural industry should be exclusively productive of it; and for the plain and obvious reason, that agricultural industry, even in the most extended sense in which that term has ever been used, is not the exclusive means by which such produce is procured. The labour of the manufacturer who fabricates the plough, is as efficacious in producing corn, as the labour of the husbandman by whom the plough is guided. There is scarcely a single article of wealth, in the production of which several different branches of industry have not concurred. We saw, in the last chapter, that without the aid of the manufacturer who prepares implements and machinery, all the spontaneous productions of nature, except fruits, roots, and a few of the more helpless animals, would have remained for ever beyond our reach; and it is equally evident, that without the aid of the instruments of production furnished by manufacturing industry, no progress could ever have been made in clearing and cultivating the soil, and thereby multiplying its useful productions. Much of the error involved in the agricultural theory of the French Economists had its origin in their indulging in arbitrary abstractions, and in their failing to remember, that though the several kinds of industry may be separated in our classifications and reasonings, they must be united in the business of production. Even upon the principles of the Economists themselves, improvements in manufactures augment the wealth of a nation; because, as we shall see in the subsequent paragraphs, they enable a given quantity of labour to extract a greater quantity of produce from the soil.

In the last chapter we perceived, that there

are no natural limits set to the effective powers
of manufacturing industry; but that, on the contrary, an increase in the quantity of labour and
capital applied, leads to the use of improved
machinery, and to a more perfect subdivision of
employment, and thus enables a given number
of workmen to produce a greater quantity of
goods. Now it is important to remark, that the
reverse of this takes place with respect to agricultural industry; and that upon every increased
quantity of labour and capital applied to the
soil, we obtain a less proportional return. This
singular and important fact it will be necessary
to illustrate.

It is self-evident that, as we extend cultivation over inferior soils, the application of any
given quantity of labour and capital will yield a
less and less quantity of produce. If a hundred
workmen, with a proportional supply of seed
and of instruments of husbandry, can raise four
hundred quarters of wheat from a given quantity of land of the first quality, it is obvious that
the same quantity of labour and capital applied
to equal portions of land of second, third and

fourth rate quality, could not raise four hundred quarters of this grain, but would produce some smaller and successively diminishing quantity of it; say three hundred and fifty, three hundred, and two hundred and fifty quarters. It is also evident, that as successive applications of given portions of labour and capital to inferior soils yield a successively decreasing produce, the ultimate limits of cultivation must be at length attained. Supposing that our hundred labourers consumed one hundred quarters of wheat while working upon the soil, and that it required one hundred quarters more to supply them with seed, and to subsist them while they prepared their clothes and agricultural implements; then, on the cultivation of a piece of ground sufficient to occupy one hundred labourers, a capital consisting of two hundred quarters of corn must be expended; and if the soil is of so inferior a quality as to be incapable of yielding two hundred quarters, it is impossible that this ground should continue to be tilled. The cultivators, not having their seed and subsistence replaced to them, must remove to a more fertile district, or perish of want. Nor could any possible rise in the price of agricultural produce prevent this result, and keep under tillage districts incapable of replacing the seed and subsistence expended. For it is only that portion of the agricultural produce which exceeds the seed and subsistence required in cultivation, that can be brought to market; and when there is no excess of this nature, then the farmer can derive no advantage from elevated prices.

That which takes place with respect to the successive cultivation of inferior soils, will be found to take place also with respect to the successive applications of additional labour and capital to superior soils. If one hundred labourers, with a proportional capital, consisting of seed, subsistence, and implements, can raise from a given extent of ground of first-rate quality a supply of subsistence and materials for four hundred persons; then, doubling the labour and capital employed upon this piece of ground would not lead to a doubling of the produce; and two hundred workmen with the proportional supply of subsistence, seed and implements, could not raise from it subsistence for eight hundred. On the contrary, instead of the quantity of produce being increased in the same ratio with the labour and capital, and of two hundred workmen being able to raise subsistence for eight hundred, three hundred for one thousand two hundred, and four hundred for one thousand six hundred; the ratio in which the produce of this given extent of soil could be increased, would diminish inversely with each additional quantity of labour and capital employed: and while one hundred labourers raised subsistence for four hundred, two hundred might be able to raise subsistence for no more than seven hundred; three hundred only for nine hundred; and four hundred only for one thousand. While in this manner each successive addition to the labour employed, effected a less proportional addition to the produce raised, we should speedily arrive at the point beyond which any farther application of labour could not add to the produce already extracted a sufficient quantity of subsistence for the workmen by whom it should be performed. Here it is evident that improvement must be arrested.

If I expend five hundred quarters of wheat in cultivating a farm of any given extent, and if I obtain a produce of six hundred quarters of wheat, then my profit will be twenty per cent. ; but if I employ six hundred quarters instead of five hundred, and in consequence raise six hundred and ninety, where I before raised six hundred, then it is self-evident, that the ninety quarters added to my produce, will be less than the additional capital expended in obtaining them ; and that I must speedily abandon such forced and ruinous improvements. No possible rise in the price of corn could render them beneficial. For, unless the quantity of subsistence which is raised, exceeds the quantity which is expended in raising it, there is no surplus to bring to market, and no price is available.

The principle, that each additional application of labour and capital to the improvement of land, effects a diminished proportional increase, is supported by the direct evidence of facts. When small capitals are laid out upon the soil, and cultivation is conducted in an unexpensive manner, the land proprietor, without trenching upon the farmer's reasonable profits, often receives half the produce as his rent: but when large capitals are invested in the soil, and the system of high farming is pursued, the proprietor, in order to leave the cultivator a reasonable return upon the stock which he employs, must be satisfied to receive as his rent, a third, a fourth, or even a fifth part of the produce. This demonstrates that each additional quantity of produce is raised at an increased expense. For, if one hundred labourers raised from a given surface four hundred quarters of wheat, and two hundred of these replaced with a reasonable profit the capital which the farmer expended in setting them to work, then the remaining two hundred quarters, or half the produce, might go to rent; and, if two hundred labourers could raise eight hundred quarters; or, in other words, if a double expenditure occasioned a double produce, then, as four hundred quarters would afford the farmer the same return on the capital which employed two hundred labourers, as two hundred quarters had afforded him on the capital which put one

hundred labourers in motion, the other four
hundred quarters would be disposable; or, in
other words, one half of the produce of the farm
might still be appropriated as rent. It is only
because the farmer cannot increase the quantity
of produce in the same ratio in which he increases the quantity of work done upon the farm,
that the proprietor receives a less proportion
of produce as his rent. Where one hundred
labourers raised four hundred quarters of wheat,
there two hundred labourers could not raise
eight hundred quarters, but would raise some
less quantity, say seven hundred. Now, the half
of seven hundred quarters could not be taken
as rent, because it requires four hundred to
replace with a reasonable return the capital
which the farmer expended in putting two hundred labourers to work; and, therefore, only
three hundred, or less than the half of the produce, remains as the land proprietor's proportion.
In the progress of improvement, the proprietor
receives a constantly diminishing proportion of
the whole produce, because the whole produce

bears a constantly diminishing proportion to the capital which raises it.

Again; it is self-evident, that the productive powers of agricultural industry must diminish in proportion as soils of an inferior quality are resorted to. Now, the very fact that in the progress of society, lands are resorted to which yield a diminishing proportional return upon the capital employed on them, is a demonstration that land even of the first quality, also yields a diminishing proportional return upon additional portions of capital employed to heighten its cultivation. For, if additional portions of labour and capital could be bestowed on fertile lands with the same advantages which attended the first portions so bestowed, then it is plain that inferior soils never would be taken in. If, on the fertile districts of a country, one hundred labourers could raise subsistence for two hundred, two hundred for four hundred, and so on, there never could exist a necessity for resorting to inferior soils, from which the labour of one hundred could extract subsistence only for one hun-

dred and fifty. But as we apply additional
portions of labour to the fertile districts of a
country, its productive powers gradually diminish; and though the first hundred men employed upon a given surface may raise subsistence
for two hundred, yet the second hundred employed on it will be able to raise subsistence for
some smaller number only; say one hundred
and fifty. In this case, the second class of
labourers will have a powerful motive to withdraw themselves from bestowing heightened
cultivation on the districts of superior quality,
and to spread over tracts on which they may be
able to raise subsistence for one hundred and
seventy, or even for one hundred and sixty. Thus,
we see, that when an additional capital laid out
on the superior soils, would yield a less return
than the same capital laid out upon soil in the
next degree inferior, then, and not till then, can
there be a motive for taking that next degree of
soil into cultivation. Capital ever seeking its
most beneficial occupation, and thereby constantly tending to a certain level, will so distribute itself upon the soil, that the last portion of

it employed upon the best lands, will yield an equal rate of return with the first portions of it employed on the worst lands under tillage. When, in consequence of the next quality of land being too inferior to replace the seed and subsistence which might be expended upon it, tillage cannot be extended over a wider field; then, additional capitals laid out upon the lands under cultivation will not occasion an additional produce equal to the additional expenditure; and it will be found ruinous to carry what is called high farming any farther. When we can no longer take in our inferior lands, we can no longer improve those of better quality. At the same time that we arrive at the ultimate limits of extended, we also arrive at the ultimate limits of heightened cultivation.

The principles, that each successive portion of capital which is employed either to bring in inferior soils, or to ameliorate those of a better quality, effects a less proportional addition to the produce than that which was effected by the capital previously applied; and that, in the progress of improvement we are constantly approaching the ultimate limits, beyond which cultivation can be neither extended nor heightened, lead to some of the most important conclusions in the science of political economy. We have already seen how intimately and inseparably one branch of industry is connected with another. In manufactures, each additional portion of labour and capital which is employed, produces not merely an equal, but a greater proportional effect than that which was previously applied; and where one hundred workmen can fabricate one thousand yards of cloth, there two hundred workmen, from being able to establish among themselves more perfect subdivisions of employment, will be able to fabricate, not merely two thousand yards, but some greater quantity; say two thousand five hundred yards. But though manufacturing industry has not in itself any natural limits, yet it is affected by those which nature has assigned to agriculture; and its advancement must necessarily be arrested when cultivation can be pushed no farther. Though additional portions of capital might still be capable of producing a higher proportional effect than those previously applied;

yet, as the productive powers of agriculture became stationary, it would be impossible that such additional portions should be attained. Manufacturing capital consists of subsistence, materials, and instruments for abridging labour; and as these implements were formed by labour employed upon other materials, and supported by other subsistence, into subsistence and material all manufacturing capital ultimately resolves itself. Now, in a country that has advanced beyond the hunting or savage state, the greater part of material, and almost the whole of subsistence, is extracted from the soil. Hence, when no additional capital can be applied to the soil, no additional capital can be obtained for manufactures; and where the progress of agricultural industry is arrested, there the progress of manufacturing industry must be arrested also.

From the principles above stated, respecting the application of capital to land, it necessarily follows, that every improvement in agricultural science removes to a greater distance the point at which the spread of tillage and the amelioration of the soil must cease. Every thing which can with propriety be termed an improvement in agriculture, enables a given quantity of labour to raise a greater quantity of produce; or, what comes to the same thing, allows a given quantity of produce to be obtained by a less quantity of labour. Let us, for the sake of illustration, suppose, that upon a given tract of soil, four sets of labourers, consisting of one hundred each, have been successively employed; and that the first hundred raised subsistence for four hundred, the second for three hundred, the third for two hundred, and the fourth for one hundred. Let us suppose farther, that the cultivator, besides the subsistence advanced to the four hundred labourers, expends in seed and implements subsistence for four hundred more; and then the whole expenditure upon the soil will be subsistence for eight hundred, while the produce will be subsistence for one thousand; or, in other words, will replace the capital which raised it, with a profit of twenty-five per cent. Now, in this case, cultivation will have been pushed too far; and the employment of the last hundred labourers, who merely replace their subsistence, without doing any thing to return the other portions of capital which contributed to set them at work, occasions a positive and unnecessary loss. If the farmer had not employed them, it is true that his produce would have been only subsistence for nine hundred; but then he would have saved their subsistence, and seed, and wear and tear equal to their subsistence; so that his expenditure would have been less by subsistence for two hundred. In consequence of employing the last set of labourers, he expends subsistence for eight hundred, and obtains a produce of subsistence for one thousand; while, by dismissing them, he might reduce his expenditure to subsistence for six hundred, and obtained a produce consisting of subsistence for nine hundred; that is, might increase his surplus or profit from subsistence for two hundred, to subsistence for three hundred. The last set of labourers, therefore, would inevitably be dismissed.

Now, let improvements be effected in agriculture,—let a better quality of seed and of manure be discovered,—let machinery for enabling the same number of labourers to execute a greater quantity of work be invented; and let the result be, that on our given extent of territory, the first hundred labourers will raise subsistence for five hundred, the second for four hundred and fifty, the third for four hundred, and the fourth for three hundred. In this case, then, the fourth and last set of labourers would raise for the farmer a produce consisting of subsistence for three hundred, while the expenditure by which it was obtained would be equal to subsistence for only two hundred. The profit, therefore, which the farmer would obtain by employing the last set of labourers would, in consequence of the improvements in agriculture, be fifty per cent. So far from cultivation being pushed beyond its proper limits, additional labour might be beneficially employed upon the soil; for if a fifth set, consisting of one hundred, could, while they expended their subsistence, and other capital equivalent to their subsistence, increase the produce of our given surface, by subsistence for two hundred and fifty, the farmer, even on this last portion of his capital, would obtain a surplus of twenty-five per cent.

The result will be precisely the same, if we consider the improvements in agriculture, as allowing the same quantity of produce to be raised by a less quantity of labour and capital. If four hundred labourers, with an expenditure of subsistence for eight hundred, can, on our given surface, raise a produce equal to subsistence for one thousand; while three hundred, with an expenditure of subsistence for six hundred, can raise a produce equal to subsistence for nine hundred; then it is evident, that by forcing a produce equal to subsistence for one thousand, the farmer diminishes his net surplus one third, and that he will consequently discontinue to cultivate so highly. Now, let improvements take place in agricultural industry, and, in consequence of these improvements, let three hundred workmen, with an expenditure of subsistence for six hundred, be enabled to perform the same quantity of work which four hundred, with an expenditure of subsistence for eight hundred, were formerly capable of performing: then this same quantity of work may be performed without pushing cultivation too far; and subsistence for one thousand may be extracted from our soil, without occasioning any diminution in the farmer's surplus produce. On the contrary, when three hundred labourers, with a proportionate capital, raised subsistence for nine hundred, the surplus was subsistence for three hundred: but now, when these three hundred labourers can do the work of four hundred, and extract subsistence for one thousand, the same expenditure creates a greater produce, and the surplus is subsistence for four hundred, instead of for three hundred.

It is unnecessary to go through the details of illustrative cases, in order to shew that those improvements in the application of agricultural labour, which allow cultivation to be carried to a greater height, also allow it to be extended over a wider surface. If four hundred labourers, with a proportionate capital of subsistence for eight hundred, could, from any given district, raise a produce consisting of subsistence for seven hundred, then it is evident that the expenditure would exceed the return, and that this district could not be profitably cultivated. But if improvements took place in agriculture, enabling three hundred labourers to perform the same quantity of work which the four hundred formerly performed, and to raise from this district a produce consisting of subsistence for seven hundred, then it is self-evident, that it might be cultivated with a profit. The expenditure would be subsistence for six hundred, and the produce subsistence for seven hundred; leaving a surplus of subsistence for one hundred, as the farmer's remuneration.

Improvements in agricultural science, as throwing to a greater distance the point beyond which cultivation can be neither heightened nor extended, necessarily remove to a greater distance the point beyond which manufacturing capital can be no farther accumulated. Manufacturing capital, as we have already seen, is resolvable into food and material; and, in advanced stages of society, these, with the exception of fish and minerals, are almost exclusively derived from the soil. Now let us suppose, that on a tract of given extent, five distinct sets of labourers are successively employed; and that besides replacing the food and material which they consume while at work,

The first hundred creates a surplus produce of food and material for . . 100

2nd ditto for 80

3rd ditto for 60

4th ditto for 40

5th ditto for 20

———

300

it being farther supposed, that this last surplus upon the employment of one hundred labourers, is the lowest for which the farmer will risk his capital in cultivation. In this case, the sum of the five different surpluses will amount to subsistence and material for three hundred labourers; and, therefore, this given district, besides subsisting the five hundred agricultural labourers employed on it, will furnish the means of employing three hundred manufacturers.

Now, let us suppose that an improvement

takes place in agricultural science; and that in consequence, when five sets of labourers, consisting of one hundred each, are successively employed upon our given surface, the surplus created by the

1st hundred, is food and material for 120

2nd ditto for 100

3rd ditto for 80

4th ditto for 60

5th ditto for 40
                              ———
                               400

The sum of these several surpluses being food and material for four hundred, our given surface, besides subsisting the five hundred agricultural labourers employed on it, would furnish the means of occupation for four hundred, instead of three hundred manufacturing labourers. But this would not be all. By the supposition, food and material for twenty is a sufficient surplus to induce the farmer to employ one hundred labourers; and each hundred successively turned upon the soil, creates the same surplus which, before the improvement in agriculture, the immediately preceding hundred was capable of creating. Consequently, a sixth set of labourers, consisting of one hundred, may now be employed upon our given surface; and these, besides replacing their subsistence, will raise food and material for twenty. In consequence of the improvement in agriculture, six hundred agricultural labourers may be employed, instead of five hundred; and the six different surpluses, amounting to food and material for four hundred and twenty, will furnish the means of employing four hundred and twenty manufacturing labourers.

But yet again. The improvement in agriculture which allows one hundred additional labourers to be employed upon our given surface, will also allow cultivation to be extended over tracts which could not before be profitably tilled. All those pieces of ground which formerly could just replace the subsistence of the first hundred labourers who might have been employed on them, but which were left waste because unable to yield a surplus, we now suppose to be each capable of replacing the subsistence of the first hundred employed on them, with the adequate surplus of food and material for twenty. These pieces of ground will consequently be sought for the purposes of tillage. Let five of them be situated on the same estate with the given surface before under tillage, and they will give employment to five hundred additional agricultural labourers; and will yield five different surpluses, amounting to food and material for one hundred; and consequently furnishing the means of employing one hundred additional manufacturing labourers. This estate, therefore, consisting of the given surface before under tillage, and of the five pieces of ground before lying waste; and which originally furnished employment only for five hundred agricultural, and three hundred manufacturing labourers; will now, in consequence of an improved mode of culture, occasioning an increased surplus of twenty per cent. upon all capital vested in the soil, allow of the employment of one thousand one hundred agricultural, and five hundred and twenty manufacturing labourers. This is a most important result. The improvement in agriculture, adding twenty per cent. to the surplus created upon capital invested in the soil, would, in consequence of allowing old land to be more highly cultivated, and new land to be brought under tillage, admit a doubling of the wealth and population of our district.

I have before remarked that in the work of production, the different kinds of industry unite, and reciprocally augment each other's effective powers. As improvements in agriculture increase the quantity of capital which can be employed in manufactures ; so improvements in manufactures remove to a greater distance the ultimate limits of agricultural prosperity, and admit of additional applications of capital to the soil. This important principle I shall endeavour to place in as clear and convincing a point of view as possible.

If, with the same set of labourers, a capitalist were at one and the same time to cultivate the soil and to manufacture its produce, the manner in which improvements in manufacturing industry contribute to the extension of tillage, would be apparent. For, it is obvious that such improvements would have precisely the same effect as the adoption of a superior course of husbandry in enabling the capitalist to obtain a remunerating surplus from soils which, before the improvements, could not be profitably tilled. If one hundred labourers were employed upon an estate, and if fifty raised food and material for one hundred and twenty-five, while the remaining fifty prepared implements and wrought necessaries for one hundred and twenty-five; then the capitalist, who advanced food and material, implements and wrought necessaries, for the one hundred, would obtain all these things for one hundred and twenty-five; that is, would gain twenty-five per cent. which we assume to be the customary rate of profit. Now, let the powers of *manufacturing* industry be so improved, that forty are able to prepare implements and wrought necessaries for one hundred and fifty; while the effective powers of *agricultural* industry continuing exactly as before, the remaining sixty labourers raise food and material for one hundred and fifty: and then the capitalist who advances food and material, implements and wrought necessaries, to the one hundred agricultural and manufacturing labourers upon our estate, will, in consequence of the improvement in manufacturing industry, obtain a surplus return of fifty, instead of twenty-five per cent. Now, it is evident that all the inferior tracts belonging to this estate, upon which the labour of fifty was unable to raise food and material for one hundred and twenty-five, could not, before the improvement in manufactures, be brought under cultivation; because the customary rate of profit is taken at twenty-five per cent., and this rate cannot be obtained except when, with a capital of wrought necessaries and implements, food and material for the fifty manufacturing, and fifty agricultural labourers, a return of wrought necessaries and implements, food and material for one hundred and twenty-five, shall be produced. But as soon as the improvement in manufactures enables forty to prepare wrought necessaries and implements for one hundred and fifty; or thirty-four to prepare them for one hundred and twenty-five; then, tracts of land so inferior as to require the labour of sixty-six, instead of that of fifty, to raise food and material for one hundred and twenty-five, might be brought into cultivation: because the capitalist, who advanced food and material, clothes and implements, for thirty-four manufacturing, and sixty-six agricultural labourers, would obtain all these things for one hundred and twenty-five; that is, would obtain twenty-five per cent. the customary rate of profit.

When industry is divided into separate and distinct operations, and one capitalist cultivates the soil, while another works up its produce, the effects of improvements in manufactures are precisely analogous to those above detailed. The products of equivalent capitals are of equal value. When the manufacturer, on advancing food and material, clothing and implements for fifty, obtains wrought necessaries and implements for one hundred and twenty-five; then the farmer, who cultivates a soil upon which an advance of food and materials, wrought necessaries and implements for fifty, yields a return of food and material for one hundred and twenty-five, will be

able to purchase the wrought necessaries and implements for fifty, with food and material for fifty:
and hence, as his whole expenditure will be
equivalent to no more than food and material
for one hundred, while his produce is food and
material for one hundred and twenty-five, he
gains twenty-five per cent. the customary rate
of profit. But when, in consequence of the
introduction of machinery, a capital of food and
material for thirty-three and one third, will produce a return of wrought necessaries and implements for one hundred and twenty-five ; then the
farmer who cultivates an inferior soil, on which it
requires a capital, of food and material, clothing
and implements for sixty-six and two thirds, to
raise food and material for one hundred and
twenty-five, will gain the customary profit of
twenty five per cent. : because, food, &c. for
sixty-six and two thirds, (the capital which
raises food and material for one hundred and
twenty-five,) being twice the amount of food, &c.
for thirty-three and one third, (the capital which
prepares clothes and implements,) the farmer will
be able to purchase clothes and implements for

his sixty-six and two thirds labourers, with food and material for thirty-three and one third; and thus, his whole expenditure in employing sixty-six and two thirds labourers, being food and material for one hundred, and his produce, food and material for one hundred and twenty-five, he will obtain the customary rate of return from tracts very far inferior to those which, before the improvement in manufactures, could be profitably tilled.

Thus, then, it is demonstrable, that every improvement in manufacturing industry which enables necessaries and implements to be fabricated with less labour and expense, extends cultivation over inferior tracts, and adds to the quantity of the surplus produce which supports and gives employment to artisans and manufacturers.

The highly important consequences which result from improvements in agricultural science will, it is hoped, prove a sufficient apology for carrying the reader through these long illustrative details. The principles evolved enable us to trace with accuracy the effects of contrivances for abridging agricultural labour; and to give a satisfactory solution to the often agitated question, whether large farms are hurtful or beneficial? Contrivances, such as threshing machines, for the abridging of labour, though to a hasty observer they may seem calculated to diminish the demand for workmen, have in reality a directly contrary operation. They allow additional portions of capital to be applied to all old lands; they drive the plough over new districts which could not otherwise be tilled; and, while they thus by a double operation enlarge the sphere of agricultural exertion, they increase the surplus produce of the soil, and thus furnish the means of employing an increased manufacturing population.

With respect to the advantage or disadvantage of large farms, the question is somewhat more complicated, and may require a brief illustration. Let the estate of a nobleman be divided into ten small farms, each cultivated by the labour of the farmer and his family; and let one of these farmers find, that if he were to conduct a large concern, he could, in consequence of employing improved machinery, and of otherwise abridging and economising labour, perform the same quantity of work with a less number of hands, and therefore bring a larger proportional surplus produce to market, and afford to pay a higher proportional rent, than while he continued on his small farm. On the expiration of leases, the nobleman, tempted by the offer of a higher rent, lets the whole estate to this single farmer; and consequently the other nine farmers, with their families, sink to the condition of agricultural labourers upon the estate. So far the effect is injurious. But, on the other hand, the employment of more efficacious machinery, and the more economical application of labour, which are found admissible into large concerns, and which enable the great farmer to tempt the proprietor with the offer of a higher rent, would also enable him, with a given expenditure, to raise a greater produce than before. This, as we have already seen, would allow old fields to receive a higher dressing, and new fields, which before lay waste, to be brought into cultivation; would cause a larger quantity of surplus produce to be brought to market, and consequently furnish the means of employing a larger number of manufacturing labourers. Let the surplus produce of this estate have been formerly food and material for ten, and let it now be food and material for fifteen, manufacturing families. The case will then stand thus:—the evil of throwing the whole estate into one large farm will consist of the loss of comfort sustained by the nine families who have sunk from the state of small farmers to that of day labourers; while the benefits resulting from the change will consist of the additional comfort enjoyed by the family which obtain the large farm, the additional enjoyments of the proprietor who receives a higher rent, and the whole enjoyments of the five additional manufacturing families, to which the increased surplus produce of the estate furnishes the means of existence. It is impossible, therefore, to doubt, that throwing the estate into one large farm produced a great balance of good. Leaving the increased comforts of the proprietor and large farmer quite out of the question, we have fourteen families subsisted instead of nine; and it may even happen that these fifteen are more abundantly subsisted than the nine could formerly have been. For, as I have endeavoured fully to explain elsewhere*, profits have, in the progress towards wealth and improvement, a constant tendency to fall in relation to wages; so, that in a high state of civilization, a family living upon daily or weekly wages, may obtain a greater quantity of the comforts of life, than if it laboured independently upon a small farm.

To guard against the possibility of misconception, it will not be improper to remark, that by improvements in agricultural science are meant, those discoveries only in the application of labour and capital, which increase not the gross, but the surplus produce of the soil. If, in adding subsistence for one hundred persons to the gross produce of my estate, I expend subsistence for one hundred and ten, it is obvious that instead of increasing, I diminish the wealth of the country, and the means of employing a manufacturing population. Such a losing system of tillage,

---

* Essay on the Corn Trade, Part ɪᴠ. chap. ɪɪɪ.

indeed, the farmer by profession will never consent to pursue; but as the amateur who cultivates his own estate, may sometimes be induced to adopt it, under the delusion that he is engaging in a work of public utility, it may be expedient to admonish him, that it is only when the experimental farmer discovers the means of raising a given produce at a less expense, that he throws the limits of prosperity to a greater distance, and is entitled to be regarded as a public benefactor.

It may also be proper to remark, that the principles we have unfolded respecting the ultimate limits set to cultivation, are applicable to those lands only which are made to produce the materials of subsistence. The materials of subsistence are the things expended in cultivation; and the corn land which does not return so great a quantity of them as was consumed in tilling it, leaves us nothing to carry to market, and must go back to its natural state. The case is different with a hop-garden, or a vineyard. Here the whole produce may always be brought to market; and, therefore, it is not the quantity of produce, but its value, as compared with that of the things expended in production, which, with respect to such lands, must determine the quantity of labour and capital which may be beneficially employed to heighten or extend cultivation.

What has here been said respecting the varying effective power of agricultural industry, serves still farther to illustrate and establish the principles stated in the preceding chapter respecting the perpetually decreasing difference between the value of produce in a raw, and in a manufactured state. As population increases, and it becomes necessary to take in new soils, or to cultivate the old in a more expensive manner, it constantly requires an augmenting quantity of capital to raise the same quantity of produce; while, on the contrary, the advance of a country in wealth and population, by giving occasion to improvements in machinery, and to more perfect divisions of employment, enables the same number of hands, and consequently the same expenditure for food, to work up a greater quantity of material. From the conjoint operation of these causes, the value of raw produce is, in the progress of society, perpetually increasing with respect to manufactured goods; or, to express the same thing in a different form, the value of manufactured goods is perpetually diminishing with respect to raw produce. But notwithstanding the operation of this two-fold cause, it is impossible that the period should ever arrive, when the manufacturer shall be unable to do more than add to the raw material the value of the subsistence which he consumes while at work. From the law of competition, the products of equal capital will be of equal value. If an agricultural capital equal to food for one hundred can raise a produce equal to food for one hundred and one, then a manufacturing capital equal to food for fifty, with material equivalent to food for fifty, will produce wrought goods which will be equal in value to food for one hundred and one; or, in other words, which will exceed in value the value of the food added to that of the material. While agricultural capital does more than replace itself, manufacturing capital will give products of more value than itself. But it is evident, that cultivation can never be permanently pushed so far that agricultural capital will be unable to replace itself; and that therefore the period never can arrive when manufacturing industry shall not be able to add to the raw material a value greater than that of the subsistence consumed in carrying it on. Thus again we find that the distinguishing tenet of the French Economists, namely, that manufacturing industry is unproductive of wealth, because the manufacturer does no more than add to the material the value of the subsistence consumed while at work, turns upon a gratuitous assumption, which is not only unsupported by evidence, but which never had, and from the nature of things, never can have, any foundation in fact.

CHAP. VI.

MERCANTILE INDUSTRY.

SECTION I.—*Origin and Effects of Barter or Trade.*

W HEN we employ labour and capital in transporting and exchanging those things which previous applications of labour and capital have acquired, or prepared, we exercise mercantile or commercial industry. The origin of this branch of industry, and the manner and degree in which it aids the formation of wealth, demand a careful consideration.

In the earliest periods of society, a sense of mutual convenience must have induced men to barter or exchange the articles appropriated by their labour. The savage who had chanced to kill a greater number of wild animals than he could consume, but who, in doing so, had expended all his implements of hunting, would naturally be desirous of giving a part of his superfluous and perishable food for a fresh supply of arrows; while he who had been unsuccessful in the chase, and who happened to have more arrows than he immediately required to use, would be equally solicitous for the exchange. Thus, in the rudest state in which men have been found to exist, we may trace the origin of a species of industry, which, as society advances, enables the inhabitants of the most distant regions to administer to each other's wants, and which exerts such mighty influence on the resources and prosperity of nations.

When we consider the nature of mercantile industry, and the manner in which it operates, we find, that it employs in proportion to the labour which it puts in motion, a much greater quantity of capital than the others. Mercantile capital consists, in the first place, of all the things employed in the conveyance of goods, and in all the packages, shops, and warehouses, used in preserving them until demanded. But this is the least part of mercantile capital. After the divisions of employment have been once thoroughly established, it is an exceedingly small portion of the product of his peculiar industry which each individual requires for himself; and, therefore, almost the whole of the articles composing the revenue of a country are brought to market, and passing through the hands of merchants and dealers, become a portion of mercantile capital before they reach the consumer. Nay, the food and material which the manufacturer, the clothing and implements which the cultivator employs, reproductively, were purchased in the market, and were portions of mercantile capital before they were portions of manufacturing or of agricultural capital. Mercantile capital, therefore, consists not only in the shops and warehouses, the carriages and vessels, by means of which it is carried on, not only of all the articles of revenue which annually pass from the producer to the consumer, but of all the articles necessary to replace the manufacturing, and (with the exception of such things as are at once raised upon and re-invested in the farm) of all those necessary to replace agricultural capital.

It may, in a few words, be defined to consist of all the things employed to circulate wealth, and of all the wealth which is circulated.

The number of mercantile labourers which this vast capital puts in motion, is comparatively small, and consists of the sailors, waggoners, bargemen, wharfingers, shopmen, with the clerks and assistants employed by merchants, bankers, and dealers. It is evident that a manufacturing capital, consisting of tools, subsistence, and materials for a thousand men, or an agricultural capital, composed of seed, subsistence, and implements for a thousand, would put a thousand labourers in motion; while, on the contrary, a mercantile capital made up of articles identical both in kind and in degree with those composing either of the former, might not give employment to more than twenty mercantile labourers. The reason is obvious. As twenty men employed about waggons, barges, and warehouses, may transport and sell tools, subsistence, and materials for a thousand, the same identical capital which might set a thousand men to work in the hands of the manufacturer or farmer, may not, in the hands of the merchant, employ more than twenty.

Dr. Smith has stated* the fact, that capital invested in trade and commerce, puts a much smaller quantity of labour in motion, than capital employed in manufactures or agriculture; and from this fact he draws the conclusion, that mercantile industry does not augment the value of the annual produce, or, as he defines the term, the riches of a country, in nearly as great a degree as agricultural and manufacturing industry. That this conclusion is fundamentally erroneous, will, it is hoped, sufficiently appear from the subsequent illustrations respecting the manner in which mercantile industry aids the formation of wealth, and increases the value of the articles upon which it is employed.

When industry appropriates the plants and animals which nature presents in a form adapted for immediate consumption; when it bestows utility upon materials which could not otherwise administer to our wants; or, when it ameliorates

---

* Wealth of Nations, b. ii. c. 5.

or multiplies the fruits of the soil, its operation in producing wealth is so obvious and direct, that with a very moderate degree of observation and reflection, it may be perceived and understood. The case is different when industry merely transports commodities, and exchanges one for another. No preceding writer with whom we are acquainted, has given a completely satisfactory explanation of the manner in which mercantile industry increases wealth. That trade and commerce enrich the country in which they are carried on, is a fact which experience forces on the belief of all; but how they bring about this desirable result, few appear to have understood. While the supporters of the theory known by the name of the " Mercantile " System," maintain that mercantile industry enriches a country, by bringing into it a larger supply of the precious metals, the disciples of the French Economists contend, that it can do so only by importing the raw produce of foreign agricultural states. Even recent writers, who have rejected the errors both of the mercantile and of the agricultural system, have not been eminently successful in solving this intricate problem in economical science, and in laying open the *modus operandi* by which commercial industry produces wealth.

We have defined wealth to consist in articles which possess utility, and on which some portion of labour has been bestowed. Now, as the possessing of utility, and the requiring some portion of labour, constitute the essence of wealth, it necessarily follows, that every operation of industry which is instrumental in bestowing utility must be instrumental in producing wealth. But many articles which possess utility in one place, do not possess it in another place ; and, therefore, the industry which conveys such articles from the latter to the former, is instrumental in conferring utility, and consequently in creating riches. The merchant, for example, who ships timber from North America, where it might otherwise have remained as an incumbrance and nuisance upon the land, and carries it to the West India Islands, where it becomes an article of considerable utility, is evidently a productive labourer. Permitted to remain on the lands of

America, the lumber would not have been wealth; conveyed to a West India Island, it is wealth. This change has been wrought by commercial industry, and, therefore, commercial industry is productive.

When mercantile industry bestows utility by conveying articles from one place to another, its operation in producing wealth is direct and obvious. But this branch of industry has also an indirect operation in the formation of riches, which is much more important, and which, as it is somewhat less obvious, will require to be illustrated at greater length.

As soon as the exchanging of commodities became familiar to the minds of a people, it must have suggested to them the utility of dividing their labour. The dextrous huntsman would perceive, that by exchanging his superfluous food for bows and arrows, he might obtain a greater number of these implements than if he fabricated them himself; while he who was slow of foot, but expert at mounting trees, and in giving the proper form to their branches, would discover, that by exchanging bows and

arrows for the wild animals of his flecter neighbour, he could obtain a more abundant supply of
them than if he personally engaged in their
pursuit. Thus a sense of mutual advantage
would establish a division of employment. The
athletic and the bold would engage in the occupations of the chase, and the timid and infirm
devote themselves to some species of domestic
and sedentary labour.

The divisions of employment to which the
exchange of commodities gives occasion, augment, to an astonishing degree, the productive
powers of human industry. As our wants and
desires are very various, the operations of labour
by which they are supplied and gratified, must
be very various also. If a man were to attempt
to fabricate for himself all the articles necessary
to comfortable existence, half his time would be
expended in shifting his tools and adjusting his
materials: distracted with a multiplicity of employments, he could become expert at none. But
where a person devotes himself to a single trade,
his time is no longer lost in shifting from employment to employment; and use and habit

give him, in the performance of his peculiar operations, a rapidity and skill, which, until the fact is forced upon us by experience, we can scarely conceive the human hand capable of acquiring. Next to the application of capital, the division of employment furnishes the most effectual means of increasing the productive powers of industry. Adam Smith has stated, that by dividing the different operations of the manufacture among them, ten persons may make forty-eight thousand pins in a day; while, if they had wrought separately and independently, they could not have accomplished the two hundred and fortieth part of the work which, by a proper division and combination of their labour, they are now capable of performing.

But it is not in mechanical operations alone that the division of employment augments the powers of industry. Nature, by giving to different districts different soils and climates, has adapted them for different productions. One tract of land is peculiarly fitted for the growth of grass, another seems as exclusively destined for the production of corn. In one country, the vine grows luxuriantly, while the animals which feed upon its pastures have but a poor and scanty covering; in another country, the grape ripens but imperfectly, while the fleeces of the animals it feeds, furnish the materials of clothing in abundance. Now, it must be obvious to the most inattentive observer, that by establishing a division of employment in these districts, and in these countries, the productions of the earth will be multiplied to an extent which cannot easily be calculated. If we sow corn on our arable land, and feed cattle on our pastures; if we cultivate the grape beneath a congenial sky, and breed sheep where their fleeces will be abundant; then shall we enjoy more corn and cattle, more wine and clothing, than if we reversed the order of nature, ploughing up our meadow grounds, and leaving our arable lands under grass, converting our vineyards into sheepwalks, and our sheepwalks into vineyards.

The view which we have here given of the advantages resulting from the division of employment, will enable us to form a just conception of the nature and extent of the benefits conferred by mercantile industry. This branch of industry, besides its direct operation in bestowing utility upon articles which otherwise could not possess it, allows each individual to confine himself to the mechanical operation in which he is most skilful and expert, or to give to his fields that peculiar mode of culture which is suitable to their soil; and thus, by an indirect operation, powerfully contributes towards the creation of that universal opulence which, as has been justly observed, gives the lowest class of labourers, in a civilized and prosperous country, a greater command over the conveniences of life, than is enjoyed by many an African king.

But, in order to shew more clearly the manner and the degree in which mercantile industry contributes to the production of wealth, let us examine for a moment the effects which would result from a suspension of all exchanges between man and man. It is self-evident that the instant the articles of wealth became untransferable, the divisions of labour, with all their advantages, would be discontinued. The weaver, for example, would no longer fabricate a greater quantity of cloth than he thought necessary for his own consumption; but would, on the contrary, be obliged to supply his wants and gratify his desires by combining in his own person a great variety of occupations. Hence half his time would be lost in shifting his tools, and adjusting his materials; and his attention being distracted by a multiplicity of employments, he could become expert at none. Again; the occupier of arable land, being, by the supposition, no longer able to exchange his surplus corn, would cultivate no more of that grain than he thought necessary for his own use. Those fields, the produce of which he formerly disposed of in the market, would now lie waste, or else be made to yield a scanty supply of some article not congenial to their soil. Similar interruptions would take place in the occupations of the grazier; we should see cattle feeding in the neglected corn-field, and the moist meadow ploughed up in order to produce grain. Man being no longer able to give his labour the direction calculated to co-operate with nature, the productive powers of agricultural industry would sustain a great diminution, and the earth would yield him but a very inconsiderable portion of the wealth which it is capable of affording.—To recapitulate.—Mercantile industry gives occasion to the divisions of employment; and these multiply to an immense extent the articles which supply our wants and gratify our desires. Prohibit trade, and the divisions of employment cease: restore it, and these divisions, with all their benefits, return. Hence, whatever may be the benefits resulting from the divisions of employment, these benefits are to be referred to trade, or mercantile industry, as their original and proper source.

Mercantile industry not only gives occasion, in the first instance, to the divisions of employment, but at all times and in every conceivable case, determines the extent to which they can be carried. When men make few exchanges, each must work at many trades. Where the market is very small, no person can have any encouragement to devote himself entirely to one employment, for want of the power to exchange all that surplus part of his own labour which is

over and above his own consumption, for such
parts of the produce of other men's labour as he
may have occasion for. In thinly-peopled districts, where families live several miles from
each other, a man must learn to perform for
himself several little pieces of work, for which,
in a more populous neighbourhood, he would
call in other workmen. We find that country
workmen are almost every where obliged to
apply themselves to all the different branches of
industry, which have so much affinity as to be
employed about the same sort of materials. A
country carpenter deals in every sort of work
that is made of wood; a country smith in every
sort of work which is made of iron. The former
is not only a carpenter, but often a joiner, a
cabinet-maker, and even a carver of wood, as
well as a wheelwright, a ploughwright, a cart
and waggon maker. The employments of the
latter are still more various. In such situations
it would be impossible for the common business
of a nailor to be carried on as a distinct trade;
for if it were, a single workman would be
enabled to make a thousand nails a day, which

would probably be as great a number as the neighbourhood required in a year.

In those interior and thinly-peopled districts, where few exchanges can be made, and where, in consequence, each individual is compelled to apply himself to several different kinds of work, we find the productive powers of industry at the lowest ebb. In such situations too, as none but the most fertile tracts are required for cultivation, the progress of wealth can be little retarded by that peculiar property of the soil which, when two equal portions of capital are applied, causes it to yield a diminished return upon the last. But the advantage of cultivating none but the best lands, is altogether insufficient to compensate the want of mercantile industry, and of the divisions of employment to which it gives occasion. Little work is dispatched, and that little in a rude unfinished manner. The produce of the soil bears no proportion to its natural fertility, and the country continues miserably deficient in the comforts and conveniences of life.

The circumstances of the people are widely

different in populous districts, situated in the
neighbourhood of the sea, or of navigable rivers.
Here the power of exchanging is unlimited, and
each person finds that in return for the surplus produce of his own labour, he can obtain
such portions of the produce of other men's labour,
as he may have occasion for. In consequence
of this extension of mercantile industry, divisions
and subdivisions of employment are established,
and each particular trade is reduced to a few
simple operations, in which time is saved, and
an almost miraculous rapidity obtained. When
the productions peculiar to the soil, and to the
acquired talents of the people, exceed what is
wanted for home consumption, the surplus is
exchanged against the productions peculiar to
all the other climates of the world; and while
each field receives that species of cultivation
which is best calculated to co-operate with nature,
and every hand is directed to the employment
to which habit has adapted it; the necessaries,
comforts, and luxuries of life are multiplied to
an extent scarcely conceivable to those who have
been always confined to situations in which

mercantile industry has little scope, and its consequents, the divisions of employment, are imperfectly established.

The great importance of mercantile industry renders it expedient that we should descend from this general statement of its results, and trace distinctively its particular operation in heightening the productive powers of the other applications of labour and capital. It has already appeared, that though in our classifications and reasonings the several branches of industry may be considered as distinct and separate; yet in the actual business of production they are always found in conjunction and co-operation. In order to appropriate the spontaneous gifts of nature, it is necessary to manufacture tools and implements: manufactures could not go on if the other branches of industry were not exerted to supply material and subsistence; and if appropriative industry did not furnish iron and timber, and manufacturing industry prepare the spade and the plough, the cultivation of the earth would cease.

Now trade and commerce are the prime

instruments which bring these different applications of labour and capital mutually to co-operate
with, and aid each other. If it were not for
mercantile industry, there could be no division
of employment; and he who wished to acquire
any article of wealth, would have to perform for
himself all the different operations concerned in
its production. Let us examine the influence
which this would have upon the effective powers
of the several branches of industry, beginning
with that which appropriates the spontaneous
gifts of nature.

Without mercantile industry, and the division
of employment to which it gives occasion, the
fisherman, for example, after having supplied himself with materials, would have to build his own
vessel, to manufacture his own line and tackling,
and by a previous exercise, either of appropriative
or agricultural industry, to provide a stock of
provisions to subsist upon while at work. Under
such circumstances, a canoe, with lines and
tackling of the most inferior description, would
be the only capital he could acquire; his exertions would necessarily be confined to the vici-

nity of the shore; and if, while so poorly
equipped, he chanced to appropriate a greater
quantity of fish than his own family could consume, the surplus could find no market, and
would perish upon his hands. Contrast these
feeble and limited productive powers with those
which the fisherman acquires when mercantile
industry enables him to borrow aid from the
miner, the manufacturer, and the farmer. The
stout ship now takes place of the skiff or the
canoe; the metallic hook and harpoon supplant
the crooked bone or pointed stick; provisions
are supplied for the most distant voyages, and
the fisherman, after visiting banks situated in
the middle of the ocean, and approaching either
pole, finds in every commercial country of the
world, a market for the cured fish, the sperma-
ceti, and the oil which he brings back.

The influence of manufacturing industry in
heightening the productive powers of the manufacturer, is still more conspicuous. It has been
already stated, that as capital accumulates, and
population multiplies, the same number of hands,
in consequence of improved machinery, and more

perfect divisions of employment, become capable
of working up a greater quantity of material.
But were it not for trade and commerce, improved machinery and the divisions of employment, which thus increase so prodigiously the
effective powers of manufacturing industry,
could never have existed. It is self-evident,
that if there were no exchanges, there could be
no division of employment; and the slightest
consideration must convince us, that without
the divisions of employment, the implements for
abridging labour would be of the rudest kind,
and the effective powers of the manufacturer at
the lowest ebb. Supposing that there were
neither trade nor commerce, and that in consequence each individual performed every kind of
work for himself; then, he who wished to fabricate a plough, would, in the first place, have to
furnish himself with instruments for felling
timber, and exploring mines. These once obtained, he would be under the necessity of going
to the forest to cut down branches for the
shaft of his plough, and then of procceding to
some mineral district to dig from the bowels

of the earth the iron for its share. But his labours would not cease here; and, after the necessary materials had been thus obtained, the branches would have to be cut down to the proper shape and dimensions, a furnace must be erected for smelting the ore, and a forge for softening the purified metal, and beating it out into the proper form. But these complicated and difficult operations no single individual,— no single family could perform; and, therefore, without mercantile industry, and the divisions of employment which it enables us to establish, a plough, in any way resembling that which is at present used, could never have been fabricated.

With respect to agricultural industry, the case becomes still stronger. The plough is but one out of many implements necessary for cultivating the soil; and if, besides supplying himself with the whole of these, the farmer with his own hands had to erect his own buildings, to fabricate his own furniture, and to make his own clothes, it is evident that nothing deserving the name of tillage could possibly be effected. Agriculture, which has been ignorantly represented as the single and only source of wealth, can scarcely have existence until trade and commerce, by establishing divisions of employment, have enabled all the other branches of industry to unite and co-operate with it in the work of production.

While mercantile industry multiplies the effective powers of labour, by causing the most dissimilar and distant operations to concur in the business of production, it occasions a highly important saving in capital. If it were not for trade and commerce, and the consequent divisions of employment, each person would have to furnish himself with all the different kinds of tools and implements. For example, if there were in any neighbourhood four persons, each of whom cultivated, wove, made shoes, and performed carpenter's work for himself, the fixed capital of each person must consist of four different sets of instruments, to enable him to carry on these four different trades; and as only one set could be employed by each at one time, three fourths of the fixed capital of this little community would be always in a state of

unproductive inactivity. But if, in consequence
of the establishment of a system of barter
amongst these four individuals, each should
confine himself to a particular occupation, then
one set of tools would be sufficient for each;
and, in consequence of the divisions of employment, an incalculably greater quantity of work
would be performed, with a fourth part of the
fixed capital formerly required. But instead of
four, there are four hundred different branches
of business, all requiring a different set of tools
and implements. The saving in the keeping up of
fixed capital, the nature of which we have here
endeavoured to illustrate, is of the highest importance; and, in our estimates of the benefit
conferred by mercantile industry, should never
be overlooked.

Having thus shewn the manner in which mercantile industry aids the production of wealth,
it will be expedient to explain the way in which
it affects the exchangeable value of the articles
it is employed to convey and to transfer.

As the products of equal capitals are equivalent, if a manufacturer and farmer, without the

intervention of a third party, were to barter their respective commodities, dividing equally the cost of carriage; then one hundred quarters of corn raised by the latter, with an expenditure of subsistence for fifty labourers, would exchange for one hundred yards of cloth fabricated by the former, with a like expenditure. But if the barter were conducted through the intervention of a dealer or merchant, the case would be otherwise; and the one hundred quarters of corn would no longer exchange for the one hundred yards of cloth. The merchant must receive the customary rate of profit upon his capital, which always consists, first, of the things necessary to transport and preserve the goods in which he deals; and, secondly, in the goods themselves. Supposing that his whole capital is equal to subsistence for one hundred labourers, then the farmer, in exchange for the one hundred quarters of corn, which he had raised with a capital of fifty days' subsistence, would receive no more than fifty yards of cloth, or one half of that which the manufacturer had fabricated with a capital of fifty days' subsistence; while, in like

manner, the manufacturer would receive in exchange for his one hundred yards of cloth only
fifty quarters of corn, or half the produce of the
equal capital employed by the farmer. The
reason is obvious. Two capitals, each consisting
of fifty days' subsistence, are engaged in the
direct production of commodities, and one capital
equal to the other two, or consisting of one hundred days' subsistence, is employed in indirect production, or in aiding, by the establishment of the
divisions of labour, the effective powers of agriculture and manufactures. Now, as the law of
competition will necessarily equalise the profits
of stock, the goods obtained must go in proportional parts to the capitals, which, whether directly
or indirectly, contributed to their production; and,
therefore, when the exchanges are perfected, the
farmer and the manufacturer, whose joint capitals
amounted to subsistence for one hundred, will
possess between them fifty quarters of corn, and
fifty yards of cloth; while the dealer whose single
capital was one hundred days' subsistence, will
have for himself fifty quarters of corn with fifty
yards of cloth. But this proportional distribu-

tion of products amongst the several capitalists engaged in the work of production, could not take place, unless the dealer obtained from the farmer one hundred quarters of corn for fifty yards of cloth, while from the manufacturer he acquired one hundred yards of cloth for fifty quarters of corn. Hence, in the hands of the dealer, commodities acquire an additional exchangeable value, which is totally distinct from that which is determined by the amount of capital directly employed in their production, and which is regulated by the customary rate of profit on the capital employed combined with the expense of carriage.

The principle, that commodities acquire an increased exchangeable power in passing through the hands of the dealer, is not inconsistent with the general fact that the products of equal capitals are equivalent, but on the contrary, is its necessary consequence. In the case just stated, indeed, the manufacturer for the product of the capital which he employs in direct production, obtains only half the products of the equal capital which the farmer employs in direct production; while, in like manner, the farmer receives in exchange for his products only one half of the articles prepared by the equal capital of the manufacturer. But then, it is to be recollected, that while the capitals of the farmer and manufacturer are employed directly, the capital of the dealer equal to the sum of the other two, is employed indirectly, and through the divisions of labour in raising the corn and fabricating the cloth. As one half of the dealer's business will consist in exchanging with the manufacturer corn for cloth, in this one half of his capital will be employed. But when one half of the dealer's capital, or fifty days' subsistence, is employed in conveying and offering for exchange a quantity of corn raised by an agricultural capital of fifty days' subsistence, then the corn thus offered is in fact the product of capitals of one hundred days' subsistence, and consequently will be worth double the quantity of cloth fabricated by a capital of fifty days' subsistence. And, in like manner, when this cloth fabricated by subsistence for fifty, is conveyed and offered to the farmer by another capital equal to subsistence for fifty, it is in fact the product of a capital of one hundred days' subsistence, and will become worth twice the quantity of corn raised by the farmer with an expenditure of subsistence for fifty. Commodities, therefore, acquire an additional value in the hands of the dealer, because, in his hands, they become the product of additional capitals.

That which the dealer gives for his commodities to the direct or immediate producer of them, is called, in the language of commerce, their prime cost, and that for which he again disposes of them is termed their selling price. The difference between the prime cost, and the selling price of commodities is the fund from which the profit of the dealer is derived; and the several circumstances which determine this difference, are the same as the laws which regulate the rate of profit, and which I have elsewhere endeavoured to explain*.

The disciples of the French Economists conceive, that the difference between the prime cost

---

* Essay on the Corn Trade, Part iv. chap. iii.

and selling price of commodities, is so much deducted from those by whom they are immediately produced; and that the dealer who exchanges the product of a given agricultural capital for the product of a greater manufacturing one, and *vice versâ*, can acquire wealth only at the expense of the farmer and manufacturer. A slight consideration of the subject is sufficient to convince us, that this is a radical error.

The existence of a distinct mercantile class employing a distinct mercantile capital, arises from, and is a branch of that division of labour which heightens, in so astonishing a degree, the effective powers of human industry. If there were no capitalists employed in buying up commodities for the purpose of selling them again in proper proportions to the consumer; then, when the farmer wanted cloth, he would be compelled to carry his corn to the weaver, and propose an exchange of their respective articles. But if the weaver had already a sufficient supply of corn, and would not part with his cloth, except in exchange for shoes, then, before the farmer could obtain the clothing of which he stood in need,

he would be obliged to effect a previous bargain
with the shoemaker; and if he also had bread
enough, and would give shoes only in exchange
for hats, then with the hatter a preliminary
barter must be effected. Under such circumstances, an incalculable portion of time and
labour would be lost, and while each sought
others with whom to exchange his particular
commodity for the various articles he wanted,
the business of production would be perpetually
suspended.

Now, all this waste of labour and suspension
of production is obviated by the intervention of
a distinct mercantile class. Let a corn-store
and cloth shop be established in the neighbourhood, and our farmer, without difficulty or delay,
will be able to sell at the former, and to buy at
the latter. Similar facilities would be given to
the weaver. When a class of dealers set up
warehouses and shops for the collecting and
vending of commodities, then every direct producer, freed from the necessity of having recourse
to circuitous and uncertain barter, and knowing
where he can at all times be supplied with such

products of other men's industry as he may require, is enabled to devote his whole time and labour to his proper calling, and becomes capable of creating a far greater quantity of wealth than he could otherwise produce.

Thus we see, that the intervention of the dealer occasions an increase of wealth, from which, without any injury to those who carry on other branches of industry, his profits are derived. All those articles constituting the greater portion of his capital which he deposits for sale in shops and warehouses are productively employed. The circumstance of their being so deposited, give a more continuous and uninterrupted motion to the plough, and to the loom, and multiplies the effective powers of the cultivator and manufacturer. It is true, that this operation of mercantile capital is indirect, but it is not, therefore, the less efficient. All mercantile industry, whether it be carried on in the way of immediate barter between the several cultivators and manufacturers, or through a distinct and intermediate class of dealers, augments production indirectly. As was before observed, the existence of a class of dealers is a branch of that division of employment which multiplies the effective powers of industry; and their several capitals, which, to the superficial and inattentive observer, may appear to lie inert and inoperative in their shops and warehouses, and to put no labour in motion, except that employed in carriage, impart an increased activity to every other application of capital, disengage and turn to direct production considerable portions of labour which would otherwise be lost, and thus create a fund which not only pays the customary profit to their proprietors, but leaves with the cultivator and manufacturer a greater quantity of products than they could otherwise possess.

Supposing, that while direct producers exchange their respective articles by the circuitous and uncertain mode of immediate barter with each other, the farmer and cultivator expending each subsistence for fifty, can raise thirty quarters of corn, and fabricate thirty yards of cloth; and that when exchanges are conducted by the intervention of dealers, they can with the same expenditure raise one hundred quarters, and

fabricate a hundred yards; then, though the
capital which the dealers employed in exchanging the corn and cloth equalled the sum of the
capitals by which those things were directly
produced, and consequently absorbed one half as
their profit, still the farmer and manufacturer
would be gainers. For, notwithstanding that the
dealers, in conducting the necessary exchanges,
have absorbed one half of their products, they
have still fifty quarters of corn and fifty yards
of cloth remaining; while, had they conducted
their own exchanges without the intervention
of the dealer, they could have by the supposition
only thirty quarters and thirty yards. Nor is
the principle of this supposition merely arbitrary.
The intervention of the dealer must always occasion an increased production of wealth, greater
than that which is necessary to pay the customary rate of profit on the capital he employs;
for, if this were not the case, his intervention
would be injurious to those who carry on other
branches of industry, and they would immediately find an interest in effecting their exchanges, not through him, but by immediate

barter with each other. Supposing that while such immediate barter was carried on, the farmer and manufacturer, by expending each a capital of subsistence for fifty, could raise thirty quarters of corn, and fabricate thirty yards of cloth; and that when their products were exchanged through a dealer employing a capital of subsistence for one hundred, they could with the same expenditure as before, raise fifty quarters, and fabricate fifty yards; then, by continuing to conduct their business through the dealer, they would sustain considerable loss. For, as the dealer's capital is equal to the sum of the capitals employed in direct production, one half of the goods, as has just been demonstrated, will be the proportion due to him, and the farmer and manufacturer who had obtained thirty quarters of corn and thirty yards of cloth when they bartered directly with each other, will have only twenty-five quarters and twenty-five yards, in consequence of the dealer's intervention It is quite evident that, under such circumstances, they would cease to conduct their business through him.

But, further, if the intervention of the dealer did not occasion an increase of wealth more than sufficient to indemnify the direct producers for that which he subtracts from them, he would himself have an obvious interest in withdrawing his capital from the business of effecting exchanges. If, when exchanges are effected by immediate barter amongst the direct producers, capitals amounting to one hundred days' subsistence, can raise thirty quarters of corn, and fabricate thirty yards of cloth; and if, when aided by the dealer's capital amounting to one hundred days' subsistence, these capitals belonging to the farmer and manufacturer can raise fifty quarters, and fabricate fifty yards; then the dealer, by continuing to exchange commodities, obtains five quarters and five yards less than if he engaged in the business of direct production. For, his capital of one hundred days' subsistence being half of the whole capital employed in direct and indirect production, would be entitled to one half of the products obtained, or to twenty-five quarters of corn, and twenty-five yards of cloth; while, if his capital of one hundred days' subsistence were withdrawn from the business of exchanging, and invested in agriculture and manufactures, its return would be, by the supposition, thirty quarters and thirty yards. The effect would be similar in every conceivable case in which the intervention of the dealer did not occasion an increase of wealth sufficient to indemnify the direct producers for that which he subtracted as the profits of his capital. If any two sets of capitals, when one is employed in direct production, and the other in effecting exchanges, do not create a greater quantity of wealth than could be created were the whole invested in agriculture and manufactures, then it would not be the interest of the proprietors of any of these capitals to employ them in mercantile industry. The fact that capital is employed in the distinct and separate business of effecting exchanges, is in itself a sufficient demonstration that the intervention of the dealer renders the whole capital of the country more productive, than it otherwise could be, and causes an increase of wealth more than sufficient to indemnify the cultivator and manufacturer for the portion of their products which the dealer subtracts as the profits of his trade.

But though the intervention of the merchant and dealer will always bestow upon the industry of the manufacturer and farmer an increased effective power, sufficient and more than sufficient to indemnify them for the articles he subtracts as his profit; yet it is obviously their interest, as well as that of the community at large, that exchanges should be conducted with the smallest possible expense which is compatible with the perfect establishment of the divisions of employment. The investing of distinct and separate capitals in mercantile industry is beneficial, only because it allows exchanges to be effected at a less expense of time, labour, and capital, than if they were carried by means of immediate barter amongst cultivators and manufacturers, and thus permits more time, labour, and capital, to be devoted to the direct production of commodities. On the very same principle, every diminution in the amount of mercantile capital, which can be effected without retarding exchanges, and checking the division of employment, tends to

increase the wealth of the community. In the
cases just stated, if the dealer employing a capital of fifty instead of one of hundred days' subsistence, could exchange the one hundred quarters
of corn, and the one hundred yards of cloth,
which the farmer and manufacturer had raised
and fabricated with two capitals of fifty days'
subsistence each, then the difference between
the prime cost and the selling price of these
commodities would be reduced from a hundred
to fifty per cent.; for the capital of the dealer
being now only one third instead of one half of
the whole capital employed in production, his
proportion of the articles obtained would also be
reduced from one half to one third. One half
of his business being with the farmer, he would
employ one half of his capital, or twenty-five
days' subsistence in offering to him the one hundred yards of cloth which the manufacturer had
fabricated with fifty days' subsistence: this cloth
when so offered being, in fact, the product of a
capital of seventy-five days' subsistence, two
thirds of it would be given to the farmer for the
corn he raised with a capital of fifty days' sub-

sistence; and thus, in consequence of the dealer being able to effect exchanges with a less expense than before, the farmer would receive sixty-six, instead of fifty yards of cloth, for his one hundred quarters of corn. On the same principle, the manufacturer would obtain sixty-six, instead of fifty quarters of corn, for his one hundred yards of cloth. But this would not be the only benefit arising from the reduction in the expense of carrying on mercantile industry. The saving effected in the business of indirect production would increase the quantity of capital available for direct production. The improvement in mercantile industry, which enabled the dealer to exchange the fruits of the soil for the fabrics of the loom, with a capital of fifty instead of one of a hundred days' subsistence, would disengage a capital of fifty days' subsistence for cultivating the earth and working up its produce. Thus, one third would be added to the capital employed in direct production, and the useful commodities raised or fabricated would be increased by fifty per cent.

In the two chapters immediately preceding,

we saw, that improvements in manufacturing and agricultural industry, throw to a greater distance those limits beyond which cultivation can be neither heightened nor extended; and by consequence, the means of supporting an increased manufacturing population no longer obtained. Effects precisely similar are produced by improvements in mercantile industry. Every such improvement must enable the dealer to transport and exchange his goods with a less expenditure of capital; or, if he employs the same amount of capital, in a shorter period of time; and in either case will allow cultivation to be both heightened and extended, and the materials for employing manufacturing industry to be increased.

It is evident, that the further progress of industry must cease, when additional capital applied to the soil can no longer replace itself with a surplus sufficient to induce the capitalist to undertake the business of cultivation. Let us suppose, that this necessary surplus is ten per cent. that it requires a mercantile capital equivalent to food and wrought necessaries for one hundred to exchange the goods produced by a manufacturing and an agricultural capital, each equivalent to food and wrought necessaries for fifty, and that a manufacturing capital equivalent to food and wrought necessaries for fifty, prepares wrought necessaries for two hundred and twenty. In this case, no agricultural capital can be applied to the soil, except where the expenditure of food and wrought necessaries for fifty will produce food for two hundred and twenty; because, no inferior rate of return upon agricultural capital would afford the necessary rate of profit. When aided by the expenditure* of a mercantile capital equivalent to

---

* In fact, that portion of the mercantile capital which consists in the subsistence of the labourers it employs, the gradual decay of buildings, carriages, and vessels, with the loss and damage of goods, is all that is expended. In the cases assumed in the text, we have supposed, that the whole of the mercantile capital is consumed in order to avoid more complex details, and to simplify our illustration of the manner in which improvements in mercantile industry allow of agricultural improvements, which could not otherwise be effected. The supposition can in no way invalidate our conclusions, as it is obvious, that in whatever degree the dealer's capital is expended, the class of direct producers must replace it with the necessary profit.

food and wrought necessaries for one hundred,
a manufacturing and an agricultural capital,
each equal to food and wrought necessaries for
fifty, can produce food and wrought necessaries
for two hundred and twenty, the necessary
profit of ten per cent. is obtained upon all the
capitals employed; the whole expenditure being
food and wrought necessaries for two hundred,
and the return for these things two hundred
and twenty. But it is evident, that if an agricultural capital of food and wrought necessaries
for fifty, could not raise food for two hundred
and twenty, the necessary profit could not be
obtained, and that tracts of soil from which the
expenditure of such a capital might extract food
for two hundred, or even for two hundred and
ten, must remain untilled.

But while the effective powers of manufacturing industry remain as before, let the employment
and expenditure of a mercantile capital, equivalent to food and wrought necessaries for fifty,
be sufficient to conduct exchanges and establish
the divisions of employment between the farmer
and manufacturer, and then tracts may be culti-

vated from which the expenditure of food and wrought necessaries for fifty can extract no more than food for one hundred and thirty. For the sum of the capitals now expended is equivalent to no more than food and wrought necessaries for one hundred and fifty, and to replace this with the necessary profit of ten per cent. requires a reproduction only of food or wrought necessaries for one hundred and sixty-five. But as a manufacturing capital of fifty can fabricate wrought necessaries for two hundred and twenty, one of thirty-seven can fabricate them for one hundred and sixty-five; or, in other words, replace, with the necessary profit, that portion of the whole capital which consisted in wrought necessaries; and if the wrought necessaries can thus be replaced by a capital of thirty-seven, instead of by one of fifty, then a capital of thirteen will be disengaged from manufactures and added to the agricultural one of fifty, destined to reproduce that part of the original expenditure which consisted of food. Consequently there will be an agricultural capital of food and wrought necessaries for sixty-three, to raise food for one hun-

dred and sixty-five; and all lands from which
an expenditure of food and wrought necessaries
for sixty-three, can raise food for one hundred
and sixty-five, may be brought under tillage.
But if sixty-three raises food for one hundred and
sixty-five, fifty will raise it for one hundred and
thirty; and, therefore, lands from which a capital
of food and wrought necessaries for fifty can
raise these things for one hundred and thirty,
may be profitably cultivated; though previous
to the improvement in mercantile industry, none
could have remained under tillage, except those
from which this expenditure could extract food
for two hundred and twenty.

In a similar manner we might demonstrate,
that those improvements in mercantile industry
which have the effect, not of reducing the expense
of transporting and exchanging commodities,
but of shortening the period in which their
transport and exchange may be accomplished,
have a reaction upon other applications of labour
and capital, and throw to a greater distance the
limits beyond which cultivation can be neither
heightened nor extended. The illustrative de

tails, however, would be somewhat more complicated and involved, and as the question relates to the theory of profit rather than to that of production, it is not necessary to enter upon an exact analysis of it in the present chapter.

From what has been said above, the reader will at once perceive the nature of the benefits which a country derives from all those improvements in roads, in navigation, or in the modes of conducting business, the effect of which is, to allow commodities to be transported at a less expense, or in a shorter period. Such improvements lower the price of goods to the consumer, increase the return upon the capitals employed in direct production, allow of heightened and extended tillage, and, by consequence, of increased resources for the maintenance of a manufacturing population.

It may also be proper to remark, that the principles which we have here endeavoured to unfold, are calculated to set at rest some controverted questions of considerable importance. The prejudice against large farms, which was noticed in the preceding chapter, has been frequently extended to the employment of large capitals in trade, which is represented as being at one and the same time ruinous to the small dealer and injurious to the consumer. This involves a contradiction. The great, or, as he is sometimes unfairly termed, the overgrown capitalist, can supplant the small dealer only by underselling him, and in whatever degree he can do this, he must in the same degree benefit the public at large. The fact is, business can be conducted in a large way at a cheaper rate than it can be conducted in a small way. A single capital of 50,000*l.* will transport and exchange a greater quantity of goods than ten separate capitals of 5,000*l.* But every saving which takes place in the capital necessary to effect exchanges and establish the divisions of employment, increases the quantity of capital available for direct production, lowers the difference between the prime cost and selling price of commodities, or, in other words, causes the several classes of cultivators and manufacturers to obtain, with the same quantity of their peculiar productions, a greater quantity of the other

products which they require. By these operations too, the smaller capitalist will be benefited,
not injured. Even if he had previously engaged
in mercantile industry, and in the first instance
found himself under the necessity of incurring
the loss which is generally the consequence of
transferring stock from one occupation to another, yet in a short time he would receive an
ample recompence in the reduced price of all the
articles of consumption, and in the increased
return obtained upon capital in all the branches
of direct production. The great capitalist cannot supplant the small dealer, except by underselling him; and he cannot undersell him, and
at the same time obtain the customary rate of
profit, unless conducting business upon an extensive scale reduces the expense of transporting
and exchanging goods. But if goods are exchanged at a cheaper rate, capital is disengaged
from indirect, and rendered available for direct
production,—the mass of commodities is increased, — the farmer and manufacturer can
purchase what they want with a smaller sacrifice
of the articles which they raise and fabricate,—

the progress of wealth is accelerated, and the ultimate limits of production removed to a greater distance.

Section II.—*On the Home Trade.*

Mercantile industry has generally been divided into three distinct branches, namely, the home trade, the colonial trade, and the foreign trade; which last has been again divided into the foreign trade of consumption, and the foreign carrying trade. In this and the following sections I intend to consider these several branches of mercantile industry in the order in which they have been enumerated.

The exchange of commodities between the individuals of the same community, constitutes what is called the home trade. In considering this branch of mercantile industry, the first things which strike us are its superior magnitude and importance. Of the commodities consumed in any country, the greater part is always produced at home. In England, for example, almost

the whole of the wealth which supplies the great
mass of our population with food, clothing, and
furniture, is the produce of our own land, raised
and prepared by our own labour. Notwithstanding our widely-extended commerce, the
foreign articles which we import, bear a very
small proportion to the articles procured directly
and without the intervention of foreign barter,
by the exercise of domestic industry. Now, it
is the home trade which, by establishing the
home divisions of employment, causes all the
other branches of domestic industry to concur
and unite in the business of production; and
thus multiplies the powers of the labour and
capital from which the revenue of the great
majority of the nation is mainly derived. Abolish
the home trade, and the home divisions of employment will cease; and the efforts of man,
uncombined and unconcurring, will no longer
be able to subdue the earth. Appropriative,
manufacturing, and agricultural industry, being
all carried on by the same unconnected individual, or, at most, by the same unconnected
family, would languish in a nearly unproductive

state. Our mines could not be explored, nor
our distant fisheries continued: each individual
being obliged to appropriate or raise his own
subsistence and materials, our manufacturing
towns would be left without an inhabitant; and
while the person who tilled the soil was compelled not only to work up his own produce,
but to fabricate all his own implements of
husbandry, our agriculture would be almost
totally suspended. Thus the destruction of the
home trade would in a manner annihilate all
the other branches of industry, and reduce the
country to a state much more destitute and
barbarous than that in which it was found at the
invasion of Julius Cæsar.

Now, as the greatest portion of the wealth
annually consumed in the country is the direct
produce of domestic industry, it necessarily
follows, that the difference between the state
just described, and that in which we are actually
placed, is mainly occasioned by the extent and
activity of our home trade, and the consequent
variety and accuracy of the home divisions of
employment. To the facilities of domestic

intercourse, to the ease, rapidity, and security, with which the peculiar products of one part of the country can be exchanged for those of another, the superior powers of our industry are in a great measure to be attributed. This is the principal cause which allows our farmers to cultivate in such a manner, that their efforts shall co-operate with nature; and which, by enabling each town to supply all parts of the kingdom with its peculiar fabric, congregates our manufacturing population into considerable masses, and thereby perfects the division and subdivision of mechanical labour, and effects a most important saving in the application of capital.

In estimating the peculiar advantages of the home trade, we should always remember that by each operation it confers a two-fold benefit. When one person gives his exclusive attention to the cultivation of the soil, while his neighbour and countryman confines his attention to working up its produce, then the mercantile industry by means of which this division of employment can alone be established, at one and the same time augments the productive powers, both of domestic agriculture and of domestic manufactures. But when any individual cultivates the soil, and exchanges its produce for wrought goods imported from abroad, then the mercantile industry by which the international divisions of employment are established, at one and the same time augments the productive powers of domestic agriculture, and of foreign manufacture. Thus then it is demonstrable, that in every transaction of the home trade, the whole of the benefit resulting from the consequent division of employment remains in the country; while in each transaction of the foreign trade, a part of this benefit will belong to foreign countries. If, under a system of unfettered intercourse, England were to send a thousand pounds worth of woollen cloth to Ireland, and to receive in return a thousand pounds worth of linen; then the United Kingdom would obtain a much greater increase to its productive powers, than if England exported to France a like value in cloth, and brought back an equivalent in lace. In the first case, the whole of the benefit derived from the exchange, and the consequent division of employment, would remain in the United Kingdom; but, in the second case, a part of this benefit would belong to France. Hence it follows, that the amount of exports and imports must always be a most imperfect and inadequate criterion of the extent of the benefit conferred by mercantile industry. When one parish exchanges a thousand pounds worth of its productions with another, the consequent increase in the productive powers of the labour and capital of the country may be twice as great as that which would result from exchanging productions to a similar amount with a foreign nation.

Natural or acquired faculties for conducting internal intercourse, give a country advantages with respect to the production of wealth, similar to those which would be conferred by an increased fertility of soil, or an increased degree of skill in the application of manufacturing labour. Diminishing the expense of carriage has the same effect as diminishing the expense of direct production. Supposing that in one district the expenditure of a hundred days' subsistence, will raise one hundred quarters of barley; that in another a similar advance of capital will obtain a return of one hundred bags of hops; while to convey these commodities to market, requires an expenditure of fifty days' subsistence, and then the whole cost of production upon the hundred quarters of barley and hundred bags of hops will be subsistence for two hundred and fifty. But if a canal were opened, which reduced the expense of bringing the barley and hops to market from fifty to ten days' subsistence, then the whole cost of their production would fall from two hundred and fifty to two hundred and ten days' subsistence, and a capital of forty days' subsistence would be disengaged, and would become applicable to some other branch of industry. Now, these effects are precisely similar to those which would result from increasing the fertility of the soil. Let the expense of carriage not be diminished, but let the soil of the districts which produce the barley and hops be so improved that an expenditure of eighty days' subsistence will raise one hundred quarters of the former commodity, and an advance of eighty days' subsistence obtain a return of one hundred bags of the latter; and then, as in the former case, the whole cost of production upon these quantities of barley and of hops will be reduced from two hundred and fifty to two hundred and ten days' subsistence. What was before saved in the expense of carriage, will now be saved in the expense of tillage; one hundred and sixty days' subsistence will be employed in growing the barley and hops, fifty days' subsistence will be devoted to transporting and exchanging them, and forty days' subsistence will be disengaged and become applicable to the growing and transporting of other articles. A saving in the expense of direct production, arising from greater fertility of soil, has in no way a more beneficial effect upon the wealth and prosperity of a country, than a saving to a similar extent in the expense of indirect production, occasioned by greater facilities in the transport and interchange of commodities.

This principle may be still more clearly illustrated. When industry no longer replaces with an adequate profit, the whole of the capital employed, the work of production cannot pro-

ceed. If there were a tract of land of such a
degree of fertility, as to enable a thousand
labourers employed in agriculture and manufactures to raise and prepare the necessaries of life
for one thousand two hundred, while the state
of communication was such as to require two
hundred and fifty labourers to transport and
exchange these necessaries, then it is quite
clear that this land could not be cultivated,
because one thousand two hundred and fifty
labourers employed upon it in agriculture, manufactures, and trade, could procure the necessaries
of life for no more than one thousand two
hundred. But if the means of communication
between one part of the district and another
were so improved, that the different articles of
food, clothing, &c. could be transported and exchanged by one hundred men, then the territory
may be profitably cultivated. For, in this case,
one thousand one hundred men employed in
agriculture, manufactures, and trade, will produce the necessaries of life for one thousand
two hundred, that is, will replace their subsistence with a profit of nearly ten per cent. The

diminution in the expense of production occasioned by improvements in the means of communication which disengage one hundred and fifty men from the necessary business of transporting and exchanging commodities, has precisely the same effect in rendering this district capable of tillage, as if its natural fertility had been so increased, that it would yield to the labour of three hundred and fifty, the same produce which it could formerly have yielded to that of five hundred. But every diminution in the expense of production, which enables us to bring in tracts which could not otherwise repay the cost of reclaiming them, allows additional portions of capital to be applied to the more fertile soils already under tillage. Improvements in the means of internal communication give occasion not only to extended, but to heightened cultivation, and, with respect to the facilities for obtaining agricultural produce, have precisely the same effect as a general increase in the natural fertility of the soil. As far as wealth and prosperity are concerned, it is exactly the same thing, whether we cultivate a country where it requires one hundred and thirty men to raise subsistence for two hundred, and only twenty to transport and exchange it, or whether we cultivate one in which subsistence for two hundred, may be raised by the labour of one hundred, but cannot be transported and exchanged without the labour of fifty.

With respect to manufactures, improvements in the means of carrying on internal intercourse have a still more beneficial influence. In these branches of industry a cheaper mode of communication diminishes the cost of production by a two-fold operation; and while they lower the price of food and material, enable the same quantity of work to be performed by a smaller number of hands. Where the means of internal intercourse are defective, the people must reside in the immediate neighbourhood of the district which furnishes them with subsistence, and will consequently be very much scattered over the surface of the soil; while, if the country were well intersected with roads, canals, and navigable rivers, food might be obtained from the most distant quarters, and all that part of the population which is not required in agriculture, might congregate itself into great towns. But we have seen, that in proportion as the population of a country is so congregated, the divisions of employment become more accurate, machinery of greater power is introduced, and the productive powers of manufacturing industry increased. In a great town like Manchester or Birmingham, the same number of hands will perform a much greater quantity of work than in a small village, where each individual would have to perform several operations, and where the business would not be sufficiently large to admit of extensive and complicated machinery for the abridgment of labour. Hence, improvements in the means of internal communication, cheapen wrought goods not merely by effecting a saving in the expense of transporting and exchanging them, but also by allowing that congregating of the population in the districts favourable to manufacture, which enables the same number of hands to finish up a greater quantity of materials.

It appeared, in a former chapter, that every improvement in manufacturing industry which has the effect of reducing the cost of production upon that class of wrought goods which enters into the subsistence of the labourer, operates as an indirect improvement in agriculture, and admits of land of an inferior quality being taken in, and of additional portions of capital being applied to the more fertile soils already under tillage. Hence, improvements in roads, railways, canals, and all the means of internal communication, have a direct as well as an indirect effect in reducing the expense of obtaining raw produce, and in admitting an extended and heightened cultivation. While they diminish the cost of transporting raw produce, they cheapen the manufactured articles, such as clothing, furniture, and implements, which must be expended on its production.

Such being the nature and magnitude of the benefits conferred by the home trade, it becomes the business of the statesman to inquire into the most efficacious means of encouraging and extending it. And here it is to be remarked, that the power of legislative enactments, in promoting the interchange of commodities and the divisions of employment between different parts of the same country, is negative rather than positive. Regulation can effect little good, but may produce much mischief; and, therefore, the first and most important lesson which rulers have to learn, is, to refrain from governing too much. When those who are entrusted with the administration of public affairs, have employed the powers of the state to secure to the individual a perfect empire over his property, and an unimpeded right to pursue whatever branch of honest industry he may prefer, they have fulfilled their legitimate functions, as far as relates to the encouragement of trade; and beyond this they cannot advance a single step without counteracting their own designs, and trenching upon that liberty which is as essential to the progress of wealth, as it is to the perfection of the human character. Every legislative restriction, which in any way interrupts the free interchange of commodities between one part of the country and another, necessarily checks the division of employment, and lowers the productive powers of labour and capital. The effect produced by laws of this nature, is precisely analogous to that which would result from intersecting a country with inaccessible mountains and impassable swamps. On the self-same principle that we should open roads, and construct bridges, and canals, we should blot from the statute book every enactment which prevents or retards the operations of internal trade. Whether the obstruction to the free circulation of commodities, and consequently to the division of employment, be natural or artificial,—whether it arise from rocks and mountains, or from mistaken laws, the effect upon wealth and prosperity is the same.

Bounties upon particular products or manufactures, have frequently been resorted to as the means of encouraging industry and increasing wealth. A little reflection, however, will be sufficient to convince us that it is not in the nature of things that bounties should produce these desirable effects. If a bounty were granted upon the manufacturing of any article, suppose silk, the avidity to participate in the benefit of such bounty, would draw competitors into the silk trade, and so increase the supply and reduce the value of the commodity, that its price, even when aided by the bounty, would do no more than return to the manufacturer the customary rate of profit upon his capital. Now, the increase in the quantity, and the reduction in the price of silks, would unquestionably be a benefit to the consumers of this elegant article, and if the effects of the bounty terminated here, no reasonable objection to it could be urged. But this could not be the case. The amount of the bounty granted to the silk manufacturers must be derived from taxes, laid either on other commodities, or on incomes. If the taxes be laid upon other commodities, then the price of these must be increased, and their consumption diminished, exactly in the same proportion that silks experience a reduced price and an increased consumption; and thus the encouragement extended to one branch of industry will be counterbalanced by the depression inflicted upon others. In like manner, if the tax were laid on income, those who paid it would have a less sum to bring to market than before; and in whatever

degree the consumption of silks might be increased, in that degree would the consumption of
other things be diminished. Supposing that the
bounty upon silks amounted to 100,000*l*. annually, then the quantity of silks brought to market
would experience a fall in price to this amount,
and the consumers of the article would thereby
save 100,000*l*. for the purchase of an additional
quantity either of silks or of other commodities.
But those who paid the tax would have their
incomes reduced, and their annual purchases in
the market diminished by the amount of the
100,000*l*. which they contributed; and thus again
the encouragement which the bounty afforded
to industry upon the one hand, would be balanced
by the depression which it inflicted on the other.
Nay, the depression would be even greater than
the encouragement. The whole of the sums
raised could not be available for the bounty, a part
of them must necessarily be appropriated to pay
the salaries of those by whom the tax was collected, and the bounty distributed. Here then
portions of the revenue and labour of the country
are thrown into a channel perfectly barren and

unproductive. Had the sum expended upon management, been left in the hands of the contributors, it would have been accumulated as capital, or laid out as revenue, and in either case would have created a demand for productive labour; whereas it is now bestowed upon persons whose occupation is altogether useless, and cannot in the slightest degree increase the wealth of the community.

Monopolies have been frequently resorted to, sometimes with the view of increasing the public revenue, and at other times with the intention of affording protection and encouragement to trade. The expediency of employing them as a means of raising the money necessary to defray the expenses of government, does not come precisely within the scope of this chapter; their effect upon industry, and the manner in which they aid or obstruct production, we will now consider.

A monopoly is a suspension of that law of competition, the tendency of which is to bring down the prices of all commodities to such a level that the rate of profit in the several branches of industry shall be nearly equal. The first effect, therefore, of all such exclusive privileges, is to enable those in whose favour they are granted, to raise the price of their goods, and thus to obtain a higher profit on their trade. If monopolies did not do this, they would be perfect nullities. If they left prices and profits at their natural level, and did not enable the individuals, in whose favour they are granted, to get a higher return upon their capital than that which might be obtained in any ordinary occupation, they could have no influence whatever upon industry, and would be objects of perfect indifference both to the consumer and producer. But experience proves that they are by no means objects of indifference; and the eagerness with which those who engage in the work of production, seek to protect themselves from the effects of competition, demonstrates that monopolies and exclusive privileges must have the effect of advancing prices and raising profits in those branches of industry to which they are extended. The question therefore to be determined, is, whether the increased rate of profit obtained by the monopolists, effects an increase in the wealth of the community of which they compose a part?

When the individuals engaged in any trade obtain a higher rate of profit, not by advancing their prices, but by effecting a reduction in the cost of production, then the increased return upon their capital is not acquired at the expense of the consumer, and is a clear addition made to the wealth of the community. But a very different result takes place when a higher profit is obtained, not by reducing the cost of production, but by advancing prices. In this case, the consumer loses all the additional wealth which the producer gains, and the quantity of useful commodities, instead of being augmented, is merely distributed in proportions different from those which prevailed before. If a silk manufacturer discover a process by which he can work up, with a capital of 90,000*l.*, the same quantity of goods on which he was formerly obliged to expend 100,000*l.*, then, by keeping his own secret, and not increasing the supply of silks, he may sell at the same price as before, and without in any way trenching on the resources of the consumer, may gain upon 90,000*l.* the same sum he had acquired upon 100,000*l.*, and thus obtain a disposable capital of 10,000*l.* to be invested in some other occupation ; and to create, at one and the same time, an addition to his own and to the country's wealth. But if a silk manufacturer, by means of some exclusive privilege, were enabled to raise his prices until he obtained, upon a capital of 90,000*l.*, the same sum formerly obtained upon one of 100,000*l.*, the same quantity of silks could not be brought to market at a less expense, there would be no capital disengaged to be invested in other branches of industry; his increased income would be a transfer from the revenue of those who paid the higher price for their goods, and would be no addition whatever to the wealth of the community.

When monopolies affect articles of convenience and luxury, their operation is to alter the distribution of the national wealth, by transferring into the pockets of the producers of such articles the additional price paid for them by their consumers. The consequences of all exclusive privileges, when they touch the necessaries of life, are infinitely more injurious. The progress of industry must always be arrested at that point where the expenses of production can no longer be replaced with a reasonable profit. But the necessaries of life being essential to the support of labour, always form a main ingredient in the expenses of production; and consequently all monopolies, privileges, and restraints which tend to enhance their price, render it more difficult to replace this expense, check the extension and improvement of tillage, and bring a country nearer to the ultimate limits of her resources. If we take three per cent. upon capital as the lowest rate of return, for the sake of which the capitalist will risk his property in production, then all lands may be occupied, provided they are of such a degree of fertility that when one hundred days' subsistence are expended on the soil, one hundred in manufactures, and one hundred more in exchanging the raw produce against the wrought goods, they will occasion a reproduction of subsistence for three hundred and nine. But if, in consequence of a monopoly,

the persons who expended one hundred days'
subsistence in exchanging the necessaries of life,
were enabled to obtain a return of one hundred
and eight, instead of one hundred and three,
then the whole reproduction being only three
hundred and nine, those who expended one
hundred days' subsistence each in agriculture
and manufactures, would obtain a return of no
more than one hundred a half each. By the supposition, however, a profit of three per cent. is
necessary to induce them to carry on their business; and, therefore, all such districts as possess
only the degree of fertility above described, will
be abandoned; and none will be retained in
cultivation except those, the soil of which is of
such a quality, that when one hundred days'
subsistence are expended in agriculture, one
hundred in manufactures, and one hundred in
trade, the reproduction will amount to subsistence for three hundred and fourteen; that is,
will afford three per cent., the customary rate of
profit on the agricultural and manufacturing
capitals, and eight per cent. the monopoly rate,
upon the capital embarked in trade.

The reader will readily perceive, that in whatever degree a monopoly affecting the necessaries of life may check the cultivation of inferior lands, it must, in the same degree, prevent the application of additional portions of capital to the superior soils already under tillage. In obtaining the necessaries of life, three distinct kinds of industry are employed; the agricultural, to procure food and material; the manufacturing, to prepare clothing and furniture; and the mercantile, to aid the powers of the former two by establishing the divisions of labour. Now, the joint products of these several branches of industry must always be sufficient to replace, with an adequate profit, the capitals expended in carrying them on. If we take three per cent. as the lowest rate of profit which will induce men to embark in business, then additional portions of capital may be applied to the soil as long as three hundred days' subsistence expended on the three branches of industry—agriculture, manufacture, and trade—will obtain a reproduction of three hundred and nine days' subsistence. But if, while three per cent. continues to be the *minimum* rate of profit, a monopoly or exclusive privilege enables the master in any one branch of industry to obtain a higher rate of return upon his stock, then the application of additional portions of capital to the soil must cease before the expenditure of subsistence for three hundred days occasions so small a reproduction as subsistence for three hundred and nine days; otherwise, the master tradesman, who derived no benefit from the monopoly, would receive a lower rate of profit than that which is necessary to induce him to continue his business. Supposing that the capital embarked in the favoured branch of industry, constitutes one third of the whole capital employed in bringing the necessaries of life to market, and that in consequence of the monopoly, the third part obtains a profit of eight per cent. and then the progress of heightened cultivation must be arrested when the expenditure of three hundred days' subsistence in the several occupations of agriculture, manufacture, and trade, ceases to occasion a reproduction of three hundred and fourteen days' subsistence. For, if the one hundred days' subsistence expended in any one branch of industry, whether it be that which raises food and material, or that which prepares clothing and furniture, or that which aids the effective powers of the former two, obtain a return of subsistence for one hundred and eight days, or eight per cent. it will require an additional reproduction of two hundred and six days' subsistence to give the remunerating profit of three per cent. upon the expenditure of the other two capitals consisting of one hundred days' subsistence each.

Monopolies may be granted in favour, either of particular individuals, or of particular districts. Their operation is as injurious in the latter case as in the former. When the supplying of any article of convenience or luxury is confined by law to a particular district, the price of such article rises above the level to which competition would have brought it, and to the district so favoured an undue proportion of the wealth of the country is thereby transferred; and when one part of the country obtains an exclusive privilege for supplying articles which enter into the subsistence of labour, then the other parts of the country not only have an undue proportion of their wealth transferred, but have the expenses of production increased on them, and the effective powers of their industry reduced. Thus, then, if monopolies are confined to superfluities, the distribution of wealth is the only thing affected, and the favoured district gains that which the others lose; but, when monopolies extend to necessaries, the production of wealth is checked, and the favoured district cannot acquire that of which the others are deprived. On the contrary, the favoured districts will generally participate in the injury inflicted on the country at large, and will be rendered less opulent than if the trade in subsistence had been left open to competition.

At the time that turnpike roads began to be introduced into England, we are told, that the land proprietors in the neighbourhood of the metropolis petitioned that they might not be extended to the distant counties, lest the improved means of communication might increase competition, and reduce the price of agricultural produce. Had the principle of this petition been

acted upon, and the supplying of the produce
of the soil been restricted to the immediately
adjacent counties, it is self-evident, that London
never could have become what she at present is;
while it is clearly demonstrable, that any given
portion of capital employed in the cultivation of
these favoured counties, would not have yielded
so large a return as it now affords. A great
manufacturing and commercial city confers upon
the neighbouring territory three distinct advantages. As it becomes necessary to resort to
more remote districts for the supply of subsistence, the produce of the adjacent lands
acquires to the amount of the increased expense
of carriage upon the food and material brought
from the greatest distance, a higher value in
the market than that which it before possessed;
in proportion as the accumulation of the population into large towns, facilitating the mechanical
divisions of employment, increases the effective
powers of manufacturing industry, and lowers
the price of clothing, furniture, and implements,
it reduces the cost of production in agricultural
industry, and thereby admits of additional por-

tions of capital being profitably applied to the soil; and in whatever degree the number of wealthy consumers augments, an increased demand will arise for milk, fresh butter, vegetables, fruits, and all those products of the soil which cannot be brought from any considerable distance, and which, as they are not strictly necessaries, can have no limits to the increase of their value, except that which the number and wealth of the consumers may determine. If the petition of the land proprietors in the neighbourhood of London had been complied with, they would have been cut off from all these sources of augmented wealth; and in whatever degree the exclusive privilege for the supplying of agricultural produce might have checked the growing population and prosperity of the metropolis, in that degree it would have retarded the cultivation and improvement of those very districts in favour of which it was proposed. Instead of a transfer, there would have been a diminished production of wealth.

Having thus shewn, that in every conceivable instance, bounties and monopolies, for the encouragement of the home trade, counteract the end they are intended to promote, and have a constant tendency not to advance, but to retard the prosperity of a country, I shall conclude this section with a few observations calculated to shew, in a yet stronger light, that, with respect to the application of capital and the direction of industry, the first duty of government is not to interfere. From the nature and extent of the benefits which a country derives from the facility of internal intercourse, it might seem, at first sight, not unreasonable to conclude, that the legislature has the power of rendering labour and capital more productive, by causing improvements in inland navigation to be undertaken at the public expense. The following considerations will prove that in all ordinary cases this conclusion would be erroneous.

For the sake of illustration, we will suppose, that the customary rate of profit is twenty per cent.; and that the annual expenditure of three thousand days' subsistence, one thousand of which is employed in a manufacturing town, preparing clothing and furniture, one thousand in an agricultural district, raising food and material, and one thousand in transporting and exchanging, occasions a reproduction of subsistence for three thousand six hundred days. Under those circumstances, let it be projected to construct a canal between the town and the agricultural district; let this canal cost two thousand days' subsistence, and on its completion let the annual expenditure for carriage between the town and district be reduced to five hundred days' subsistence.

Now, in such a case, it is quite plain that it would be unnecessary for government to undertake to open the canal. By the previous supposition, one thousand days' subsistence were annually expended on carriage; and, to replace this with a profit of twenty per cent. required a return of subsistence for one thousand two hundred days. Without, therefore, trenching in any way upon the customary rate of profit in agriculture and manufactures, one thousand two hundred days' subsistence are now available for paying the reduced expenses upon carriage, and the interest of the capital sunk in the canal. But the

expense of carriage, as now reduced, amounts
to no more than five hundred days' subsistence,
and to replace this, with a profit of twenty per
cent. requires only subsistence for six hundred;
consequently there remains six hundred days'
subsistence to pay the interest of the two thousand invested in the canal. This gives a return of thirty per cent. It would, therefore,
be superfluous and absurd in the government
to lay contributions on the public, for the construction of a work which would yield ten per
cent. more than the common rate of profit, and
which would consequently excite amongst individuals the most ardent competition to invest
their capital in so beneficial a concern. Nay, it
would not only be superfluous and absurd, it
would be positively pernicious in the government
to undertake the opening of the canal; because,
when works are carried on at the public expense,
they are never performed so economically and
well, as when carried on at the risk of private
individuals, watching over the expenditure of
their individual fortunes.

But supposing that our canal were to cost

eight thousand days' subsistence, instead of two thousand, and that as the return on the concern would be thereby reduced ,from thirty to seven and a half per cent., individuals could not be found to engage in it. Would it not then be expedient for government to undertake the work at the public expense? Certainly not. By the supposition, the customary rate of profit is twenty per cent. and, therefore, it would be highly prejudicial to force capital into a channel in which the return could be only seven and a half per cent. When a new mode of communication will afford an adequate return on the capital which must be expended on it, individuals will undertake to open it ; and when it will not afford the customary rate of return, it should not be opened at all. In either case, nothing but mischief can result from the interference of government. With respect to the internal trade of a country, the whole art of governing is comprised in giving security to property, and in opening an uninterrupted field to individual exertion.

SECTION III.—*On the Colonial Trade.*

HAVING considered what seems important and peculiar in the home trade, I will proceed to examine the colonial trade. This, like every other branch of mercantile industry, gives occasion to divisions of employment, and thus heightens the productive powers of labour and capital. England, for example, abounds with land peculiarly adapted to the feeding of sheep; but as a part of such land is sufficient to supply us with all the mutton and wool we require, the remaining part of it must be employed in producing something else for which we have a demand. Let us suppose that our demand is for sugar; and then the remaining part of the land peculiarly adapted to the feeding of sheep, will be employed in the cultivation of saccharine plants. Neither the soil nor the climate of England, however, is congenial to plants abounding with saccharine matter; and were we to lay out our grounds in plantations of the beet or of the parsnip, we should obtain only a small supply of sugar at a great expense. But let a tropical island, in which the sugar-cane grows luxuriantly, be discovered and taken possession of, and the proprietor of the English beet plantations will immediately perceive, that by feeding sheep upon the grounds which nature adapted to pasture, and exchanging his wool for the sugar of the colonist, he can obtain a much more abundant supply of this article than by raising it at home. The colonist too, in whose warmer climate nature has given the sheep a thin and scanty covering, will find it his interest to raise more sugar than he requires for his own consumption, and to send the surplus to England in exchange for clothing. Hence, between the mother country and the colony a mutually beneficial territorial division of employment will be established; and the home and the colonial proprietor, in consequence of their co-operating with nature, will augment, in a very high degree, the productive powers of their respective industry.

Here, perhaps, it may be asked,—If it is by

establishing divisions of employment that the colonial trade promotes the formation of wealth, what can be the utility of incurring the expense of maintaining colonial establishments? Might not the trade which is carried on between a mother country and her colonies, be equally extensive and beneficial, though the connexion between them were dissolved, and the colonies acknowledged as independent states?

One answer to these questions is, that the territories in which colonies are generally established are inhabited by tribes of savages, possessing neither the inclination nor the skill to render their soil productive; and that before any beneficial divisions of employment can be established with such territories, they must be taken possession of by a civilized people.

This answer, however, applies only to the policy of sending out colonists in the first instance to cultivate tracts inhabited by savage tribes, and does not go to shew that any increase of national wealth is derived from retaining sovereignty over colonies which have been once thoroughly established, or over nations already sufficiently industrious. The proper answers to these questions are the following :—

In the first place, the colonial resembles the home trade, in the two-fold benefit which it confers, and in the security and permanence which it possesses. When England trades with an independent island, a part of the wealth created by the consequent division of employment goes to enrich foreigners. But when England carries on traffic with Jamaica, the whole of the increased wealth, brought into existence by the divisions of employment hereby established, is the property of British subjects, and adds to the strength and resources of the British empire. Besides, when we exchange our commodities with an independent state, the beneficial divisions of employment to which this traffic gives occasion, are liable to be suspended by a declaration of hostilities, or by the enacting of those restrictions and prohibitions which commercial rivalry is perpetually suggesting. But when a mother country and her colonies, particularly if they possess a commanding marine, interchange their surplus products, nothing short of a dismemberment of the empire can suspend their intercourse, or interrupt those divisions of employment by which they are enabled to make the most of the natural peculiarities of their soil, and of their acquired advantages in the application of labour.

In the second place, from the relative proportions, according to which population and capital have, in all old countries, been hitherto found to increase, the supply of labour has such a tendency to exceed the demand for it, that the labouring classes, even when there is no extraordinary stagnation or revulsion in the channels of industry, are commonly reduced to a degree of distress and temptation, for which, in the actual state of knowledge and of morals, there is no conceivable remedy except in a system of colonization, sufficiently extensive to relieve the mother country from superfluous numbers. The question of colonization, however, with respect to its influence in mitigating the evils of excessive population, will fall more properly under our consideration when we come to examine the several circumstances which regulate wages, and affect the interests of the labouring classes. It is alluded to in this place merely for the purpose of exhibiting, in a stronger light, the futility of the objections which have sometimes been urged against the extension of the colonial system.

It is extremely improbable that the objections against colonial establishments, even were they as valid as in reality they are futile, should ever have the effect of inducing princes and sovereign states voluntarily to resign such dependencies. A question of much greater practical importance presents itself for our consideration;—namely, can any accession of wealth be derived from those restrictions which, in modern times, parent states have almost uniformly imposed upon the commerce of their colonies? Such restrictions have generally had for their object, either to grant to particular companies, and particular ports, an exclusive privilege to trade with the colonies; or, to compel the colonies to make the mother country the mart, or *entrepôt,* for effecting all their transactions with foreign countries; or, to secure to the domestic producer the monopoly of the colonial market. I shall examine the effects of these restrictions in the order in which I have enumerated them.

When a particular company, or a particular town, obtains the exclusive privilege of trading with the colonies, home-made goods become dearer in the colonial market, and colonial goods dearer in the home market than they would be if the law of competition were allowed to operate unchecked. It is only by being enabled to dispose of their commodities at prices above the level which would be determined by free competition, that the merchants of a particular company or town can receive any benefit from the exclusive privilege of trading with the colonies.

But raising the price of home-made goods in the colonial market, and of colonial goods in the home market, above the level of free competition, brings no additional wealth into existence, but merely enhances the profits of the merchant at the expense of the consumer. Nay, this mode of raising prices, and of enhancing the profits of the privileged merchant, instead of increasing the general mass of wealth, will tend to diminish it. Enjoying considerable profits by the aid of their exclusive privilege, the merchants trading between the mother country and the colonies will not be compelled to shut out competitors by taxing their ingenuity to the utmost in order to discover the cheapest and most expeditious modes of conducting their business. A greater quantity than would otherwise be necessary, of the labour and capital of the country, will therefore be employed in exchanging commodities, a d consequently a less quantity will remain to be employed in directly producing them. But this is not all. Many of those articles which the mother country sends to the colonies, and which the colonies send to the mother country, will consist of the necessaries of life, or of the articles expended in raising and fabricating the necessaries of life. But we have seen, that whatever increases the expense of bringing such articles to market, lowers the return upon capital throughout all the departments of industry, sets narrower limits to the extension and improvement of tillage, and diminishes the quantity of food and of raw material which can be obtained for manufactures. Granting, therefore, to particular companies, or even to particular towns, the exclusive privilege of trading with the colonies, not only enriches the favoured individuals at the expense of the home and colonial consumers, but at one and the same time checks the prosperity, both of the colonies and of the mother country.

The effect is different with respect to those restrictions on the colonial trade which have for their object to render the mother country the mart, or *entrepôt,* for conducting the commercial intercourse between the colonies and foreign countries. These increase the wealth of the mother country by diminishing that of the colonies. If we suppose that the British colonies consume a quantity of Russian linens, while Russia, in return, takes a quantity of their sugars; then it will be the clear and obvious interest, both of the colonies and of Russia, that their respective commodities should be carried and exchanged with the smallest possible expense. But if England restricts her colonies from holding a direct commerce with foreign countries; and if, in consequence, the sugars and the linens must be first consigned to the port of London, and thence reshipped for their final destination, then the London merchants to whom the consignments are made, and by whom the reshipments are effected, will charge their commission upon these transactions; and this commission, paid by the Russian and colonial consumers in the increased price of their goods, will be a clear addition to the wealth of England, obtained by the restrictive system imposed upon the colonies.

It may perhaps be objected, that if the British colonies were permitted to hold a direct traffic with Russia, the London merchants to whom the consignments were made, and by whom the reshipments were effected, would employ their capitals in some other direction, and, by making the customary rate of profit, would effect the same addition to the national wealth as before. We answer, that mercantile capital consists, first and mainly, of the commodities which are circulated; and, secondly, of the vessels, docks, wharfs, and warehouses, by means of which their circulation is effected. If the restrictive system were abolished, and a direct trade permitted between our colonies and Russia, all that portion of mercantile capital consisting of the sugar to be consumed in Russia, and the linen to be used in the colonies, which was consigned to the London merchant, and upon which he obtained a commission, would disappear altogether from the port of London, and no longer pay England a per centage. Besides, that portion of mercantile capital which consisted of docks, wharfs, and warehouses, though it remained in the country, yet could not be transferred to agriculture or manufactures, and when London ceased to be the *entrepôt* between the colonies and Russia, the dues, profits, and rents paid for the use of these things by the colonial and Russian consumers, would be so much net revenue which England would lose by the abolition of the restrictive system.

The principles here stated, enable us to trace one of the sources of the great prosperity of England during the late war. Her conquests, her naval superiority, and her restrictive system, aided as it was, by the anti-commercial decrees of the French Government, rendered the United Kingdom the *entrepôt* for the colonial trade of Europe. The consignments from all the colonies of produce for the purchase of foreign goods, and from all the countries of Europe of foreign goods for the purchase of colonial produce, constituted an immense mercantile capital, circulating throughout the ports of the United Kingdom, paying a regular commission to the British merchant, with dues, profits, and rents, for the use of docks, wharfs, and warehouses. When peace returned, and England resigned her colonial conquests, this immense floating capital was no longer attracted to her ports. The British merchant ceased to receive his accustomed commission, and the proprietor of docks and warehouses, the dues and rents paid by the colonial and continental consumer; and the cessation of hostilities, instead of giving, as some persons seemed to expect, a new impulse to commercial prosperity, was followed by a diminution of trade, and a loss of wealth.

Those restrictions which have for their object

to secure to the productions of the mother country a monopoly in the colonial market, may also
have the effect of enriching the mother country
at the expense of the colonies. Supposing that
Scotch and Irish linens cannot be sold with an
adequate profit at so low a price as those of
Germany; and that England, by protecting
duties and prohibitions, compels her West India
Islands to purchase the more costly articles;—it
will be evident, that the wealth of these colonies
must be diminished by the amount of the difference between the price which they pay for
British, and that, at which, under a free trade,
they might obtain German linens. A little
consideration will also render it evident, that
this loss sustained by the colonies, will be a
source of gain to the mother country. Under
the circumstances supposed, if it were not for
the artificial protection afforded to them, Scotch
and Irish linens could not be manufactured for
the colonial market; and the manufacturers
would be compelled to transfer their capital to
the production of other articles with which to
purchase the colonial produce required for the

home market. But why, in the first instance, was colonial produce purchased with linens, instead of with the other articles now fabricated for that purpose? For no other reason, assuredly, but because the merchant found that linens, when sold in the colonies at the prices secured by the restrictive system, enabled him to bring back a more valuable return in colonial goods than he could have purchased with any other article produced at home, by an equal expenditure of labour and capital. Had there been any article, obtained at home at the same expense, which could have purchased in the colonies a greater, or even an equal quantity of their produce, this article it would have been the interest of the merchant to have exported. The fact of his having preferred the exportation of linen proves, that this article, when protected against foreign competition, will purchase in the colonies a greater quantity of their produce than any other obtained at an equal expense. The restrictive system, therefore, which prevents foreign from beating home-made linens, out of the colonial market, enables the mother country to purchase her colonial produce with a less sacrifice of labour and capital than she otherwise could do. While the colonies would be impoverished by giving a greater quantity of the produce of their labour and capital for the linens they required, the mother country would be enriched by giving a less quantity of her products for the sugar and rum which she consumed.

The principle, that restrictions compelling the colonies to receive those commodities which other countries could furnish to them cheaper, increases the wealth of the mother country by diminishing that of the colonies, is so important, and at the same time so inadequately understood, that it may be expedient to illustrate it by an analytical detail.

It is quite evident, that no legislative restrictions would be required for forcing the consumption of British linens in our West India Islands, unless other countries could furnish them cheaper; and that even after the imposition of the restrictions, the British merchant would not export linens to these Islands, unless the state of the

market were such, that he obtained a better
return, either in money or in colonial produce,
than he could obtain by exporting additional
supplies of other things. We will, therefore,
assume, as the basis of our illustration, 1*st*, that
Jamaica pays the United Kingdom one hundred
and ten stone of sugar for that quantity of linen
which, if trade were free, she could obtain from
Germany for one hundred stone. 2*d*, that the
markets of Jamaica being already supplied with
all British goods except linen, the additional
exportation to that Island of a quantity of woollens or of hardware, &c. &c. which had been
produced by a capital of one hundred days' subsistence, would cause a glut of these things, and
so lower their exchangeable value, that the venture brought back a return of only one hundred
stone of sugar; while a venture consisting of
a quantity of linen produced by a capital of one
hundred days' subsistence, obtained a return of
one hundred and ten stone.

In this case it is evident, that the commercial
restrictions forcing the colonies to take British
instead of German linens, diminish the wealth

of Jamaica to the extent of ten stone of sugar on every one hundred yards of linen she consumes; while they increase the wealth of the United Kingdom to the extent of ten stone of sugar upon every portion of capital equal to one hundred days' subsistence employed in supplying the colonial consumer with the linen for which he has a demand. Thus we see exactly the *modus operandi* by which the monopoly of the colonial market gives to the mother country the products of a greater quantity of colonial industry in exchange for the products of a given quantity of domestic industry.

While the restrictions on the colonial trade which give the products of domestic industry a monopoly in the colonial market, increase the wealth of the mother country at the expense of the colonies, those restrictions which secure to colonial productions an exclusive privilege in the home market, enrich the colonies at the expense of the mother country. When England imposes an unequal duty upon the sugars of the East Indies, in order to encourage the trade with the West India Islands, she renders herself tributary to her own colonies, and makes a voluntary sacrifice of wealth to the amount of the difference between the quantity of her products which she gives for her supply of West India sugars, and the quantity for which she might obtain an equal supply of sugars from the East. Again; when the legislature recently laid heavy duties on the importation of Norwegian timber, in order to force the people of England to purchase the dear and inferior timber of Canada, the interests of England were blindly sacrificed to those of Canada, and the wealth of the country diminished by the difference between the price we are forced to pay for American timber, and the price for which we might obtain the article from the North of Europe. But this is not the worst; with the single exception perhaps of iron, timber is the most serviceable article in aiding human labour. It enters, more or less, into every portion of capital employed in production. Now, increasing the difficulty of obtaining the ingredients of capital, and thereby raising their exchangeable value with respect to other things, necessarily reduces the rate of profit. Hence, the monopoly which England has granted to Canada in the timber trade, not only compels her to sacrifice a greater portion of her wealth in exchange for the timber she requires, but tends to lower the return upon capital throughout all the departments of her industry. By the duties on Norwegian timber, the mother country loses incalculably more than the colonies can gain.

In concluding this section on the colonial trade, it may be expedient to shew, that the principle, that restrictions may benefit the mother country by injuring the colonies, or enrich the colonies by impoverishing the mother country, is in no way inconsistent with the doctrine established in the preceding section, that the utmost freedom of internal intercourse promotes the wealth of a country. When a mother country and her colonies are regarded as one empire, there can be no doubt that the aggregate wealth of this empire will be increased by establishing an entire freedom of trade between all the countries composing it; in the same way as the aggregate wealth of a country is increased by permitting unrestricted intercourse between its several provinces. But, as in any country a monopoly, or exclusive privilege, in favour of a particular set of persons, or of a particular town, might enrich those persons, or that town, at the expense of the community; so, in an extensive empire, commercial regulations may be devised which will have the effect of rendering one country tributary to another. In revising our colonial system, if the object of the legislature should be to increase the wealth of the British dominions, the utmost freedom should be extended to the trade between the several countries of which these dominions are composed. But, should the object be to cause the greatest possible portion of the general wealth to centre in the United Kingdom, as a compensation for the expense of protection; then restrictions should be imposed, rendering the mother country the *entrepôt* for the foreign transactions of the colonies, and securing to her productions a monopoly in their markets. We cannot conceive, that it is ever the real object of legislators to enrich a colony by impoverishing the parent state;

because this would be to counteract the only end for which colonial possessions are maintained; and therefore regulations, similar in principle to those under which England imports her timber from Canada, must have their origin either in ignorance, or in a corrupt compliance, in return for parliamentary support, with the wishes of some powerful junta of ship-owners and merchants, whose private interest is opposed to that of the public.

Section IV.—*On Foreign Trade, or Commerce.*

WE have now to examine the peculiar and distinguishing effects of foreign trade, or commerce. The manner in which this branch of mercantile industry augments the wealth of a country, is precisely analogous to that in which the home and the colonial trades occasion a similar effect. The divisions of employment augment in a wonderful degree the productive powers of land, labour, and capital. By the mechanical division, each person acquires, in his peculiar calling, an expertness and skill which would otherwise be unattainable; by the territorial division, cultivation is made to co-operate with nature ; and by both, capital is economised, and all its products are multiplied.   Now, these beneficial divisions of employment may be established between individuals residing in different nations, as well as between individuals residing in the same nation.   If the people of England have acquired greater skill than their neighbours in working up cotton, while those of France excel in manufacturing silk, then, between the two countries a mechanical division of employment, mutually beneficial, may be established. By England's confining herself to the fabricating of cottons, and France to the fabricating of silks, these articles of clothing may be produced in greater abundance than if each country directed its labour and capital to the occupation more peculiar to the other.   Again; while the mines and coal pits of England give her peculiar facilities in procuring and working up tin and iron, and while the soil and climate of France

give her peculiar advantages in producing wine
and fruit, a territorial division of employment,
mutually beneficial, may be established between
the two countries: England, by working her
mines, and exchanging her metals for the produce of the French vine-yards, will obtain a
much greater quantity of wine, than if she
attempted to cultivate the grape at home,
beneath an uncongenial sky; and France, by
exchanging her wine for the hard-ware of England, will obtain a much more abundant supply
of these articles, than if she attempted to work
the metals for herself.   Now, as it is the home
trade which gives occasion to the home divisions
of employment, so it is foreign trade, or commerce, which gives occasion to the foreign divisions of employment. All the increase of wealth,
therefore, which nations derive from the foreign
divisions of employment, are to be referred to
commerce as their original and proper source.
Having thus shewn the manner in which foreign
trade heightens the power of production, and
increases wealth, we proceed to point out what
is peculiar to this branch of mercantile industry.

As in the operations of the home and colonial trades, the benefit is always two-fold; so, in the operations of foreign trade, the benefit is always reciprocal. The opinion so frequently urged by economists, and acted upon by statesmen, that what one nation gains by commerce, some other nation must lose, is totally destitute of proof, and directly contrary to fact. When England, availing herself of her natural advantages, prepares more tin and iron than is necessary for her own consumption, and exchanges the surplus for the wines and fruits of France, she obtains a much greater quantity of these articles than the labour and capital expended upon the equivalents with which they are purchased, could have raised at home. But, in this case, the gain of England is not the loss of France. On the contrary, the latter country, by availing herself of the natural peculiarities of her soil and climate, and exchanging her surplus wine and fruit for the tin and iron work of England, obtains a much larger and better supply of these useful commodities, than the labour and capital expended upon the fruit and wine by which they were purchased, could otherwise have procured for her. Again; while, in consequence of more accurate divisions of mechanical employment, and of the application of better machinery, England can manufacture cloth cheaper than Poland; and while Poland, in consequence of having none but her first-rate soils under cultivation, can raise corn cheaper than England; then, England, by exchanging cloth for corn, will obtain a much greater quantity of corn than the labour and capital expended on the cloth could have extracted from her own soil. But this gain of England is not acquired at the cost of Poland. On the contrary, Poland obtains in exchange for her corn, a much larger and better supply of cloth than the labour and capital expended on the corn could have manufactured for her at home. The advantages are mutual and reciprocal. In both countries the productive powers of industry are multiplied. England has more food, and Poland has more cloth, than if a fettered commerce destroyed the international divisions of employment.

Another most important consequence of

foreign trade is, that it accelerates prosperity in
new countries, while in old countries it removes
the natural check to prosperity, and throws the
stationary state to a greater distance. In new
countries, where it is not necessary to cultivate
inferior lands, or to cultivate the better soils in
an expensive manner, the productive powers of
agricultural industry are extraordinarily high;
while, from the population being thin and scattered, and from capitals being little accumulated,
the application of machinery, and the division
of mechanical employment are imperfect; and
consequently, the productive powers of manufacturing industry are extraordinarily low. The case
is reversed in old countries. In these, the necessity of resorting to inferior soils, and of applying
additional portions of capital to the best, renders
it daily more difficult to raise an increased supply
of agricultural produce; while, in consequence
of denser population, and larger accumulations
of capital, employment is more subdivided, and
machinery better applied; so that the productive
powers of manufacturing industry increase, rather
than diminish. Hence, we perceive, that in new

countries, prosperity is retarded by the difficulty of converting raw produce into wrought goods; while, in old and populous countries, prosperity is checked, and ultimately the stationary state brought on, by the difficulty, not of working up, but of procuring agricultural produce. Now, the difficulty of working up raw produce in the one case, and of obtaining it in the other, may be completely obviated by those international divisions of employment which foreign trade establishes. This important principle we will proceed to demonstrate by one or two illustrative cases.

Let us suppose, that in America, the labour of one family is, in consequence of none but the best lands being under cultivation, sufficient to raise the raw produce necessary for the consumption of six families; and that, owing to the thinness of the population, and to the consequent imperfection in manufacturing industry, it requires the labour of three families to prepare the wrought goods necessary for the consumption of six. In this case, a surplus, or net revenue, amounting to fifty per cent. upon capital, would be annually created; the expenditure of raw material and wrought goods for four families, reproducing material and wrought goods for six. Now, if we suppose that four fifths of this net revenue, or forty per cent. upon the capital employed, is expended unproductively, and that one fifth, or ten per cent. upon the capital employed, is reserved for accumulation and repro- duction; then, without calculating the compound ratio of increase, the capital of America will be doubled every ten years.

We must now make a further supposition, in order to shew in what manner foreign trade might increase the net revenue, and shorten the period in which the accumulation of one fifth of such revenue would double capital. While the productive powers of agriculture remain as be- fore, let the labour of two families, employed upon the new lands of America, raise a quantity of agricultural produce sufficient to purchase of the cheaper manufactures imported from Eng- land, the wrought goods necessary for the con- sumption of six families; and then, as soon as this international division of employment is esta- blished, the surplus, or net revenue annually created in America, will amount to a hundred per cent. on the capital she employs. For by the supposition, the labour of three produces that which is equivalent to the raw material and wrought goods consumed by six. Now, if, as before, four fifths of this net revenue (being now eighty per cent. on the capital employed) are expended unproductively upon superfluities; and if the remaining fifth, now twenty per cent. upon capital, be reserved for accumulation and reproduction, then the capital of the country, without calculating the compound rate of increase, will be doubled in five years, instead of in ten. Nor will this accelerated march of prosperity be obtained by frugality and self-denial. On the contrary, while capital is made to double in five, instead of in ten years, the expenditure and enjoyments of those who live upon net revenue are, by the supposition, twice as great as before.

Having thus illustrated the manner in which the prosperity of a new country, where agricultural products are raised at little expense, is accelerated by a commerce with an old country, where wrought goods are prepared with little

expense, we have now to shew, how the ultimate limits to the progress of an old country are
thrown to an indefinite distance, by trading
with a new country.

We will suppose, that cultivation has been
pushed so far in England, that, upon the next
quality of land which remains to be taken in, it
would require the labour of five families to raise
the raw produce necessary for the consumption
of six; while, in consequence of the accumulation of capital, and the subdivision of employment, the labour of one family will prepare the
wrought goods necessary for the consumption of
six. Now, it is plain, that if in this case England cannot import raw produce, she will have
arrived at the stationary state. If she attempted
to raise an additional quantity of food and material from her own soil, the labour of six families,
five being employed in cultivating, and one in
manufacturing, would just produce the quantity
of food, material, and wrought goods necessary to
the consumption of six families; and no surplus
would be created to remunerate the capitalist
for the employment of his stock. But it is

evident, that before capital ceases to replace itself with a surplus or profit, production must be arrested. While it required the labour of one family to supply the wrought necessaries consumed by six, land requiring the labour of five, to raise the raw produce required by six, could not be taken into cultivation; and England would find it impossible to extract an increased quantity of food and material with which to subsist and employ an additional population. The ultimate limit of her prosperity would be attained.

Now, let the commerce of America be opened to England, and let the manufactured goods prepared by the labour of three families bring from that country a return, consisting of agricultural produce for six families; and immediately the limits to the wealth and population of England will be removed to a greater distance. For the labour of one prepares the wrought goods, and by means of this exchange, the labour of three procures the raw produce necessary to the consumption of six. But when four produce what is expended by six, the surplus or profit is fifty per cent. The most rapid accumulations of capital might be made, and the manufacturing population of England might continue to multiply while there remained in America a fertile and well situated district to be reclaimed. Thus commerce, and the consequent division of employment, between the old and the new country, while they rolled with redoubled velocity the tide of civilized population from the Atlantic to the Pacific Ocean, would give the wealth and resources of England the capability of an almost infinite increase.

Such being the advantages which foreign trade is calculated to bestow, as well on new countries, in which the progressive state is retarded by the high value of wrought goods in relation to raw produce, as in old countries in which the stationary state is approached in consequence of the high value of raw produce as compared with wrought goods; it must fill us with astonishment to see the governments of England and America rivalling each other in their efforts to contract within the smallest compass, that species of intercourse between the two countries, which, were it freed from restraint, would enable them to confer reciprocal and almost infinite benefits upon each other. This furnishes a melancholy proof of the small portion of wisdom with which the affairs of nations are administered. The circumstance that the advantages of foreign trade are reciprocal, and equally divided between the nations carrying it on, instead of inducing ministers and legislators to allow it a free and unimpeded course, furnishes them with an argument (if such it may be called) for restricting the importation of all those articles which it may be possible to produce at home. The home trade, it is affirmed, confers a two-fold benefit; and any given capital employed in conducting it, increases the effective powers of two other capitals invested at home in direct production, and thus secures to the country the whole of the benefit resulting from the division of labour; while foreign trade confers only a single benefit, any given portion of capital employed in conducting it, increasing the effective powers of but one other capital invested at home in direct production, and bestowing upon the foreign producer one half of the additional wealth which the division of labour creates. Hence, it is contended, that the foreign trade, which confers the lesser benefit, should not be permitted to interfere with the home trade, which confers the greater benefit; and that England should exchange her manufactured goods, not against American, but against British produce ; and that America, instead of bartering her raw produce for the wrought goods of England, should give it to support manufactures to be established within her own territory.

This argument, for discouraging the foreign in favour of the home trade, turns upon an entire misconception of the nature and effects of mercantile industry. It is no doubt true, that a mercantile capital, employed in the home trade, and giving occasion to the home divisions of labour, would increase the effective powers of two other British capitals invested in direct production ; while a mercantile capital, employed in the foreign trade, and giving occasion to international divisions of labour, could increase the effective powers of only one other British capital.

But to conclude from this, that the foreign must be less beneficial than the home divisions of labour, is to mistake words for things, and to suffer our understandings to be swayed by the expressions two-fold and reciprocal, instead of by the actual quantity of wealth which the different kinds of mercantile industry are instrumental in creating. The surest way of obviating this source of ambiguity and error, is to descend from general terms, and to argue analytically from particular cases.

If England were to expend a manufacturing capital of food and wrought necessaries for one hundred, in fabricating wrought necessaries for five hundred; an agricultural capital of food and wrought necessaries for two hundred, in raising food for five hundred; and a mercantile capital of food and wrought necessaries for one hundred, in exchanging the wrought necessaries of her artisans, against the food of her cultivators; then the mercantile capital engaged in conducting this home trade, would increase the effective powers of two other British capitals invested in direct production, and the whole expenditure of food and wrought necessaries for four hundred, would be replaced by food and wrought necessaries for five hundred, or with a profit of twenty-five per cent.

Now, while England employs the same quantity of industry as before, let its direction be changed; let a capital of food and wrought necessaries for two hundred be expended in fabricating wrought necessaries for one thousand, and another capital of food and wrought necessaries for two hundred in exchanging wrought necessaries for four hundred, with the American farmer for food for six hundred, and then the additional capital of food and wrought necessaries for one hundred, required in conducting the foreign and more distant exchanges will be withdrawn from direct production, and this double mercantile capital, instead of conferring, as when employed in the home trade, the two-fold benefit of increasing the effective powers of the British manufacturer and British farmer, would bestow the reciprocal benefit of heightening the effective powers of the British manufacturer and the American farmer. But it is plain, that notwithstanding this nominal loss, England would gain a real advantage by this change in the direction of her industry. The whole capital of food and wrought necessaries for four hundred, expended in direct and indirect production, instead of obtaining a return of food and wrought necessaries for five hundred, or an increase of twenty-five per cent. will now acquire a reproduction of food and wrought necessaries for six hundred, or an increase or profit of thirty-three per cent.

It may be objected, perhaps, that these cases are not fairly stated, and that when the agricultural capital of food and wrought necessaries for two hundred, is transferred from the soil to be partly employed in manufacturing for the American market, and partly in conducting foreign and more distant exchanges, it may obtain, instead of a greater, such a less quantity of food, as will render the aggregate profit upon the whole capital employed lower than before. I answer, that this is impossible; because, if the transference of capital from agriculture to manufactures and commerce, brought a less instead of a greater return of food, such transference never could have taken place. By the supposition, when all the capitals amounting to food and wrought necessaries for four hundred, are expended within the country either in direct production, or in the home trade, the rate of increase upon them is twenty-five per cent. When, therefore, the merchant engages in foreign trade, and expends food and wrought necessaries for two hundred, in exchanging wrought necessaries for four hundred against American corn, he must retain in his own hands, in order to replace his capital with the same rate of return which he obtained while engaged in the home trade, food and wrought necessaries for two hundred and fifty. But if the merchant who exports wrought necessaries for four hundred, brings back less than food for five hundred, say only food for four hundred and fifty, and retains in his own hands food for two hundred and fifty, in order to replace his capital; then the food for two hundred which remains, and which is to be paid for wrought necessaries, will not be sufficient to replace with a profit the capital expended by the manufacturer. For, by the supposition, the manufacturer expended food and wrought necessaries for two hundred in fabricating wrought necessaries for one thousand, and in order to replace his expenditure with a profit of twenty-five per cent. he must be enabled to retain wrought necessaries for two hundred and fifty in his own hand, and to exchange the remainder, or wrought necessaries for seven hundred and fifty, for food for two hundred and fifty. But there is disposable in the hands of the merchant, only food for two hundred. Hence, while that part of the manufacturer's capital, consisting of wrought necessaries for two hundred, is replaced with a profit of twenty-five per cent., the other portion of it is replaced without any increase whatever, and thus the rate of return upon his aggregate expenditure will be less than when the supply of food was grown at home*. But if

---

* Our merchant who employed food and wrought necessaries for two hundred in exporting wrought necessaries for four hundred, and bringing back food for four hundred and fifty, and who, after retaining in his own hands food for two hundred and fifty, gave the remaining food for two hundred for the manufacturer's wrought necessaries

the capital which had been transferred from the soil to manufactures, brings a less return in its new than in its old occupation, it will inevitably flow back to domestic agriculture. When the product of any given capital invested in manufactures will purchase only a less quantity of food from the foreign farmer than the same capital could raise at home, it is impossible that food should continue to be imported. In like manner, when a country is so circumstanced, that the product of a given capital invested in agriculture will purchase from abroad a less quantity of manufactured goods than the same capital could fabricate at home, it will be impossible to continue to import such goods. The fact that Eng-

---

for seven hundred and fifty, would gain seventy-five per cent. upon that portion of his capital which consisted of wrought necessaries for two hundred, as four hundred would be exported, and seven hundred and fifty remain in his hands. But the greater surplus obtained upon that portion of the merchant's capital which consisted of wrought necessaries, would not balance the loss of all surplus upon that portion of the manufacturer's capital which consisted of food; because, the exchangeable value of food for two hundred, so greatly exceeds that of wrought necessaries for two hundred.

land and America barter wrought goods and raw
produce, is in itself a sufficient demonstration
that the international division of employment
confers upon the two countries the reciprocal
benefits which I have attempted to describe.

It is frequently contended, that however beneficial a free trade might be, if all countries
could be prevailed upon to admit and act upon
the principle, it would be highly inexpedient in
any one country to abandon the restrictive system while her neighbours continued to enforce
it. According to this doctrine, it would be injurious to England to admit the free importation
of American produce, unless America were to
consent to a free importation of British goods in
return; because, were America to refuse this,
the labour and capital thrown out of employment by our receiving from abroad that quantity
of produce which was before raised at home,
could not be reinvested in the production of an
increased quantity of goods for exportation.

This objection against the free admission of
those things which can be brought cheaper
from abroad, turns upon the supposition that

foreign countries will give their productions, not for an equivalent, but as a gratuity or tribute. Nothing can be more erroneous or absurd. Commerce is an exchange of equivalents, a bartering between nations of one commodity for another. As no people will consent to give away the fruits of their industry as a voluntary tribute to their neighbours; the country which permits her commodities to be exported to another country, imposes on herself the necessity of allowing that other country to export to her their price, or equivalent, in other articles. When America sends the produce of her soil to England, and refuses to receive British goods in return, she does not obviate this necessity, she only obliges England to export her commodities to some other country, in order to purchase the article which America may consent to receive. The process is more circuitous, but the result is precisely the same.

To recur to our former case; if, on the establishment of a free trade between England and America, England instead of continuing to employ her capital of subsistence for two hundred upon an inferior soil, which yields in return only food for five hundred, were to employ it in manufacturing cloth, and exchanging her fabric with the American cultivator for food for six hundred, it is self-evident that the portion of her labour and capital disengaged from the soil by the importation of American produce so far from being thrown into a state of inactivity would find a more beneficial occupation than before. But if upon the establishment of a free trade upon the part of England, America refused to receive British goods, while England withdrew from the soil a capital which raised food for five hundred, and employed it in manufacturing cloth, exchanging this cloth for the gold of Portugal, and purchasing with the gold so obtained food for six hundred from the American farmer; then it is equally self-evident, that the capital disengaged from British agriculture by the importation of American produce, so far from being thrown into a state of inactivity, would be reinvested in a more profitable occupation.

The advocates for protecting domestic industry by restrictions on the importation of foreign articles, urge, as a further objection, that the foreign market may be glutted with our fabrics, and that, if we allow the importation of foreign produce, it may be found impossible to increase our exports so as to afford, in the extension of manufactures and commerce, a beneficial investment for the capital displaced from the soil.

I answer,—that under this supposition, the whole controversy is set at rest. If America will not receive our goods, and if we cannot increase our exports to other foreign countries so as to obtain a quantity of foreign commodities or of gold, with which to pay for American produce; then, as America will not give it to us for nothing, not one quarter of her produce can be imported into England, and the home grower will be as effectually protected against foreign competition, as if the British Islands were encompassed with Bishop Berkeley's wall of brass. The objection is destroyed by the very supposition upon which it is founded. In the case of England adopting a free trade with respect to America, while America adheres to a restrictive system with respect to England, if England cannot invest a greater quantity of capital in manufactures and commerce so as to purchase in other foreign markets the equivalent which America may consent to receive in exchange for her produce, then no American produce can be imported into England, and no capital turned from domestic agriculture to seek reinvestment in the extension of trade and commerce. All things would remain precisely in the same position as before; the self-same cause which rendered it impossible to reinvest in manufactures and commerce the capital which might be disengaged from the soil by the importation of foreign produce, depriving us of the means of purchasing that produce, and preventing the occurrence of the circumstance which might dislodge capital from domestic agriculture.

I have dwelt upon the interchange between old and new countries of wrought necessaries against raw produce, because it is the species of commerce which has the greatest influence upon national prosperity, and that concerning which the most inveterate prejudices prevail. It is by

no means my intention, however, to undervalue
the importance of foreign trade in superfluities
and luxuries, or to extenuate the absurdity of
those who imagine they can give encouragement
to domestic industry by encumbering this branch
of traffic with restrictions. The more perfectly
the international divisions of employment are
established, the more entirely each country can
confine itself to those occupations in which it
possesses natural or acquired advantages, the
more abundant the supply of commodities will
become. If England, with two capitals, each
consisting of subsistence for one hundred, fabricates one hundred and fifty bales of cotton, and
one hundred bales of silk, while France, with
two similar capitals, manufactures one hundred
and fifty bales of silk, and one hundred bales of
cotton; then between both countries, two hundred and fifty bales of cotton, and two hundred
and fifty bales of silk will be produced. But if
England withdraws one of her capitals from the
fabrication of silk to that of cotton, she will produce three hundred bales of that article, and if
France withdraws one of her capitals from the

manufacture of cotton to that of silk, three hundred bales of silk will be produced; and when, according to the law of competition, the half of the one product is exchanged against the half of the other, England will obtain an increase of wealth to the extent of fifty bales of silk, and France an increase to the extent of fifty bales of cotton. An unrestricted commerce in these articles would be reciprocally and equally beneficial.

Now, supposing that France should become so blind to her own interest as to employ one of her capitals of subsistence for one hundred in manufacturing one hundred bales of cotton instead of devoting it to fabricating the silks with which she could purchase one hundred and fifty bales of cotton from England, this mistaken policy on the part of France could furnish no conceivable reason why England should imitate the absurd example. The refusal of France to take our cheaper cottons, would not render it less our interest to receive her cheaper silks. If one hundred and fifty bales of French silks continue to be imported, something must be exported to pay for them, and in preparing this something, the capital disengaged from the manufacturing of silk at home, will find a more beneficial occupation than before. Should France refuse to receive every species of British fabric, then the capital displaced from the silk manufacture by the introduction of her cheaper article, would be employed in preparing a greater quantity of goods to be sent to other foreign markets in order to bring back a return in money with which to liquidate our debt to France; and should the state of all other foreign markets be such, that we could not export to them a greater quantity of goods, and thus obtain an equivalent with which to purchase French silks, then as France would not give her fabrics for nothing, no French silks could be imported into England, and no domestic industry displaced. It never could become necessary for the protection of domestic industry, that we should retaliate upon any foreign country the restrictive system which it may ignorantly enforce against us. For as no country can export, unless she consents to import the equivalents which other countries may be able to return, the only injury the enforcement of the restrictive system against our commerce can inflict, is to prevent the introduction of those articles which the foreigner can furnish cheaper than ourselves, and thus to leave the domestic producer as completely in possession of the home market, as if the most rigorous measures of retaliation were resorted to for his protection.

There is one case in which a free foreign trade might impoverish and depopulate a country. When countries have arrived at that ultimate point, beyond which no additional capital can be employed with a profit in raising food and the materials of wrought necessaries, then, if one country were to acquire superior facilities in the production of superfluities and luxuries, the free importation of such articles into the other countries would dislodge a great portion of their capital without presenting any possible opening for reinvestment, and would cause their manufacturing population to emigrate or perish. As I do not remember that any preceding writer has attended to the peculiar effects which, under these circumstances, a free foreign trade would produce, I shall endeavour to present a clear and precise analysis of the manner in which they would be brought about.

Let us suppose, that England and France have each arrived at that point of improvement at which the expenditure of a capital of food and wrought necessaries for one hundred, will raise food for one hundred and fifty-three; and a capital of food and wrought necessaries for fifty prepare wrought necessaries for one hundred and fifty-three, and then the rate of increase or profit will be just two per cent. Let this two per cent. be the lowest rate of profit for the sake of which the capitalist will engage in production, and let it be impossible to increase the quantity of food, because the next land to be taken in cannot yield the necessary increase of two per cent. upon the capital expended on it. Now, while such continues to be the situation of the two countries with respect to necessaries, let France acquire the power of manufacturing all articles of superfluity and luxury for half the cost at which they can be prepared in England.

Under such circumstances, the French manufacturer might sell his superfluities, and obtain
a handsome profit at a price which would be
altogether inadequate to replace the capital of
English manufacture. For, the French manufacturer who expended food and wrought necessaries for one hundred, in working up fifty bales
of silk, would gain twenty per cent. if he sold
his commodity in the English market for food
and clothing for one hundred and twenty, while
the British manufacturer who expended food
and wrought necessaries for two hundred in
preparing a similar article, and afterwards sold
it for the same price of food and wrought necessaries for one hundred and twenty, would lose
nearly fifty per cent. by the transaction. If a
free trade, therefore, were permitted with France,
it would be impossible for the English producer
to sell his fabrics at so low a price as the French,
and consequently all the food and wrought
necessaries which had formerly purchased superfluities fabricated at home, would now be exported to pay for the cheaper fabrics of France.
Nor could the labour and capital dislodged by

the introduction of the foreign goods, formerly
made at home, find any other profitable occupation. By the supposition, no additional supply
of food and material can be extracted from the
soil to replace that exported in exchange for the
increased quantity of foreign articles imported,
and to afford support to the manufacturing
population thereby thrown out of work. The
distress would be great and extensive. For,
when cultivation had thus attained its ultimate
limits, the rent on all the good and middling
lands would be extremely high, and proprietors
would have a large demand for the fabrics which
administer to convenience and luxury, and consequently, the number of persons thrown out of
work by the supply of these things being received
from abroad, would bear a very considerable
proportion to that of the whole population. A
free foreign trade would be the greatest cala-
mity which could befal the country.

Other and analogous cases might be stated,
in which the unrestricted admission of foreign
manufactured articles would be the antecedent
of similar distress. In all such cases, the condi-

tion essential to the production of the effect I have described, is, that the country importing foreign fabrics, shall have so nearly attained the limits of her agricultural resources, that the labour and capital dislodged from domestic manufactures shall be unable to extract from the soil an additional supply of food and material equal to that which is sent out in exchange for the foreign fabric. We are never to forget, however, that in a country which has advanced so far in wealth and population as to have approached the limits of her agricultural resources, the exchangeable value of raw produce will be very high as compared with wrought goods, and that such a country cannot export the former in exchange for the latter, until all the other countries with which she has dealings, have so pushed their agriculture, and so improved their manufactures, that the difference between the exchangeable value of raw produce and wrought goods shall be greater in the foreign than in the home market. But when will this state of things arrive upon the shores of the Baltic, and of the Euxine, and in the almost boundless tracts of fertile land yet unappropriated throughout the vast continents of North and South America? The case supposed of a country approaching the ultimate limits of her agricultural resources, and at the same time exporting raw produce in exchange for wrought goods, so as to deprive herself of the means of employing her manufacturing population, cannot occur in practice for centuries to come.

While there are hypothetical cases in which an unrestricted importation of foreign articles would lead to a diminution of wealth, there are actual cases in which restrictions on the exportation of domestic articles would lead to an increasing wealth. The foreign consumers who take our commodities must return to our exporting merchant such a quantity of other things as will replace, with some increase or profit, all the expenses he incurs in sending these commodities out. If government increase the merchant's expense by imposing a tax on the commodity he exports, then the foreign consumer must either pay our merchant an additional price equal to the tax, or go elsewhere for his article. But if the commodity taxed were peculiar to our own country, and could not be obtained elsewhere, then the foreign consumer would have no alternative but to receive it, and would be compelled to pay our merchant the increased price necessary to cover the tax. Thus a country which possesses commodities peculiar to herself, and generally desired, may render other countries tributary to her by imposing duties on the exportation of those things in the production of which she has a natural monopoly, either partial or complete. If, however, the monopoly should be only partial, then the tax imposed on exportation should be less than the difference between the expense of producing the article at home, and the expense of producing it in less favoured countries, so as still to leave our merchants in a situation to undersell competitors in the foreign market.

In the preceding section, when considering the effect of restrictions on the colonial trade, I endeavoured to shew, that by one set of regulations a mother country might enrich herself at the expense of the colonies, and by another set of regulations increase the wealth of the colonies by diminishing her own. The principles there unfolded apply equally to the foreign trade. If England, by power or by persuasion, can render herself the mart and *entrepôt* for conducting the external trade of another country, she will gain by the rent paid for her docks and warehouses, and by the commission due upon consignments, whether that other country be Jamaica a colony, or the Brazils an independent state. And again; should England, by a treaty of alliance and commerce, bind the South Americans to receive from the United Kingdom, or oblige herself to receive from South America, goods which other countries could supply at a cheaper rate; then her gain in the former case, and her loss in the latter, would be precisely analogous to the gain which she acquires and the loss which she suffers when an Act of Parliament imposes similar regulations upon the intercourse between the United Kingdom and the West India Islands.

No additional argument can be requisite to prove, that when government, by the imposition of unequal duties, compels the consumer to

receive the inferior and dearer wines of Portugal,
instead of the superior and cheaper wines of
France, England suffers a loss of wealth equal
to the difference between the price which she
now pays for Portugal wine, and the price
which, under a system of equal *ad valorem*
duties, she would pay for French wines. It is
true, indeed, that when Portugal consents to
receive from England fabrics which other countries could supply cheaper, she not only suffers a
diminution of wealth in her turn; but, upon the
principle stated in the preceding section, enables
England to obtain the wines of Portugal in exchange for a smaller portion of the products of
her industry, than she would otherwise be compelled to give for them. But the benefits thus
reciprocally conferred, do not altogether balance
the evils reciprocally inflicted. When two countries, for the mutual encouragement of their
industry, agree to receive from each other articles
which might be obtained cheaper elsewhere, they
place themselves to a certain extent in an
artificial and precarious state; and on the
interruption of their commercial treaty, either

from a misunderstanding between themselves, or through the preponderating influence of some powerful neighbour, the revulsion and derangement which succeed are more considerable than they would have been, had industry been left to flow in the more natural, and therefore more permanent channels, which it would have worked out for itself.

But, though the policy of purely commercial treaties, binding the contracting parties to receive from each other articles which can be procured cheaper elsewhere, is always more than doubtful; the same objections do not apply to those partly commercial and partly political arrangements, by which a great naval power may obtain exclusive privileges in the markets of a minor state, in return for protecting her trade, or sustaining her independence. During the period of the formidable family compact between the different branches of the house of Bourbon, Portugal, in giving peculiar encouragement to the trade and navigation of England, recruited the force which preserved her from becoming a dependency of Spain; and the increase of wealth which England obtained by being enabled to purchase a larger portion of the productions of Portugal with a smaller portion of her own, was but a fair and moderate equivalent for the additional expenses she incurred, and ought not to have been attended with the drawback arising from her being obliged to give for the inferior wines of her ally a greater quantity of her commodities than that for which she might have obtained the superior wines of France. A country may grant exclusive privileges to the trade and marine of a natural ally, just on the same principle on which she may grant them to her own. In either case, it may be sound policy to sacrifice some portion of wealth in order to increase security.

A remarkable instance of the propriety of occasionally departing from economical principles, in order to provide for national security and power, is exhibited in the Navigation Act of England. When this famous Act was passed, enormous taxes upon the necessaries of life had reduced the rate of profit in the republic of Holland very much below the level of the rest of Europe; and consequently her ship-owners were content with receiving lower freights than those of other countries, and were engrossing the carrying trade of the world. As far as mere wealth is concerned, there can exist no doubt that England, under such circumstances, would have been a gainer by paying the low freight of the Dutch, and turning her own capitals from the carriage of goods to those branches of direct production in which she could realise a higher profit. Assuming, for illustration, that the rate of profit was fifteen per cent. in England, and only ten per cent. in Holland, then whatever amount of capital England might disengage from her carrying trade and invest in agriculture or manufactures, would reproduce itself, not only with the ten per cent. profit, to be paid upon the same amount of Dutch capital which supplied the place of British capital in the carrying trade, but also with an additional surplus of five per cent. But if Holland had been suffered to engross our carrying trade, her mercantile marine would have covered, and her military marine commanded the seas; and England, for the sake of a comparatively trifling accession of wealth, would have lost her place in Europe.

As the several nations of the world advance in wealth and population, the commercial intercourse between them must gradually become less important and beneficial. I have already shewn that the species of foreign trade which has the most powerful influence in raising profits and increasing wealth, is that which is carried on between an old country in which raw produce bears a high value in relation to wrought goods, and a new country where wrought goods possess a high exchangeable power with respect to raw produce. Now, as new countries advance in population, the cultivation of inferior soils must increase the cost of raising raw produce, and the division of labour reduce the expense of working it up. Hence, in all new settlements, the increasing value of raw produce must gradually check its exportation, and the falling value of wrought goods progressively prevent their importation; until at length the commercial intercourse between nations shall be confined to those peculiar articles, in the production of which the immutable circumstances of soil and climate give one country a permanent advantage over another.

On this ultimate and necessary limitation of foreign trade Mr. Malthus has founded an argument against the extension of the most beneficial of all branches of commerce, namely, that which is carried on between old and new countries. But surely there is no sound wisdom in refusing to enjoy a decided advantage at the present time, because in the lapse of ages we must lose it. On the same principle we ought not to live because hereafter we must die. When we consider the situation of the countries bordering on the Baltic and the Euxine,—when we look to Southern Africa and to the vast continents of North and South America, we shall be convinced that centuries must roll away before the full peopling of the world interposes difficulties in the way of England's exchanging her cheap manufactured goods for the cheap agricultural produce of less advanced countries.

SECTION V.—*On Money, and Paper Currency.*

THROUGHOUT the illustrations and reasonings contained in the preceding chapters, I have in general excluded money from consideration, and taken the interchange of commodities as a system of direct barter. This was necessary, in order to simplify complicated questions, and to enable us to arrive at our conclusions by the shortest and most obvious process. When the hypothesis which we employ for the purpose of tracing out and elucidating the principles of economical science, has a reference to money, we are apt to be involved in confusion and error, in consequence of our attention being directed, not to what is essential and inherent in the case before us, but to some circumstance or accident connected with the commodity which happens to be employed as the medium of exchange, and practical measure of value. Having, therefore, in the former divisions of this work, alluded as little as possible to the operation of a circulating medium, it becomes necessary that I should, in the present section, give some account of the origin and nature of money, and of the manner in which it aids production.

As soon as the divisions of employment became tolerably well established, and individuals began to supply their wants and gratify their desires by transferring the surplus products of each other's industry, the necessity of having some medium of exchange must immediately have been felt. If the transfer of commodities were performed by means of barter, the business of life would be subject to the most inconvenient interruptions and delays. A farmer, for example, who had in his barn a larger quantity of wheat than he required for the consumption of his family, and who destined the overplus to purchase for them a supply of shoes, would be obliged to proceed with a quantity of his wheat to the shoe-maker, and to endeavour to negociate an exchange. Now, it might probably happen that the first shoe-maker whom he accosted, had already obtained all the wheat he meant to consume ; and, therefore, the farmer would be under the necessity of remaining without shoes, until he could find a shoe-maker who wanted wheat.

If unfortunately the whole trade were already supplied with wheat, the farmer would be under the necessity of endeavouring to ascertain what was the article the shoe-maker wished to procure; and if this article was beer, then, as a preliminary to his future negociation with the shoe-maker, he would be compelled to apply to the brewer to exchange a portion of beer for wheat. But the brewer might also be supplied with wheat ; and, therefore, the farmer would be obliged, in the first instance, to endeavour to exchange his wheat for some commodity desired by the brewer, in order that with it he might purchase the beer with which he afterwards meant to procure shoes.

Tedious as this process may appear, it is one of the simplest cases which could be stated for the purpose of pointing out and explaining the laborious path which, if the circulating medium were withdrawn, and all transactions performed by barter, every man would be compelled to tread, in endeavouring to supply his wants by parting with the surplus products of his industry. It must be obvious to any one who will take time to examine the question, that the course would often be far more tedious and intricate, before the repeated interchange at length procured for the individual the particular commodity which he wanted.

Neither is this the sole source of the labour which would be imposed upon man, if transactions were conducted in the way of barter. As in this case there would exist no acknowledged practical standard, by which the value of commodities could be measured; in adjusting the terms of exchanging them, an inquiry would have to be undertaken for the purpose of determining their relative worth. If the brewer, to whom the farmer applied, wished to have some wheat, and it so happened, that neither the farmer had antecedently exchanged wheat for beer, nor the brewer beer for wheat, they would be at a loss to fix the quantity of wheat that should be given for a gallon of beer. If, indeed, each had luckily already procured a leg of the same sheep, in exchange for the commodity he possessed, they might then discover the relative value of the wheat and the beer; because, two things equal to one and the same thing, are equal to one another: but as it would probably happen that the farmer and brewer had not exchanged wheat and beer for the same commodity, they could not have recourse to this easy mode of deciding the portion of wheat which ought to be parted with, for the acquisition of a given quantity of beer. The course, therefore, which the farmer would have to pursue, even after he had undergone the labour necessary to discover a brewer who wanted wheat, might be exceedingly laborious, before he could trace out, by the examination of various exchanges, some one interchange which afforded a comparison between the value of the wheat and of the beer.

If this, however, could not be discovered, the farmer would be obliged, as the only means of determining the terms of the exchange, to institute an inquiry into the quantities of labour or of capital which wheat and beer respectively required for their production. Now, this being done, and the beer obtained, it is plain that the farmer might be under the necessity of repeating the same operation in negociating the exchange for the shoes. The exertion and expense attending the interchange of commodities might equal, and, perhaps, on some occasions exceed, the exertion and expense required for their production.

To avoid these circuitous operations, and to save the time and labour required when the transactions of mercantile industry are carried on by way of barter, each individual, as soon as the divisions of employment were tolerably well established, must have found an interest in keeping constantly by him some commodity, which being of known value and of universal consumption, would be readily received by his neighbours in exchange for such portions of their surplus productions as he might occasionally require. Now, when men had seen this commodity frequently employed as the means of exchanging other commodities, they would become willing to receive a greater quantity of it than might be necessary for their own consumption, under the confidence, that whatever articles they wanted, might at any time be procured for it. Passing freely from hand to hand, its value would be universally known; it would be employed to compute or measure the value of all other things; and in this manner a medium of exchange, a rude species of money, would be established.

Various commodities have, at different times, and in different countries, been employed for the purpose of measuring the value of other articles, and exchanging them against each other. In the rude ages, cattle are said to have been the common medium; and accordingly we find, that in old times, things were frequently valued according to the number of cattle which had been given for them. But cattle must have been a most inconvenient instrument of exchange. The person who wished to purchase a supply of cloth, and who had nothing to give in exchange for it but a sheep or an ox, would be obliged to buy cloth to the value of a whole sheep, or a whole ox, at a time. He could not buy less, because his medium of

exchange, his money, could not be divided without loss; and if he wished to purchase more, he
would for the same reason be obliged to take
double or treble the quantity,—the value of
two or three sheep, or two or three oxen. Now,
it is evident, that a medium so bulky, so unport-
able, and indivisible as cattle, would frequently
obstruct the interchange of commodities. Finding it often difficult, and sometimes impossible,
to exchange by means of cattle, the surplus products of their respective industry, for the precise
quantity of other articles which they might
require, the inhabitants of the country in which
cattle formed the only acknowledged measure of
value, would on many occasions be compelled to
supply their various wants by combining in their
own persons, a variety of occupations. The divisions of employment would therefore be very imperfectly established; the productive powers of
industry would be checked; and the country
withheld from the acquisition of that general
opulence which, if it possessed a more perfect
instrument of mercantile industry, it would be
capable of acquiring.

A knowledge of these inconveniencies seems at length to have led all nations to employ the precious metals as the measure of value and medium of exchange. For these functions they are admirably calculated. They can not only be kept without waste, and without expense, for any length of time which may be necessary, but they can be divided into any number of parts, and reunited without loss. Hence, the person who possesses gold and silver can, when general consent has rendered them the instrument of exchange, at all times proportion their quantity to the precise quantity of the commodity which he wants; and thus make what purchases he pleases.

But though the metals are thus admirably adapted for facilitating the transactions of mercantile industry, their utility as a medium of exchange was, in the early periods of society, limited by two very considerable inconveniencies, —the trouble of weighing, and of assaying them. As a small difference in the quantity of a piece of gold or silver makes a great difference in its value, weighing the metals with proper exactness becomes an operation of much nicety; and if performed previously to every purchase, would very much obstruct the exchange of commodities, and thus prevent the divisions of employment from being thoroughly established. Ascertaining the fineness of the precious metals is an operation still more difficult and tedious, and cannot be performed without exposing them to the action of proper solvents. To do this previous to every purchase would be impossible. The trader, therefore, while bullion continued to be the sole instrument of exchange, must have been compelled to guess from external appearance the fineness of the metals which he received for his goods. This would expose him to the grossest impositions, and often oblige him to receive, instead of a pound of pure silver or gold, an adulterated composition of the cheapest materials, which had, however, in outward appearance been made to resemble one or other of those metals. Now, while the profits of the merchant continued in this manner at the mercy of every knave in the community, it must have been difficult for him to have carried on any very active or extensive operations. The inter-change of commodities must have been obstructed; and, therefore, the productive powers of industry reduced to that languid state which is ever the consequence of individuals combining in their own persons a variety of occupations.

The inconveniencies which were felt while bullion continued to be the sole medium of exchange, gave occasion to the establishment of coined money. In all countries which have made any advance towards improvement, it has been found necessary to ascertain by a public stamp, the weight and the fineness of those pieces of the precious metals which are commonly employed in the market to purchase goods. The first public stamps which were impressed on the current metals, seem to have been intended to ascertain their fineness or purity, and to have resembled the sterling mark which is at present affixed to plate, and bars of silver; or the Spanish mark sometimes affixed to ingots of gold. By this mark, base adulterated metals were excluded from the market; and hence, while the merchant, no longer exposed to the risk of receiving, instead of gold and silver, compositions of cheaper materials resembling these materials, acquired confidence and ability to extend his speculations, the exchange of commodities became more frequent, and the divisions of employment were more accurately established.

But the difficulty and inconvenience of weighing the metals with sufficient exactness still continued, until a public stamp was devised, which covering both sides of the piece, and sometimes it edges also, ascertained not only its fineness, but the quantity of metal it contained. In this was effected the last improvement of which metallic money seems susceptible; and coin, from its superior utility and convenience, became, with respect to the internal transactions of every country in which it was established, the universal measure of value, and medium of exchange. At first, the name or denomination of the coin expressed the quantity of metal which it contained. In England, for example, the pound sterling contained originally a real pound weight of silver, of known fineness; and a penny, a real penny weight, the twentieth part of an ounce, and the two hundred and fortieth part of a pound. This relative value between the different denominations of our coined money still continues; but, in consequence of repeated deterioration, the denomination has long since ceased to express the quantity of metal which our coins contain. This is of no very material importance at present; though the debasing of the coin at the periods when it took place, must have effected an unjust and ruinous violation of the spirit of all existing contracts. If the stamps affixed by the authority of the state to the gold and silver pieces which are circulated through the country, certify faithfully, that those pieces are of a given weight and fineness, it seems immaterial whether the weight of each piece be implied in the name. All that the public good requires is, that in the daily and hourly operations of trade, the time and expense of weighing and assaying the metals shall be saved. When public stamps assure us that the pieces circulating in the market, no matter by what name they may be called, contain a certain quantity of gold or silver, this is effectually done; and this being done, mercantile industry receives all the facilities which the establishment of coined money seems capable of affording it.

From what has been said in the preceding paragraphs, respecting its origin and nature, money may be defined to be, a commodity possessing intrinsic value, and rendered, by general consent, the medium of exchange, and the practical measure for computing the relative exchangeable value of other things.

These circumstances, the possession of underived exchangeable value, and the being rendered by general consent the medium of exchange, and the practical measure for computing the relative value of other things, are essential to money; and in these every article which has been employed as money, from the most barbarous to the most polished times, have equally partaken. According, indeed, to the degree of improvement, and to the extent to which the division of employment has been carried, the articles constituting this instrument of mercantile industry, will be found more or less convenient; but in the essential properties which we have mentioned, they all must have agreed. Cattle, the money of ancient times, possessed a high exchangeable value; by cattle, purchases were made; and we read, that in cattle the relative exchangeable value of the armour of the ancient heroes was computed. Every other article which, in the dawn of civilization, may at any time have been employed as money, must have performed similar functions; and functions precisely similar are, though with incalculably more facility and convenience, performed by the coined money of European States.

In the business of life, the term money is seldom used in its most extended sense. When a merchant tells his foreign correspondent that he will pay him in money, the expression has a reference to bullion, the commodity which general consent has rendered the criterion of value, and the medium of exchange, in the great commercial republic; and when he engages to discharge a domestic debt in money, the signification of the term is still farther limited, and implies the coined metal only which general consent and the law of the land may, in his particular country, have made the instrument of exchange, and the practical measure of exchangeable value. Thus the term, money, with respect to the civilized commercial world, means gold and silver; with respect to any particular nation, it means that nation's current coin.

In tracing the origin of money, and stating the functions it performs, we were necessarily led to notice the manner in which it aids the production of wealth. Without some article of known exchangeable value, readily received as an equivalent for other things, and serving as a practical measure of their relative worth, the interchange of commodities must have been very limited, and consequently the divisions of employment very imperfectly established. Now, money obviates these evils, and by a two-fold operation augments production. In the first place, it saves all that time and labour which, while the intercourse between man and man is carried on by barter, must frequently intervene before a person can be supplied with the quantity of the commodity which he wants. In the second place, and in consequence of its saving the time and labour which must otherwise be spent in effecting exchanges, it multiplies the transactions of mercantile industry, and thus allows the divisions of employment to be more thoroughly established. By the first operation, it disengages a very considerable portion of labour from an unproductive occupation, and enables it to receive a more useful direction. By the second operation, it increases in a very high degree the productive powers of the labour already usefully employed; it assists every man in availing himself of the dexterity and skill which he may have acquired in any particular calling, and promotes cultivation in a manner suitable to the climate and soil of different districts and of different countries. And by both these operations, money increases, to an extent not easy to be calculated, the wealth of the communities in which it is established.

But, though money performs these important functions, the employment of it is attended with certain inconveniencies which considerably limit its utility as an instrument of mercantile industry. In the first place, however portable the materials of which it is composed may be, in comparison with other articles, it cannot be conveyed to distant places without considerable labour and expense. In the next place, the country which employs metallic money, must be at considerable expense in acquiring and supporting it; must devote an important portion of her productive industry either to the working of mines, or to the fabricating of articles with which to purchase the metals from other countries in which they are worked. And, in the third place, when money constitutes the only medium of exchange, the most opulent merchant may frequently find it impossible to turn his stock into cash, with sufficient promptitude to enable him to seize the opportunities of the market.

The inconveniencies and delays to which mercantile industry was exposed, while metallic money continued to be the only medium of exchange, would naturally suggest the expediency of employing some substitute for gold and silver. The substitute which most readily presented itself was paper credit. Traders desirous of purchasing goods, and possessing the necessary capital for doing so, finding it impossible to call in their debts, or to turn their stock into money with sufficient celerity to carry their speculations into effect, would endeavour to make the purchases they desired, by giving a note or bond payable on some future day. Now, if the people in the neighbourhood had such confidence in the wealth and probity of the issuer of such note or bond, as to believe he would be able to discharge it as soon as it became due, the person who might receive it, would find no difficulty in paying it away, either in the discharge of a debt, or in the purchase of other goods. Thus this paper security might circulate from hand to hand, supplying the place of a more expensive instrument of exchange, and of one too, which could not be transported without labour, nor procured with sufficient promptitude to meet the unforeseen opportunities of the market.

As confidence and credit were established, bills of exchange became the principal medium by which the more distant operations of mercantile industry were carried on. These bills were found so beneficial, not only in supplying, by a most convenient substitute, the sudden demands for money, but also in obviating the labour, risk, and delay, incident upon the transmission of the precious metals; that first the usage of merchants, and afterwards the laws of commercial states, encouraged their circulation by peculiar privileges.

The circulation of bills of exchange was greatly extended, and their utility, as an instrument of trade and commerce, very much increased, by their being made payable some time after date. *A*. might wish to purchase a quantity of goods which *B*. was desirous of. selling; but if *B*. had occasion for ready money, and if *A*. though a thriving and opulent trader, could not call in his debts, or dispose of his stock, so as to procure an immediate supply of cash, this transaction, though mutually beneficial and mutually desired, might never take place. But if *A*. gave a bill payable at three months upon a substantial merchant who happened to owe him the money, and *B*. from the confidence reposed in the drawer and acceptor of the bill, could readily dispose of it in the market, then the obstacle to their dealing would be at once removed. For this bill being easily turned into cash, would to *B*. answer all the purposes of ready money; while the circumstance of its not being payable until after the expiration of ninety days, would enable *A*. to avail himself instantaneously of the sum then falling due to him, and to prosecute what he conceived to be a profitable speculation. Thus, in a country where credit is understood and established, every debt which one solvent trader owes to another may, by making bills of exchange payable some time after date, be transferred from hand to hand; and, as a substitute for money, supply any sudden demand which happens to arise for a medium of exchange.

But the circumstance which gave bills of exchange the utmost degree of circulation and utility which they seem capable of attaining, was the establishment of banks. The operations of banking, as connected with bills of exchange, are of a two-fold nature. In the first place, every respectable banker keeps cash accounts with the banking-houses of the principal trading towns with which the merchants in his neighbourhood have intercourse—gives bills of exchange drawn upon these houses, and accepts the bills which they in return draw upon him.

By this operation of banking, the debts and credits of different countries, and of different districts of the same country, are balanced without the intervention of the precious metals;— facility is imparted to all the transactions of trade; and the risk and expense of transmitting the precious metals are avoided.

In the second place, banks freely discount good bills of exchange, and by this means greatly extend their circulation, and increase their utility. For though a good bill of exchange will readily pass in payment from one merchant to another,—yet in the general market they cannot enter freely into circulation, nor serve for the small and retail purchases of daily expenditure. The holder of many such bills, if he were unable to discount them, might be put to serious inconvenience. But by the operations of banking this inconvenience incident upon the holding of bills is completely obviated; and the possessor of them, confident that they may enable him to answer all calls for small sums, and to make what retail purchases he pleases, feels as much security as if he had money to a similar amount actually in his coffers.

Bankers at first discounted bills in the current coin of their respective countries; and afterwards, as confidence increased, they adopted the practice of discounting in their own promissory notes. This effected the last improvement of which paper currency seems susceptible. When the inhabitants of any particular neighbourhood have such confidence in the honour and wealth of any set of bank proprietors, as to believe that they are ready at all times to pay upon demand, such of their promissory notes as are likely to be presented to them, these notes come to have the same currency as money, from the confidence that the value which they represent may always be procured for them. Now, though some of these notes are daily returned to the bank for payment, yet a considerable part of them may continue in circulation for months and years together. Ten thousand pounds in money may be sufficient to answer the casual demands occasioned by the issue of a hundred thousand pounds in promissory notes. In this case, therefore, ten thousand pounds in the precious metals, may perform all the functions which a hundred thousand pounds could otherwise have performed; and bills of exchange may be discounted to almost any extent which the transactions of trade may require.

But paper currency is not confined to bills of exchange, and the promissory notes of bankers. This instrument of trade may be defined, after the Abbé Morellet, to consist of every acknowledgment of debt or obligation; every stipulation by writing between a debtor and creditor, which obliges the former to pay, and authorises the latter to exact, a value; and which, being capable of conveyance, becomes the means of transferring the property of these values from one to another, without transporting the things valuable in substance. More simply, as money is that which possesses an independent exchangeable value, and which is rendered, by general consent, the medium of transferring, and the practical measure for valuing other things; so paper currency is that which represents exchangeable value, and which is admitted by general consent and confidence, as an instrument for exchanging, and as a measure for computing the value of other things.

In explaining the principle which occasioned the establishment of paper currency, and in tracing the steps by which it has been improved and perfected, it was impossible not to make some allusion to the nature and extent of the benefits which it confers. These benefits, however, demand a more specific examination.

As the inconveniencies attending the employment of metallic money have been seen to be three-fold, the advantage resulting from the use of this substitute for money, is three-fold also. In the first place, a paper currency saves all the labour and capital which would otherwise be expended in transporting the metallic medium, and enables them to be employed in direct production. In the second place, it saves and turns to the business of direct production, all the labour and capital which would otherwise be absorbed in procuring and maintaining a metallic currency. And, in the third place, it bestows upon the circulating medium an elastic principle which multiplies the transactions of mercantile industry, and improves the productive powers of all the labour and capital employed throughout the country.

Though gold and silver contain great value in small bulk, yet transporting them backward and forward for the purpose of effecting each particular transaction of trade, would be attended with a very considerable expense of labour and capital. In an industrious and opulent nation, each town and each district is perpetually selling to, and buying from, every other town and district; and if purchases could not be made without the immediate agency of money, the metals would be in a perpetual state of flux and reflux through the country. While the shopkeeper of London was sending guineas to purchase fabrics from the manufacturer of Manchester, the shopkeeper of Manchester would be transmitting them to pay for goods obtained from the manufacturer in London. And while one merchant in Liverpool was conveying gold to Birmingham, in order to purchase iron work for exportation, the retail dealer in Birmingham might be transmitting that metal to another merchant in Liverpool, to purchase the foreign or colonial goods he had imported. Now, by means of bills of exchange, and the operations of banking, the risk and expense of transporting the metals is almost altogether saved. Debts and credits are balanced without the immediate instrumentality of money, and a considerable portion of labour and capital is disengaged from conducting circulation, and turned to the work of direct production.

In the second place, bills of exchange, the promissory notes of bankers, and the other written engagements of which paper currency is composed, have scarcely any intrinsic value, and may be fabricated at little or no expense; while coined money, on the contrary, consists of very costly materials, and very curious workmanship. When, therefore, a paper, is substituted for a metallic currency, a very considerable saving is produced. Now, it is evident, that every saving which can be effected in the capital employed in conducting the circulation of commodities, will allow of an increase in the capital employed in producing them. As the undertaker of a great manufactory, who employs a thousand a year in the maintenance of his machinery, will, if he can reduce this expense to five hundred, employ the other five hundred in purchasing an additional quantity of materials, to be wrought up by an additional number of workmen: so a great country, which expends annually a million sterling, in maintaining the circulating medium, if that expense can, without impeding the transactions of trade, be reduced to a hundred thousand pounds, will apply the remaining nine hundred in direct production ;— will procure and work up a greater quantity of raw produce ; —will extend her agriculture, — increase her manufactures, and thus augment the mass of commodities.

As it is impossible to ascertain, with any precision, the amount of the circulating medium, which a country at any time employs, we can

form no correct estimate of the extent of the
saving effected by substituting paper currency
for coin. Even if we knew the amount of all
the promissory notes uttered by the several
banking companies, we should not thence be able
to ascertain the quantity of the precious metals
supplanted by paper currency. Of that paper
currency the notes of bankers form a small part.
In an opulent country, where credit is established, all mercantile transactions of any considerable magnitude are conducted by bills of
exchange; and every good bill which is received
in payment for goods—every security which
passes in the market,—supplies the place of
money, and enables us to appropriate to direct
production, capital which would otherwise be
required to support the circulating medium.
Now, when we reflect for a moment on the
enormous amount of the bills of exchange, and
other paper securities which enter annually into
the circulation of a great commercial country;
when we consider that every debt which one
solvent trader owes to another, may be drawn for
by a bill payable at some future day, and thus

converted into a species of paper currency, ready to supply any sudden demand which may arise for cash, we must be struck and astonished at the almost incalculable amount of capital which is saved and turned to direct production, by thus supplanting the metallic medium. If a country were to withdraw from the business of direct production,—from agriculture and manufactures, a quantity of capital sufficient to purchase and keep up the metallic medium, which the different kinds of paper securities now so conveniently supplant, industry would receive an alarming check, and the mass of commodities sustain a fatal diminution.

But, in the third place, if we were even to withdraw from direct production,—from agriculture and manufactures, a portion of capital sufficient to purchase and to coin the quantity of metal which credit now supplants, we could not bestow upon the circulating medium the convenience and utility which it derives from being in a great measure composed of paper currency. For, to omit the repetition of what we have already said respecting the risk and

expense of making large and distant payments
in the metals, a well-regulated paper currency
bestows upon the circulating medium an elastic
principle, which supplies instantaneously each
sudden and unexpected demand for cash. This
part of the benefit obtained by substituting
a paper for a metallic currency, is precisely
analogous to that which is derived from substituting money transactions for those of barter.
When money transactions are substituted for
those of barter, the exchange of commodities is
facilitated, the divisions of employment are more
thoroughly established, and the productive powers
of industry are heightened in a degree not easy
to be calculated. When a paper, is substituted
for a metallic currency, similar effects are produced. All the merchants and dealers throughout the country are, by means of bills of exchange
and the operations of banking, enabled to convert
the sums falling due to them into a convenient
representative of money, and to effect purchases
and interchanges of commodities, which could
not otherwise take place. The facilities thus
afforded to the operations of mercantile industry,

enable each individual to devote himself more
exclusively to his particular calling, to husband
his time, and acquire increasing dexterity and
skill, or to bestow upon his field a cultivation
better calculated to co-operate with nature ; while
these more accurate divisions of mechanical and
territorial employment give, in every occupation,
increasing energy to the productive powers of
labour and capital, and swell from a thousand
springs the stream of human happiness.

The nature of the several benefits conferred
upon a country by the establishment of a well
regulated paper currency, is sufficiently obvious
and easy of comprehension ; but the precise
extent of these benefits it would be difficult,
nay, impossible, to ascertain. To calculate the
amount of the different paper securities, whether
public or private, which in a great commercial
country serve as instruments of exchange, and
disengage, for direct production, the capital
which would otherwise be expended in transmitting money, and in procuring and supporting a
metallic medium; to examine with accuracy, how
far these paper securities are calculated to meet

those sudden and temporary demands for cash, which a less elastic medium could not supply; and to trace out the additional exchange of commodities, the improved divisions of employment, and the heightened powers of production incident thereon, are all necessary preliminaries which must be disposed of before we can form a correct conception of the extent of the benefit which a country may derive from a paper currency. But though the precise amount of the benefit cannot be ascertained, its magnitude is sufficient to fill the imagination, and to excite the surprise of all who turn their attention to this important branch of economical science. Though we cannot estimate the amount of the paper securities which at any given period enter into circulation, nor calculate precisely the saving of capital,—the additional exchanges,—the new divisions of employment, — and the consequent increased production to which they give occasion; yet, on the most superficial view of the subject, we must be struck with the advantages arising from all the sums which in a great commercial country, one solvent trader owes to another, becoming, in consequence of bills of exchange, and the notes of bankers, capable of being thrown into the channels of circulation, and of instantaneously supplying, as a substitute for money, every sudden increase in the demand for an instrument of exchange. Mercantile industry is facilitated in a thousand ways. The great wheel of circulation, revolving unimpeded, with a rapid motion distributes to the several members of the community the surplus products of each other's industry. No man is compelled to waste his time, and throw away his acquired skill, by combining in his own person, a variety of callings; or to cultivate an ear of corn, or a blade of grass, upon an uncongenial soil. Labour is subdivided and abridged in a thousand ways; and by consequence, the productive powers of industry, and the quantity of all useful commodities, are increased.

Having thus shewn the manner in which money and paper currency aid the acquisition of wealth, I shall now endeavour to trace the effects which a diminution and increase in the value of

the circulating medium are respectively calculated to produce.

The first, and certainly the most injurious
consequence of a fall in the value of the circulating medium, is the reduction which it effects in
the real wages of labour. A fall in the value of
money is the same thing as a rise in the price
of all the necessaries of life; and experience
proves to us, that the rate of wages is somewhat
tardy in proportioning itself to the price of necessaries. In almost all trades the sum which is
paid for labour is regulated by a contract, tacit
or implied, between the masters and the workmen; and, notwithstanding the fluctuations in
the value of money, and in the price of necessaries, it varies but little for considerable periods.
The tardiness with which money wages adjust
themselves to the price of subsistence, is, in
England, increased by the operation of the Poor
Laws. The reward of labour has a constant
tendency to settle down to that quantity of
subsistence which, from climate and custom, is
necessary, to enable the labourer to bring up

such a family as will keep the supply of labour even with the demand: for, if he receives more than this, the quantity of labour will increase, and its value fall; and if he receive less, its quantity will diminish, and its value rise. But if the parish undertake to support the labourer's family, either wholly or in part, the masters will no longer be compelled, by the law of supply and demand, to give their workmen a sum sufficient to purchase this quantity of subsistence; and a fall in the value of money, or a rise in the price of provisions, will be followed, not by an advance in money wages, but by an increase in the poor rates.

These evils, however, could only be of short duration, and would be counteracted by the other effects of an increased circulation. When the value of money falls, there is nothing to prevent the price of labour from rising in the same proportion with that of other things, except the compact, expressed or implied, which regulates the rate of wages in the several trades. The laws against combination have probably the effect of rendering this compact less flexible than it otherwise would be, and of preventing the money rate of wages from conforming to the price of subsistence, so as to keep their real rate at the level marked by the proportion between the supply of labour and the demand for it. However, notwithstanding these laws, a fall in the value of money would gradually force upon masters a proportional rise in the wages of their workmen—unless, indeed, a diminution in the demand for labour were to take place. But a fall in the value of money, instead of diminishing, would, for some time, increase the demand for labour. As long as this fall raised the price of goods, without effecting an equivalent rise in the rate of money wages, the profits of stock would be increased; and thus the master's capital would accumulate more rapidly, while he would have a stronger motive to employ upon productive labour all the stock which his wealth or credit enabled him to command.

The alterations, too, which a fall in the value of the currency would effect in the distribution of wealth, would all be in favour of the productive classes, and tend to encourage industry, and to increase the demand for labour. During the currency of his lease, the farmer receives an important benefit; the amount of his rent remaining stationary, while the price of his produce rises. So far, indeed, as the landlord is concerned, it is unjust and injurious that the rent should be paid in a currency of diminished value. What the farmer gained, he would lose. But wealth, in the hands of the farmer, is more beneficial to the country than wealth in the hands of the landlord. By the one, it is expended productively—as capital; by the other, unproductively—as revenue. While, therefore, we cannot defend the injustice of violating the spirit of the contract between landlord and tenant, by causing the stipulated rent to be paid in a depreciated currency, we must admit, that increasing the farmer's profits, though it be at the landlord's expense, gives him at once the power and the inducement to cultivate with more spirit, and to afford employment to a greater number of hands.

In the other branches of industry, a diminution in the value of the currency would also be, in some respects, favourable. Until wages rose in proportion to the necessaries of life, all would obtain a rate of profit, somewhat higher than before. Besides, a rising scale of prices has a kind of magical effect upon trade, and inspires that confidence and credit, which give an heightened power to all the springs of production. Confidence, like those prophecies which occasion their own fulfilment, creates that increased demand which it anticipates. The masters in every trade fabricate that quantity of their respective commodities, for which they expect a profitable sale. Increase this expectation, inspire them with more confidence in obtaining a favourable market, and the supply of all sorts of goods will be immediately augmented. Now, if a single individual were to be seized with an unusual confidence, and, under its influence, were to fabricate a more than customary quantity of his peculiar article, then the other individuals of the community not having an enlarged power of purchasing, the supply of this article would be increased beyond the demand, and its producer's expectations of advantage would be disappointed. Very different is the result when the increase of confidence becomes general. In this case there is a greater quantity of commodities produced in all the branches of industry, and each class, having more goods to dispose of, will enlarge the market for the others. For example; if, in consequence of a growing and universal confidence, commodities in general were increased by a fourth, then the shoe-maker would have more shoes to dispose of; but as the consumer would have a greater quantity of the ingredients of capital to exchange against them, the demand for shoes would increase, in an equal proportion with the supply. The other industrious classes having a greater quantity of their respective commodities to exchange, these would also meet an enlarged demand, proportioned to their augmented supply, and would consequently retain the same value as before. It is easy to see, that if the general confidence had occasioned an improvement in the quality, instead of an increase in the quantity of commodities, the effect would be the same. In this manner, confidence, when general, always creates that enlargement of the market which it anticipates; and hence a rising scale of prices imparts a brisker flow to industry, through all its varied channels.

With respect to those engaged in commerce, a depreciation in the currency is beneficial to the debtor, and injurious to the creditor. But as every considerable trader must have bills to pay, as well as to receive, and is, at one and the same time, both a debtor and a creditor, the injury and the benefit will in some degree balance each other. Even he who is exclusively a creditor will receive some compensation for his loss. The brisker flow of trade will render the backward more prompt in their payments, and enable some to make good their engagements, who could not otherwise have paid at all; and will thus ensure him a quicker return, and diminish the number of his bad debts. The greater facility in obtaining discounts, which an increased issue of currency bestows, is also to be taken into the account. To the rash and gambling trader this may be an injury; encouraging him to engage in speculations ultimately ruinous to himself, and prejudicial to the country. But this objection proves too much. It might be urged with equal force against every species of commercial credit. An advantage is not to be disregarded, because imprudent people may use it to their own destruction. A few may make over-sanguine calculations, and undertake losing speculations, but the great majority of those who engage in mercantile pursuits will profit by every facility of discount and increase of credit which enables them to extend their transactions.

A diminution in the value of the currency would have the effect of lowering the salaries of all the servants of the state, whether civil or military. Now the labour of these persons, however useful and important, effects no direct addition to the wealth of the community. The salaries advanced to them are not expended productively, as capital; and if their services are as efficiently performed, when they are paid in a depreciated currency, as when paid in one of undiminished value, the difference is a clear gain to the public. With respect to all other annuitants, to the mortgagee, and to the fund-holder, their case would be nearly the same as that of the land-owner. The diminution effected in their real income would be manifestly unjust, but it would in no way obstruct production, or retard the prosperity of the country. It would have rather a contrary effect. What was taken from the annuitant would be turned into the channels of profit and wages, and would thus give a new stimulus to industry, and ameliorate the condition of the great mass of the population.

But in a country oppressed with debt and taxes, the most beneficial effects resulting from a lowering of the value of the circulating medium, would be the diminution of the public burdens. If, in the science of political economy, there is any one proposition more capable of demonstration than another, it is, that excessive taxation dries up the spring of production. When taxes raise the necessaries of life, and cause the labourer to pay a higher price for his subsistence than before, then, if his wages do not rise, they will be insufficient for his support; and his family must go upon the parish, or starve. But if, in order to place the labourer in the same independent circumstances as before, wages are raised in an equal ratio to the increased price of necessaries, then the capitalist must either raise the price of his goods in proportion to the higher wages which he pays, or receive a lower rate of profit upon his trade. Suppose that he raises the prices of his goods, and then he will be undersold in the foreign market; the commerce of the country will be destroyed; and all those to whom it afforded employment, will be thrown out of work. On the other hand, supposing, what is more probable, that the capitalist cannot increase the price of his goods in proportion to the higher wages which he pays, and then the diminished profits of his trade will tempt him to transfer his capital to countries where it will fetch a higher return, the funds for the mainte-nance of industry will be diminished, and our people deprived of the means of earning an inde-pendent livelihood. Thus we see, that heavy taxation, by rendering wages inadequate, by raising the prices of goods in the foreign market or by driving capital abroad, is the great parent of pauperism.

Having thus traced the effects of a diminution, I will now endeavour to point out the consequences of an increase in the value of the circulating medium.

As a depreciation of the currency would, in the first instance, occasion a fall in the real wages of labour; so a rise in the value of the medium in which he is paid, would give the labourer a greater command over the necessaries of life than before, and thus reduce the number of paupers, and lower the amount of the poor rates. Unfortunately these beneficial effects could not be permanent. Masters can lower wages much more rapidly than workmen can raise them. In proportion as their numbers are smaller, a combination among them becomes more easy; while, as they can always subsist for a considerable time upon their capital, their competition to obtain workmen can never be so active and urgent as that of the workmen, whose labour is their daily bread, to obtain employment. Besides, a rise in wages always diminishes, by a two-fold operation, the demand for labour. It lowers the profits of stock, and thereby checks the accumulation of capital, and takes from the inducement to engage in productive industry; while, at the same time, its prevents any given quantity or amount of capital, from putting so great a number of hands in motion as before. If the labourer receives two shillings a-day as wages, and if he daily works up material to the amount of two shillings more, then a capital of two thousand shillings will put in motion five hundred days' labour; but if wages rise to three shillings a-day, then a capital amounting to two thousand shillings would not give employment to more than four hundred days' labour, five shillings instead of four being required to furnish the labourer with wages and material for each day. Thus the combination of masters, the competition of workmen, the less rapid accumulation of capital, and its diminished power of putting industry in motion, would irresistibly tend, not only to bring the real wages of labour down to their former level, but to depress them somewhat lower than they would have been, had the rise in the currency never taken place.

We have seen that a fall in the value of the circulating medium alters the distribution of wealth in favour of the productive classes. A rise in its value has a contrary effect, enriching the class whose revenues are expended unproductively, at the loss of those by the agency of whose labour and capital the wealth of the community is created. A greater portion of the farmer's produce would be required to pay his rent, and a less portion would remain to be re-invested in cultivation and improvement. The salaries of public functionaries, the wages of all the civil and military servants of the state, though nominally the same, would in reality be increased. The mortgagee, the annuitant, and the fund-holder, all those, who, without actively engaging in the work of production, live upon the interest of money, would have their revenues increased at the expense of those funds which pay the profits of stock, and the wages of labour.

In all the transactions of trade, the creditor

would be benefited at the cost of the debtor.
The diminution in the amount of the circulating
medium, would compel the monied capitalist,
and banker, to restrict their discounts, and thus
deprive the merchant of the accustomed accommodation on which he calculated. Credit would
encounter a shock, and as an increase of confidence creates the extension of demand, which it
anticipates; so a diminution of confidence occasions that narrowing of the market which it
fears. One individual under the apprehension
that he will be able to sell less, employs fewer
workmen in preparing goods, than before; but
the diminished quantity of his goods will not
enhance their price, because, as a similar im-
pression caused less business to be done in other
trades, there will be fewer articles to offer in
exchange for them, and the demand will be contracted in the same proportion as the supply. The
shock which injures credit, suspends production.

But to a country circumstanced like England,
the most injurious effect of a rise in the value
of money, undoubtedly is the addition which it
occasions in the real amount of our debt and

taxation. Excessive taxation banished manufactures and commerce from the republic of
Holland, and we are not to expect that in our
own country a similar cause will be followed by
a dissimilar effect. In the deficiency of employment, in the amount of the poor rates, and in
the millions of capital sent out of the country as
foreign loans, England may discover the awful
truth, that exorbitant taxation is bringing her
to the limits of her resources, and to the verge
of decline.

From the brief sketch which has here been
given of the effect, which a fall and a rise in the
value of currency are respectively calculated to
produce, it must be sufficiently apparent, that
the consequences of the latter would be beyond
all comparison more injurious than those of the
former. With respect indeed to an unjust alteration, in the distribution of property, both would
be upon a par. The proprietor who had granted
leases, the creditor who had made advances
either to the public, or to individuals, with all
those whose income was estimated, or whose
capital was invested in money, would suffer by

the one; while the tenant, the debtor, and the payer of taxes, would be surcharged by the other. But though a fall and a rise in the value of currency, might inflict equal injustice upon individuals, they would produce very different effects upon the general wealth and prosperity. The violations of private property in the former case, would be accompanied by an increase of confidence, of production, and of trade; in the latter, would be aggravated by a universal stagnation, and revulsion, and, perhaps, in an over-taxed country, by a national bankruptcy.

SECTION VI.—*On the Principles of Demand and Supply.*

BEFORE the divisions of employment are established, and while each individual raises and prepares for himself all the several articles he consumes, the society will possess an advantage which will compensate, in some slight degree at least, for the low effective powers of industry In this rude and early state there can be no anxiety with regard to finding a vend or market for the goods which may be produced. Every increased exertion of labour will have a direct and immediate effect in improving the condition of the labourer, and the amount of every man's wealth will be in exact proportion to the quantity of industry he employs, and the skill with which he directs it.

On the other hand, those divisions of employment which almost miraculously increase the effective powers of human labour, are accompanied by a counterbalancing disadvantage. When they are once thoroughly established, the machine of society becomes infinitely artificial and complex, and a derangement in any of its nicer parts, not unfrequently impedes the working of the whole. Increased exertions on the part of the labourer, instead of increasing may now diminish his command over the necessaries of life; and the amount of wealth acquired by each individual will depend, not so much upon the energy and skill with which he applies his industry, as upon the numbers and the means of those who may be desirous of purchasing the peculiar commodity which he furnishes. Manufacturers may starve, not in consequence of idleness, but of doing too much work; and agriculture become a losing occupation, not from the deficiency, but from the abundance of its products. While in the rude and simple stage of society, the only object was to produce; in the improved and complex state, the object is not merely to produce, but to produce in such proportions that the peculiar articles furnished by each class may be readily and profitably exchanged for the peculiar articles prepared by the others.

In the language of political economy, the production of commodities in such proportions that each may be readily and profitably exchanged for others, is called limiting the supply to the effectual demand. The preservation of these proportions is of the utmost importance, not merely to the individual who furnishes particular articles, but to the general industry and wealth of the community. Indeed, there are scarcely any principles in economical science which come so frequently into practical operation, and which at the same time are so imperfectly understood, as those which are termed the laws of supply and demand. I shall, therefore, in concluding this long chapter upon mercantile industry, endeavour to furnish that which I conceive has hitherto remained a *desideratum* in political economy; namely, an accurate and complete analysis of the important principles of supply and demand.

In the production of every commodity certain portions of some other commodities are consumed. Effectual demand must therefore consist in the power and the inclination to give for a commodity, either by direct or circuitous exchange, a quantity of the other commodities required in their production, somewhat greater than their production actually costs. If the quantity of commodities offered in exchange for a given quantity of another commodity, does not equal the quantity expended on its production, it will be physically impossible that its production should be continued; and if the quantity offered does not somewhat exceed the quantity expended, it will be morally impossible to continue production, because the producer can have no motive to advance his capital; or, in other words, to expend one set of commodities in raising or fabricating others.

It is no solid objection to this account of effectual demand, to say, that in the profitable transactions which are daily and hourly effected in the market, an instance is scarcely ever found to occur, in which the price of an article sold consists in a quantity of all the other articles required in its production, somewhat greater than its production actually cost. If this somewhat greater quantity of these articles is never given directly and immediately, it is always given indirectly and mediately. Wherever a sale takes place, which realises a profit to the producer, and enables and induces him to continue his business, the price of the article sold must necessarily be sufficient to purchase some greater quantity of the other articles expended upon its production, than its production actually cost. No price, however high, as expressed in money or in other things, can be a remunerating price, or constitute that effectual demand which enables and encourages the producer to continue his occupation, unless it will suffice to purchase

for him some greater quantity of the ingredients
of capital than that which he expended in production. On the other hand, no price, however
low, as estimated in money or other things, can
cease to be a remunerating price, and to constitute the expression of effectual demand, unless
the quantity of money or of other things in
which it consists, be inadequate to repurchase
some greater quantity of the ingredients of
capital than that expended in the production of
the commodity sold. The effectual demand for
any commodity is always determined, and under
any given rate of profit, is constantly commensurate with the quantity of the ingredients of capital,
or of the things required in its production, which
consumers may be able and willing to offer in
exchange for it.

An effectual demand for an increased quantity of any commodity may be created by two
several circumstances, namely, by an increase in
the quantity of the ingredients of capital offered
in exchange for it, or by a diminution in the
quantity of these ingredients required for its
production. Thus, assuming that the rate of

profit is ten per cent. and that the ingredients of capital consumed in preparing a bale of muslin are one quarter of corn, and one suit of clothing; then, if the persons desirous of consuming muslin, offer one hundred and ten quarters of corn, and one hundred and ten suits of clothing in exchange for it, there will be an effectual demand or profitable vend for one hundred bales of muslin. But if, while the quantity of things required to be expended in producing muslin remains the same, the quantity of these things offered in exchange for it should be increased to two hundred and twenty quarters of corn, and two hundred and twenty suits of clothing; the effectual demand for the article would be doubled, and there would be a profitable vend for two hundred bales of muslin, instead of one hundred. A precisely similar effect would be produced if, while the consumers continued to offer no more than one hundred and ten quarters of corn, and one hundred and ten suits of clothing, for their supply of muslin, the quantity of the ingredients of capital necessary to the fabrication of one hundred bales, should be reduced from one hundred quarters of corn, and one hundred suits of clothing, to fifty quarters, and fifty suits. In either case, there would be an effectual demand for two hundred bales of muslin, instead of for one hundred.

In like manner, an effectual demand for a diminished quantity of commodities will be occasioned by two several circumstances; first, by a diminution in the quantity of the ingredients of capital offered in exchange for them; secondly, by an increased quantity of these ingredients becoming necessary to their production. If the rate of profit be ten per cent. and if it requires a capital of one quarter of corn, and one suit of clothing, to fabricate a bale of muslin; and if the ingredients of capital offered in exchange for muslin be diminished to fifty-five quarters of corn, and fifty-five suits of clothing, it is evident that no more than fifty bales of muslin can obtain a profitable vend. The same result will follow if, while one hundred and ten quarters of corn, and one hundred and ten suits of clothing are offered for the supply of muslin, the cost of producing a bale of this article should be increased to two quarters of corn, and two suits of clothing. The quantity of any commodity for which a profitable sale can be obtained, must necessarily be diminished, either by an increase in the quantity of the ingredients of capital required in its production, or by a diminution in the quantity of these ingredients brought to market to be exchanged for it.

These illustrations will be found sufficient, I trust, to establish the important principles that that which increases the effectual demand for commodities, is increased production; and that that which diminishes effectual demand, is diminished production. Wherever there is a profitable sale for an increased quantity of commodities, one of two things must necessarily have occurred;— either the consumers must have acquired a greater quantity of the ingredients of capital to replace the greater quantity of these ingredients expended in increasing the supply of other commodities; or else improvements must have been effected in industry, admitting of increased production without an increase of cost. In the former case, a greater quantity of the ingredients of capital is produced; in the latter, a greater quantity of the things, in the acquisition of which capital is expended; and in both, increased supply is the one and only cause of increased effectual demand.

It may be proper to remark, that there are cases in which an increased production of the ingredients of capital will not occasion an increased effectual demand for the articles upon which capital is expended; and conversely, in which a diminished production of the ingredients of capital will not lead to a diminution in the quantity of other things for which there is a profitable vend. In all such cases, however, the increase or diminution of production, on the one hand, is counterbalanced by a diminished or increased production on the other. Thus, to recur to our former illustration, were the quantity of the ingredients of capital offered in exchange for muslin increased from one hundred and ten quarters of corn, and one hundred and ten suits of clothing, to two hundred and twenty quarters, and two hundred and twenty suits; while the cost of producing one hundred bales of muslin rose from one hundred quarters, and one hundred suits, to two hundred quarters, and two hundred suits, then the double quantity of the ingredients of capital would not furnish an effectual demand for any increased quantity of muslin. And again; should the quantity of the ingredients of capital produced and brought to market be diminished one half, while the expense of producing muslin were diminished one half also, then fifty-five quarters of corn, and fifty-five suits of clothing would afford the same profitable vend or effectual demand for one hundred bales of muslin, as was formerly afforded by an equivalent consisting of one hundred and ten quarters, and one hundred and ten suits.

Effectual demand consists in the power and inclination, on the part of consumers, to give for commodities, either by immediate or circuitous barter, some greater portion of all the ingredients of capital than their production costs. If this be a correct account of the matter, it follows that there is a very important limitation to the principle, that increased supply is the occasion of increased demand; and it will appear, that an increased production of those articles which do not form component parts of capital, cannot create an increased effective demand, either for such articles themselves, or for those other articles which do form component parts of capital. No increased production of silks, for example, can give rise to an increased effectual demand either for muslins or for corn. The reason is obvious. In fabricating muslin or in raising corn, a great variety of articles of capital, such as food and clothing, material and implements, must be expended, and these ingredients of capital no supply of silks or of other superfluities can replace. Whatever may be the quantities of the ingredients of capital expended in production, they can be replaced only by the same quantities of themselves. When we expend any additional quantity of capital in producing muslin, such additional expenditure connot be replaced by an equivalent expenditure directed to the production of silks; but, on the contrary, must be replaced by an additional production of those identical articles of which capital is composed. If, without diminishing the quantity of capital employed in the other branches of industry, we employ in the manufacturing of muslin an additional capital consisting of food and material, clothing and implements, for a thousand workmen ; then, for the increased supply of muslin thus obtained, no effectual demand, no profitable vend, or replacement, with an adequate surplus, of the articles expended, can by possibility be found*, unless the production of the ingredients of capital be contemporaneously increased to the extent of food and material, clothing and implements, for a thousand.

It may be objected, perhaps, that if articles which do not form any component part of directly productive capital, cannot create an effectual demand for those other articles which did form component parts of capital, then the capital destined to be employed in direct production, must constitute the effectual demand for itself. But as effectual demand consists in giving

---

* In treating of the causes of increased effectual demand, I purposely exclude from consideration the increased effective demand for one article, which may arise in consequence of a diminution in the demand for another. This is a transference, and not an increase of effectual demand.

in exchange for a commodity some greater quantity of the things expended in its production, than that production actually cost, saying, that capital contributes the effectual demand for itself, involves the absurdity that a thing may be given in exchange for itself.

The absurdity here contemplated is not real, but nominal, and can present itself only in consequence of our failing to consider that the term, capital, is a general term, comprising a great variety of heterogeneous products, which are classed under one and the same denomination, on account of the accidental circumstance of their being destined to aid in the business of production. The capital destined to be employed in direct production must consist of raw produce, such as food and material; and of wrought goods, such as clothing and implements. These several things are produced by different individuals, and exchanged against each other, and when produced and exchanged in the proper proportion, each contributes to create the effectual demand for all. Thus, when the farmer expends food and clothing for one hundred in raising food for two hundred and fifty, and the manufacturer lays out food and clothing for one hundred in preparing clothing for two hundred and fifty, then by the exchange of half the corn for half the cloth, the farmer will have a greater quantity of the ingredients of capital than that which produced the corn, and the manufacturer a greater quantity than that which fabricated the cloth; that is, the several ingredients of capital will occasion an effectual demand for each other.

Were one and the same individual to produce all the several articles composing directly productive capital, then, indeed, there could be no effectual demand or profitable vend for such articles, and for the plain reason, that when the divisions of employment are thus suspended, the replacement of capital with a surplus is effected, not by exchanging the particular article produced against the several articles expended in its production, but by each individual raising and fabricating for himself greater quantities of all things than the quantities he consumes in carrying on the different branches of industry in which he engages. Where there is no division of employment, there will be no market, no profitable vend, no effectual demand.

As a considerable portion of the commodities which are brought to market are exchanged, not for other commodities, but for labour, it is necessary that we should ascertain, 1*st*, in what way the supply of commodities may affect the demand for labour; and, 2*dly*, in what way the supply of labour may affect the demand for commodities.

Labour, like commodities, requires the expenditure of several articles to produce it and bring it to market. When the quantity of other things required to maintain a given quantity of labour is offered in exchange for it, then this quantity of labour is effectually demanded; and it is self-evident, that there cannot be an effectual demand for an increased quantity of labour, unless there is an increased production of the several articles by which labour is maintained.

An effectual demand for labour differs, in some respects, from an effectual demand for commodities. As in the production of every commodity which is brought to market, some portion of labour must be employed, those ingredients of capital, the offer of which constitutes the effectual demand for commodities, must comprise the subsistence of the labourers employed, as well as the material upon which they operated, and the wear and tear of the tools with which they wrought. The effectual demand for labour, on the contrary, consists merely in the offer of an adequate quantity of subsistence. Productive labour, indeed, cannot be put into operation unless the labourers, in addition to their subsistence, are furnished with tools and material. But an increased supply of the necessaries of life is of itself sufficient to enable us to engage an increased number of menial servants and unproductive retainers.

A distinction of more importance is, that the effectual demand for labour may consist in the offer of the exact quantity of things consumed in bringing it to market; while the effectual demand for commodities includes the offer, not merely of the quantity of other things expended on production, but also of some additional quantity, enabling the capitalist, after the complete replacement of all his original advances, either to employ an additional number of workmen, or else to indulge in unproductive expenditure.

Those commodities which are brought to market by independent labourers, with little or no capital beyond their daily subsistence, will, like labour, be effectually demanded when the quantity of other things offered in exchange for them just replaces without any surplus the quantity expended in their production. The exchangeable value of such commodities cannot permanently exceed that of the subsistence of the labour which procures them. Were an article acquired with little or no capital by a day's common labour to exchange for less than a day's ordinary wages, the labourer would not continue to bring it to market; and were it to exchange for more than a day's ordinary wages, then those who lived by wages would have an interest in becoming independent workmen, and in bringing this commodity to market, until the increasing supply reduced its exchangeable value, and rendered the quantity procured by a day's labour equivalent to a day's subsistence.

The reason why those commodities which are brought to market by independent labourers, with little or no capital beyond their daily subsistence, find an effectual demand in the offer of a less quantity of other things than that which affords an effectual demand for commodities supplied with an equally moderate cost by labourers who have their subsistence advanced to them by a capitalist, is sufficiently apparent. When an independent labourer advances a day's subsistence to himself, and goes out to gather wild fruits, or to catch shell-fish, he cannot charge *profit* upon the article he brings home, because if he did, he would be better off than those who work for a master, and would immediately excite their competition; but when it is necessary that a capitalist should advance subsistence, the customary rate of profit upon such advance must be charged upon the commodity produced, otherwise the capitalist would withdraw to some other occupation in which the usual profit might be obtained.

Having shewn in what manner, and under what limitations, commodities afford an effectual demand for labour, I shall proceed to examine the question, whether labour can furnish an effectual demand for commodities, premising that I exclude from my consideration that small and unimportant class of commodities which may be brought to market by independent workmen without the aid of capital.

The ingredients of capital, or the things expended in production, consist of raw produce, as food and material; and of wrought articles, as clothing and implements; and cannot, it is self-evident, be replaced, except by articles identical to them in kind and quantity. But labour is not identical with any one of the things expended in giving it employment. Offering it in exchange for commodities cannot by possibility replace the ingredients of capital with which the commodities were produced. The supply of labour therefore, however abundant, cannot, in the first instance, constitute effectual demand, which is essentially the replacement by way of exchange, and with some surplus, of the things advanced by the capitalist in order to bring other things to market.

If labour does not constitute an effectual demand for commodities, it may be asked, what advantage the capitalist can derive from the advances he makes in exchange for labour? I answer, that the advantage of the capitalist is derived, not from the immediate exchange of capital against labour, but from the subsequent reproduction which labour and capital occasion. When I exchange for one hundred and ten days' subsistence a quantity of silks, for the production of which I had advanced one hundred days' subsistence, my capital is immediately replaced to me with a surplus of ten per cent.; but when I exchange one hundred days' subsistence for labour, my capital is in no way replaced; nay, even when the labour has produced me the same quantity of silk as before, no expenditure is returned, no surplus realised, and it is not until I have exchanged my silks for a greater quantity of subsistence than their production cost, that I find a profitable vend, and am furnished with the means, and presented with the motive to renew my operations. Now, what is it which in this case constitutes the effectual demand?

Not, assuredly, the labour for which I advance my subsistence, nor the article which that labour prepares, but the production in some other quarter of a greater quantity of subsistence than that which I advanced, combined with the will of its possessor, to exchange it for my silks.

I shall now endeavour to give some account of the relation which exists between effectual demand and supply. The supply of a commodity consists of the quantity of it which is brought to market in order to be sold. We frequently meet, both in discourse and in writing, with such expressions as the following,—the supply exceeds the demand,—the supply falls short of the demand,—and—the supply is equal to the demand. Economical writers, however, have been neither very careful nor very successful in explaining the precise nature of those relations between demand and supply, to which they apply these terms.

Effectual demand and supply are in the relation of equality when the ingredients of capital offered in exchange for commodities exceed, by the customary rate of profit, the ingredients of capital expended in producing them. It follows that supply is deficient in relation to effectual demand, when the ingredients of capital offered in exchange for commodities exceed the cost of producing them by more than the customary profit; and that supply will be in excess as relates to effectual demand, when the ingredients of capital offered in exchange for the commodities brought to market, do not exceed by the usual profit the ingredients of capital expended in bringing them there. Thus, assuming the rate of profit to be ten per cent. the supply of silks will equal the effectual demand, when, for every portion of this article brought to market with the expenditure of one hundred days' subsistence, one hundred and ten days' subsistence, or one hundred days' subsistence with other things equivalent to ten days' subsistence, is produced in some other quarter, and brought to market to be exchanged, directly or circuitously, for silk. In like manner, the supply of silk will be deficient in relation to the effectual demand, when, for every one hundred and ten days' subsistence, or for every one hundred days' subsistence with other things equivalent to ten days' subsistence which are produced and offered in exchange for silk, a quantity of silk requiring for its production one hundred days' subsistence, has not been brought to market : and, upon the same principle, the supply of silk will be redundant, as compared with the effectual demand, when, for every one hundred days' subsistence expended in producing it, one hundred and ten days' subsistence, or one hundred days' subsistence, with something equal in value to ten days' subsistence, is not produced elsewhere, and offered as its equivalent.

From what has been said, it will be apparent that the relations between effectual demand and supply, depend upon the comparative cost of production, and not upon the quantity of other commodities brought to market to be exchanged against the ingredients of capital. If, the rate of profit being ten per cent. the ingredients of capital to the extent of one hundred and ten quarters of corn, and one hundred and ten suits of clothing, are offered in exchange for silk, then the quantity of silk which can be brought to market with an expenditure of one hundred quarters of corn, and one hundred suits of clothing, will equalize the supply to the effectual demand, whether that quantity be great or small. Should the expenditure of one hundred quarters of corn, and one hundred suits of clothing, fabricate one thousand yards of silk, then one thousand yards would be required to proportion the supply of the article to the effectual demand; but should this expenditure fabricate only one hundred yards, then would one hundred yards be sufficient to keep the supply even with the demand; and should the advance of one hundred quarters of corn, and one hundred suits of clothing, bring only one yard of silk to market, still between the supply of silk and the effectual demand for it, the relation of equality would be preserved. No alteration in the quantities of those commodities which are offered in exchange for the ingredients of capital, can effect an alteration in the relations between supply and effectual demand; because effectual demand consists essentially in the power and the will to give in exchange for commodities, whatever the quantity of them may be, that portion of the ingredients of capital which their production cost, together with such surplus, whether in the form of capital or of other things, as may yield the capitalist the customary rate of profit.

The foregoing remarks must have rendered it apparent, that no absolute increase of demand can alter the relation of supply to demand, provided such increase of demand be accompanied with a similar increase of supply. As I have already shewn, an absolute increase in the effectual demand for a commodity may arise from two distinct causes,—an increase in the quantity of the ingredients of capital offered in exchange for it, or a diminution in the quantity of those ingredients required in its production. Now, supposing that demand and supply are in the relation of equality, that is, that the quantity of the ingredients of capital which may be obtained for a commodity by direct or circuitous exchange, is just sufficient to replace, with the customary rate of profit, the quantity of these ingredients expended in its production ; and supposing further, that a double quantity of the ingredients of capital come to be offered for this commodity, while, at the same time, a double quantity is expended in bringing an increased supply of the commodity to market; then it is evident that the relation of equality between the demand and supply can be in no way disturbed. Were the same quantity of the ingredients of capital to become sufficient to produce a double quantity of the commodity, while the consumers continued willing and able to offer the same quantity of these ingredients in exchange for it, still the relation of equality between the demand and the supply would continue to be preserved. The actual relation which at any time exists between supply and demand, can be altered only when the quantity of the ingredients of capital offered in exchange for other commodities, is increased or diminished without a corresponding increase or diminution taking place in the ingredients of capital employed in bringing the other commodities to market; or when the quantity of these ingredients employed in bringing the other commodities to market, is increased or diminished without a corresponding increase or diminution in the quantity of the other commodities offered in exchange.

A relative increase or diminution of effectual demand, occasions, as the terms denote, an alteration in the previously existing relation between effectual demand and supply. When both the quantity of a commodity and the quantity of the ingredients of capital expended in bringing it to market remain the same, while the quantity of the ingredients of capital offered in exchange for it is increased; then, though there would be no absolute increase of effectual demand, as regards the quantity of the commodity actually purchased and consumed, yet there would be a relative increase of effectual demand, as regards the expense of furnishing it to the consumer. And if the quantity of a commodity brought to market, and the expense of bringing it there, were to remain the same, while the quantity of the ingredients of capital offered in exchange for it should be diminished, then, though there would be no absolute diminution of effectual demand, as regards the quantity of the commodity purchased and consumed, there would be a relative diminution of effectual demand, as regards the expenses of production and the profits of those who bring the commodity to market*.

---

* When there is an absolute increase of effectual demand, a greater quantity of commodities may be sold with the same rate of profit; and when there is a relative increase, the same quantity will be sold at a higher rate of profit. In his work upon the Principles of Political Economy, however, Mr. Malthus lays great stress upon a species of effectual demand, which is neither absolute nor relative; and which neither admits of increased sales with the same profits, nor of the same sales with higher profits. This he denominates an increased intensity of demand. When the expense of producing a commodity is permanently increased, and when, in consequence, the consumer takes the same quantity of the commodity at a higher price, Mr. Malthus tells us, that the expression of a greater intensity of demand is called forth, and that a most important change is effected in the relation between the supply and the demand of such commodity. According to the definition of effectual demand which I have given in the text, it is impossible that giving an increased price for a commodity, proportional to the increased cost of its production, should be the expression of an increased intensity of demand, or should make any change in the relation between effectual demand and supply. Effectual demand is the power and the will to give for a commodity some greater quantity of the ingredients of capital than its pro-

There may also be an absolute and relative increase in the supply of a commodity.   If both

---

duction cost ; and, therefore, when an increased price is given for a commodity, there can be no increased intensity of demand for the commodity, or, to substitute the definition for the term defined, there can be no greater intensity in the power and the will to give for the commodity some larger portion of the ingredients of capital than its production cost, unless this cost of production should not have increased in an equal proportion with the increase of price.   When, in preparing a yard of muslin, two days' subsistence are expended instead of one, and when, in consequence, I give in exchange for this article twice the former quantity of the ingredients of capital, the intensity of effectual demand, or of the power to give for a yard of muslin something more than its production cost, is in no degree increased.   But what must strike the reader as much more extraordinary is, that Mr. Malthus' doctrine of intensity of demand is inconsistent with the definition of demand which he himself has given.   He defines demand to be the will combined with the power to purchase.   Now, when the cost of producing a yard of muslin is doubled, and when, in consequence, the price given for it is doubled also, this increased price is not the expression of a more intense power to purchase a yard of muslin. Mr. Malthus says, " If a given number of commodities attain-
" able by labour alone, were to become more difficult of
" acquisition, as they would evidently not be obtained
" unless by means of increased exertion, we might surely
" consider such increased exertion, if applied, as an evi-
" dence of a greater intensity of demand, or of a power

the quantity of a commodity brought to market, and the quantity of the ingredients of capital offered in exchange for it remain the same, while the quantity of these ingredients expended in producing it is diminished; then, though there will be no absolute diminution in the supply of the commodity, as regards the actual quantity brought to market, there will be a relative diminution of supply with respect to the quantity which the consumer is able and willing to purchase at a price returning average profits. And if both the quantity of a commodity brought to market and the expense of bringing it there,

---

" and will to make a greater sacrifice in order to obtain " them." Here Mr. Malthus uses the term, demand, in a sense altogether different from that expressed in his own definition. A greater intensity of power to purchase commodities, is essentially different from a power to make a greater sacrifice in order to obtain them. When the cost of producing commodities increases, we lose the power of purchasing them, unless we possess the power of making a greater sacrifice in order to obtain them. Therefore, to call that power to make a greater sacrifice which is necessary to the retaining of the same power to purchase, " a " greater intensity of power to purchase," is manifestly inconsistent and absurd.

were to continue the same, while the quantity of the ingredients of capital offered in exchange for it diminished, then, though there would be no absolute increase in the supply of the commodity, with respect to the quantity of it produced and sold, there would be a relative increase of supply, with regard to the power of purchasing and the price at which the commodity could be sold.

The great practical problem in economical science is, so to proportion production that supply and demand shall be in the relation of equality; or, to express the same thing in particular rather than in general terms, that the quantity of the ingredients of capital brought to market to exchange against other commodities, shall be equal at the least to the quantity of these ingredients expended on the other commodities. So long as this proportion is preserved, every article which the industrious classes have the will and power to produce, will find a ready and a profitable vend. No conceivable increase of production can lead to an overstocking of the market; but, on the contrary, every addition which can be made to the supply of commodities, will immediately and necessarily occasion an increase in the effectual demand for them. Whatever may have been the previous state of the market in regard to abundant supply, increased production will create a proportionally increased demand. The only limits to the increase of effectual demand will be the limits which are set to increased production, by the scarcity of fertile land, or by a rate of wages so high as to deprive the capitalist of that *minimum* rate of profit which is necessary to induce him to continue his advances.

This happy and prosperous state of things is immediately interrupted when the proportions in which commodities are produced are such as to disturb the equality between effectual demand and supply. When the supply is deficient in relation to the effectual demand, the consumer is less abundantly supplied with the conveniences of life than he otherwise might be; and when the ingredients of capital expended in the production of commodities are in excess with respect to the ingredients of capital brought to market to exchange against other commodities, then gluts and regorgements are experienced.

The great importance of these principles, both theoretically and practically, renders it expedient that they should be more fully explained and demonstrated. I shall therefore endeavour to shew, through some illustrative cases, the particular mode in which they operate; premising that when speaking of the ingredients of capital, I shall employ the terms, corn, and clothing, in a general sense, the one as standing for all the several kinds of raw produce, and the other as denoting the various wrought articles of which directly productive capital may be composed. This will conduce to brevity and clearness, while it can in no way affect the accuracy of our conclusions.

Let us suppose that there exists a society consisting of one hundred cultivators, and one hundred manufacturers, and that the one hundred cultivators expend one hundred quarters of corn and one hundred suits of clothing, in raising two hundred and twenty quarters of corn, while the one hundred manufacturers expend one hundred quarters of corn and one hundred suits of clothing, in preparing two hundred and twenty suits. In this case, the offer of half the corn of the cultivator would constitute an effectual demand for half the clothing of the manufacturer; or, reciprocally, the offer of half the clothing of the latter, an effectual demand for half the corn of the former; because, when the two classes exchanged half their respective products, the things expended in production would be more than replaced. The class of cultivators, and the class of manufacturers, instead of one hundred suits of clothing, and one hundred quarters of corn, would each possess one hundred and ten quarters, and one hundred and ten suits; and this surplus, or profit of ten per cent. they might employ either in setting additional labourers to work, or in purchasing luxuries for immediate enjoyment. It will be immediately perceived, too, that the effectual demand which allows the clothing to be disposed of with a profit, is created by the production of the corn; and that the effectual demand for the corn, is created by the production of the clothing.

Now, while the productive powers of industry remain as before, let us suppose that our society has doubled its numbers, and that two hundred cultivators, expending two hundred quarters of corn, and two hundred suits of clothing, produce four hundred and forty quarters; while two hundred manufacturers, by expending two hundred quarters, and two hundred suits, produce four hundred and forty suits. In this case, when one half of the corn of the farmers is brought to market and exchanged against one half of the clothing of the manufacturers, each class will, as before, have the things expended in production replaced with a profit of ten per cent.; and the only difference will be, that there will now be an effectual demand for double the former quantity both of corn and of clothing. But it will be quite obvious, that the double demand for corn will be created by the double production of clothing, and that the double demand for clothing will be created by the double production of corn.

Now, let us suppose, that while the society doubles its numbers, the productive powers of industry are doubled also, and that two hundred cultivators, expending two hundred quarters of corn and two hundred suits of clothing, can raise eight hundred quarters of corn; and two hundred manufacturers, expending two hundred quarters and two hundred suits, can prepare eight hundred suits. In this case, if the love of ease prevails over the desire of luxurious enjoyment, and no additional quantity of commodities is obtained, then, as there is no increase of production, there can be no increase of demand; and the only effect resulting from the improved powers of industry will be, that the society will work a shorter space of time than before. But should our little society acquire a taste for luxuries, and be willing to work the same number of hours as before, in order to obtain sugar and tobacco, ribbons and lace, then an increased production would take place, and consequently a proportionally increased demand. Of our two hundred cultivators, one hundred, expending one hundred quarters of corn and one hundred suits of clothing, would raise four hundred quarters of corn; and the other one hundred, with a like expenditure, raise a quantity of sugar and tobacco; and of our two hundred manufacturers, one hundred, expending one hundred quarters of corn and one hundred suits of clothing, will fabricate four hundred suits; and the other one hundred, with a like expenditure, work up a quantity of ribbons and lace. Now, let us mark the way in which this increased production creates a proportionally increased demand. When the several commodities are brought to market to be exchanged against each other, according to the expenses of their production, the one hundred farmers, after giving one hundred quarters of corn to one class of manufacturers for one hundred suits of clothing, one hundred quarters to the other for a fourth of their ribbons and lace, and one hundred quarters to the growers of sugar and tobacco, for a fourth of these products, would retain one hundred quarters in their own hands, and thus have their expenditure of one hundred quarters of corn and one hundred suits of clothing, replaced to them, together with a quantity of sugar, tobacco, ribbons, and lace, equal in productive cost, and therefore in exchangeable value to the capital they expended. In like manner, the one hundred fabricators of clothing, after giving one hundred suits for one hundred quarters of corn, one hundred for a quarter of the ribbons and lace produced, and one hundred for a quarter of the tobacco and sugar, would have one hundred suits remaining; and consequently would have their expenditure of one hundred quarters of corn, and one hundred suits of clothing, replaced with a quantity of luxuries equivalent thereto. By these exchanges too, the one hundred cultivators who expended one hundred quarters of corn and one hundred suits of clothing, in raising sugar and tobacco, as well as the one hundred manufacturers who, with a like expenditure, prepared ribbons and laces, would have their capitals replaced to them by the sacrifice of half their products, and would have the other half as a surplus for their own expenditure. For every article brought to market there would be a profitable vend. Each class would find that a part of the things it produced would replace the whole of the things it expended in production. But this is exactly what is meant by effectual demand; and the more accurately we analyse the operations of industry and the transactions of the market, the more clearly we shall perceive, that while the due proportions are preserved between the quantity of the ingredients of capital and of other things, increased production is the one and only cause of extended demand.

It is no solid objection to the theory of effectual demand here unfolded, that I have not taken into consideration the influence of so general and important a principle in human nature as indolence or the love of ease. This principle has no connexion whatever with the doctrine I have endeavoured to establish. That doctrine is, that while the quantity of the ingredients of capital brought to market, is equal, at the least, to the quantity of these ingredients expended in bringing other commodities there, then, increased production will be the cause of increased effectual demand. If the love of ease prevents an increase of production, an increase of effectual demand cannot follow. But surely it is most absurd to contend, that an assigned cause is inadequate to the effect, because the effect disappears when a circumstance occurs to suspend the operation of the cause.

When our two hundred cultivators and two hundred manufacturers acquire double productive powers, and are enabled with an expenditure of four hundred quarters of corn and four hundred suits of clothing, to bring to market eight hundred quarters and eight hundred suits, then one of three things must take place. The whole of the society will employ the same quantity of industry as before, in order to procure luxuries; or, the whole will prefer ease to the enjoyment of luxuries; or, one part will employ the same quantity of exertion as before, while the other part will indulge the love of ease. Now, if the whole make the same exertions as before, then the increased production, provided it be proportioned in the manner above described, must create increased effectual demand; and if the whole community prefer doing half their former quantity of work to the enjoyment of luxuries, then production will remain as before, and consequently effectual demand will remain as before. But were one part of the community to prefer ease to luxuries, and the other part luxuries to ease, the result would be somewhat different. Let us therefore inquire, whether this partial indulgence in the love of ease affords any ground of objection against the principle, that proportionally increased production occasions increased effectual demand.

Supposing that our cultivators are the class preferring ease to luxury, and that instead of one hundred raising four hundred quarters of corn, and the other one hundred a quantity of sugar and tobacco, the whole two hundred work half their time and raise only four hundred quarters of corn. In this case, they would have two hundred quarters of corn to exchange against two hundred suits of clothing, but no sugar and tobacco to exchange against ribbons and lace. What would be the result of this state of things with respect to the class of manufacturers, which by the supposition performs the same quantity of work as before, in order to enjoy luxuries? Of this class, one hundred expending one hundred quarters of corn and one hundred suits of clothing, can fabricate four hundred suits of clothing, and as two hundred of these suits are exchanged with the cultivators for two hundred quarters of corn, they will have, after replacing their own advances, one hundred quarters and one hundred suits, to give in exchange for luxuries. The other one hundred manufacturers, however, will not now be able to expend one hundred quarters of corn and one hundred suits of clothing in preparing ribbons and lace, because, by the supposition, the first two hundred manufacturers who have obtained the disposal of the ingredients of capital, offer fifty quarters and fifty suits for ribbons and lace, and fifty quarters and fifty suits for sugar and tobacco. The consequence will be, that fifty out of the second one hundred manufacturers must change their occupation, and, instead of preparing ribbons and lace, must raise sugar and tobacco. When this has been done, then production will be duly proportioned; the supply of all commodities will be in the relation of equality with respect to the effectual demand for them, and every article brought to market would find a ready and profitable sale. The distribution of the wealth produced would be as follows :—

Our two hundred indolent cultivators who expended two hundred quarters of corn and two hundred suits of clothing, in raising four hundred quarters, would have their whole expenditure replaced to them by exchanging two hundred quarters for two hundred suits, and instead of luxuries in the form of sugar and tobacco, ribbons and lace, would enjoy the absence of labour during half their time. The hundred manufacturers of necessaries, who expended one hundred quarters and one hundred suits in fabricating four hundred suits, and exchanging two hundred suits for two hundred quarters, would have, after the replacement of their advances, fifty quarters and fifty suits, to offer for sugar and tobacco, and fifty quarters and fifty suits to offer in exchange for ribbons and lace. The cultivators, therefore, who expended fifty yards and fifty suits in raising sugar and tobacco, and the manufacturers who, with a similar advance, furnished ribbons and lace, would replace their capitals, even if they gave the whole of their products for the corn and clothing offered. But by the law of competition they would obtain the whole of the fifty yards and fifty suits thus offered for half their products. For while the cultivator of corn can replace his expenditure, and work only half his time, and the manufacturer of clothing, by working all his time, can replace his expenditure with a surplus of one hundred per cent. the cultivator and the manufacturer of luxuries will betake themselves to the more beneficial branches of industry, if they cannot obtain the replacement of their expenses in exchange for half their products.

Thus we see, that in no conceivable instance, can the love of ease so operate as to prevent effectual demand from being commensurate with that duly proportioned production which renders the quantity of the ingredients of capital offered in exchange for commodities equal, at the least, to the quantity expended in bringing them to market. The love of ease may prevent the powers of production from being brought into full operation. But when production takes place, the love of ease is overcome, and it can therefore no longer narrow effectual demand.

To the theory of effectual demand which I have attempted to establish, an objection more plausible but not more solid may be urged. It is contended* that " though no permanent and " continued increase of wealth can take place, " without a continued increase of capital; yet, " under a rapid accumulation of capital or con- " version of unproductive into productive labour, " the demand, compared with the supply of " materials and products, would fall. In the case " before alluded to, while the farmers are disposed " to consume the luxuries produced by the ma- " nufacturers, and the manufacturers those pro- " duced by the farmers, all will go on smoothly ; " but if either one, or both of the parties, should " become disposed to save, with a view of bet- " tering their condition, and providing for their

---

* Principles of Political Economy, by Mr. Malthus, chap. vii. sect. iii.

" families in future, the state of things will be
" very different. The farmer, instead of indulg-
" ing himself in ribbons and lace, will be disposed
" to be satisfied with more simple clothing; but
" by this economy he will disable the manufac-
" turer from purchasing the same amount of his
" produce, and for the returns of so much labour
" employed upon the land, there will evidently
" be no market. The manufacturer, in like
" manner, instead of indulging himself in sugar
" and tobacco, may be disposed to save with a
" view to the future, but will be totally unable
" to do so, owing to the parsimony of the
" farmers, and the want of demand for manu-
" factures."

When we examine with any degree of accuracy into that which takes place when savings
are made from revenue in order to be added to
capital, we shall find this objection vague, falla-
cious, and inconsistent throughout. The previous supposition is, that of two hundred cultivators expending two hundred quarters of corn
and two hundred suits of clothing, one hundred
raises four hundred quarters of corn, and one

hundred a quantity of sugar and tobacco; that of two hundred manufacturers expending capital to the same extent, one hundred fabricate four hundred suits of clothing, and one hundred ribbons and lace; and that the two classes exchange their respective products according to the cost of production, and after replacing all the ingredients of capital expended, consume an equal portion of the surplus which appears in the form of luxuries. The subsequent supposition is, that while the powers of production remain as before, the consumption of luxuries is altogether abandoned for the purpose of adding to the existing capital the whole of the surplus it annually creates. The question is, what, under such circumstances, would be the effect of this passion for accumulating capital upon effectual demand?

The object of the whole class of capitalists is to increase capital. The cultivators of corn, and the fabricators of clothing, therefore, will no longer give any part of their productions for sugar and tobacco, ribbons and lace; but by exchanging two hundred quarters of corn against two hundred suits of clothing, will increase the ingredients of capital with a surplus of cent. per cent. And the cultivators of sugar and tobacco, and the manufacturers of ribbons and lace, having no longer any desire for these luxuries, and finding that they cannot replace their expenditure by exchanging them with the other two classes for corn and clothing, will change the direction of their industry, and with their expenditure of one hundred quarters and one hundred suits, will raise and fabricate four hundred quarters and four hundred suits, and by exchanging one half of one product against one half of the other, will also replace these capitals with a surplus of one hundred per cent. So far then there is no interruption of effectual demand. By the supposition, the passion is for accumulating capital. When the two hundred cultivators, who with an expenditure of two hundred quarters of corn and two hundred suits of clothing raise eight hundred quarters, and exchange four hundred quarters for four hundred suits, their capital is doubled; and when the two hundred manufacturers, who, with a like expenditure fabricate eight hundred suits of clothing, exchange four hundred suits against four hundred quarters of corn, they also find an advantageous market, or profitable vend, which places a double portion of the ingredients of capital in their hands.

If we suppose, that while the passion for accumulating capital thus increases the funds for maintaining productive labour, the supply of labour increases at an equal rate, and prevents any rise in wages from taking place, then twice the former quantity of labour might be employed; the expenditure of four hundred quarters of corn and four hundred suits of clothing in agriculture, and of four hundred quarters and four hundred suits in manufactures, would occasion the reproduction of one thousand six hundred quarters, and one thousand six hundred suits; and exchanging one half of one sort of articles for one half of the other sort, would open a profitable vend, an effectual demand for both, which would again place in the hands of each producer a double quantity of all the ingredients of capital expended. This process might be again repeated, and on the supposition that wages did not rise, and that abundance of fertile land could be obtained, might be carried on *ad infinitum* without the passion for accumulation ever once interfering with effectual demand. It is quite certain, however, that with such a passion for accumulation, the supply of labour could not increase so rapidly as the funds for maintaining it; and that wages would therefore rise. Let us then inquire, what effect this necessary rise on wages would have upon effectual demand?

After the first doubling of capital, and when the farmer and manufacturer are each enabled to expend in production four hundred quarters of corn and four hundred suits of clothing, instead of two hundred quarters and two hundred suits, we will suppose, that in consequence of population not increasing in the same ratio with capital, the competition of the capitalists to procure workmen so raises wages, that an advance of four hundred quarters of corn and four hundred suits of clothing, instead of employing four hundred labourers, gives employment to no more than three hundred. Now, as two hundred agricultural labourers had raised eight hundred quarters of corn, and two hundred manufacturing labourers prepared eight hundred suits of clothing, three hundred agricultural and three hundred manufacturing labourers will raise and fabricate one thousand two hundred quarters and one thousand two hundred suits; and when six hundred quarters and six hundred suits are interchanged, the class of agricultural, and the class of manufacturing capitalists which had each advanced four hundred quarters and four hundred suits, will have all the ingredients of capital replaced with a surplus of fifty per cent. But the rapid accumulation of capital which in this manner reduced the rate of profit from one hundred, to fifty per cent. could have no influence whatever in narrowing the effectual demand for the commodities produced. Lowering profit is essentially different from narrowing effectual demand. Any rate of profit, however low, which is sufficient to stimulate the capitalist to produce, is also sufficient to constitute an element of effectual demand.

Should the increase of capital beyond the proportional increase of population so elevate wages, that profit altogether disappeared, then, indeed, there would be no effectual demand for commodities; because, in effectual demand some species of profit is always an essential element. If our three hundred agricultural and three hundred manufacturing labourers, while raising and fabricating one thousand two hundred quarters of corn and one thousand two hundred suits of clothing, were to receive these quantities of corn and clothing as their wages, then the interchange of six hundred quarters and six hundred suits between the farmers and master manufacturers, would just replace to them the precise quantity of the ingredients of capital which they had advanced, without any surplus furnishing them with a motive to renew their operations. But it is self-evident that this want of effectual demand, or profitable vend, would be occasioned, not by an excess, but by the deficiency of products. Increase the effective powers of industry—enable the six hundred labourers, while receiving one thousand two hundred quarters of corn and one thousand two hundred suits of clothing as their wages, to raise and fabricate one thousand three hundred quarters and one thousand three hundred suits, and then the interchange of one half of each against one half of the other, will replace, with a surplus, all the ingredients of capital advanced. In every conceivable case, it is the deficiency, not the excess of products which prevents our finding a profitable vend. A rapid accumulation of capital interrupts effectual demand, only when, under a very high rate of wages, the quantity of the ingredients of capital produced and brought to market is deficient in relation to the quantity of those ingredients advanced in production.

When wages have so risen that the labourer reproduces the advances which are made to him, with that lowest rate of profit, for the sake of which the capitalist will continue his business, then there can no longer exist a motive to increase capital more rapidly than population; and supposing, that notwithstanding the high rate of wages,—the prevalence of moral restraint, or of prudential contrivances, should keep population and the supply of labour stationary, then the passion for accumulation must be extinguished in its own excess. By the supposition, however, some small surplus still appears in the form of profit, and were there, as probably there would be, any scarcity of land, a more consider-able surplus would appear in the form of rent. In what manner could these surpluses be disposed of, and where would be the effectual demand for the articles composing them? The answers to these questions are obvious.

If, on the extinction of the passion for accu-mulation, a taste for luxuries were revived, then in the form of luxuries all surplus would appear, — the effectual demand for them would be created as before explained; and should the commodities brought to market be in the due proportions, the extent of the demand would be precisely commensurate with the extent of production. But should the love of ease prevail over the desire of luxurious enjoyment, nothing beyond the necessaries of life would be produced; and in this case what would become of our profits and rents? and where would be the effectual demand for the articles composing them? The reply is still obvious.

On the assumption that no individual in the community will produce and consume any thing beyond the necessaries of life, the capitalist will advance to his labourers just that quantity of capital which, at the existing rate of profit, will yield the necessaries of life for his family. Thus, taking the rate of profit to be one per cent. the farmer or manufacturer who advances subsistence for one hundred families, would obtain in return subsistence for his own family; and no individual would employ a larger capital than one hundred days' subsistence.

Respecting rent, as our supposition in strictness excludes that species of luxury which consists in a retinue of menial servants and retainers, the proprietor, however extensive and fertile his territory might be, could have no wish to require for the use of his land a greater portion of the produce than that which sufficed to furnish his own family with the necessaries of life. Every portion of his estate over and above that, the rent of which was sufficient to afford the necessaries of life to his family, would be of no utility or value to him whatever. Thus the prevailing love of ease, which prevented the proprietor of capital from conducting a larger concern than that which was sufficient to yield necessaries, would prevent the proprietor of land from using any exertions to defend and retain these valueless possessions. All the portions of his estate, over and above that, the rent of which might be sufficient to give his family the necessaries of life, he would allow his children, his friends, and his neighbours to occupy; a continued occupancy would establish a title to these portions of land, which the original proprietor could have no motive to litigate, or even to question. Hence, landed property would become as much subdivided as capital. As no capital would exceed what, under the existing rate of profit, was necessary to yield the necessaries of life to the capitalist, so no estate would exceed that portion of territory which, in the actual degree of competition for land, yielded a rent sufficient to supply the necessaries of life to the family of the proprietor who let it out to farm.

In the state just described, there would certainly be no effectual demand for any articles beyond the bare necessaries of life for a stati-

onary* population. By the supposition, the
quantity of the ingredients of capital produced
is exactly equal to the quantity of these ingredients expended in reproducing the necessaries
of life; and therefore there are no ingredients of
capital in existence to replace, by way of exchange, the quantity of such ingredients which
might be expended in the production of luxuries.
But it is self-evident that the want of effectual
demand; or, in other words, the want of the
power to give in exchange for luxuries some
greater quantity of the ingredients of capital
than that which might be expended in bringing
them to market, would be occasioned, not by the
excess, but by the deficiency of production.
Production would not be checked by the want
of effectual demand, but effectual demand would

---

* The population would be stationary, because, under
the existing rate of wages, the labouring class is supposed
to be too prudent to increase their numbers, and because
no advance of wages inducing them to enlarge their
families, can take place, without reducing profits below
that *minimum* rate, for the sake of which the capitalist will
make advances.

be narrowed in consequence of the want of production.

Thus, in every conceivable case, effectual demand is created by and is commensurate with production, rightly proportioned. A universal passion for accumulating capital converts, during its continuance, the effectual demand for luxuries into an effectual demand for the necessaries of life; and when this passion is extinguished in its own excess, if it is replaced by a desire for luxurious enjoyment, then effectual demand will arise for every article which the country may have power to produce; and if this passion be succeeded by the prevalence of the love of ease, then an effectual demand will exist for every article which the community may have the inclination to produce. Vary our suppositions as we will, increased production, provided it be duly proportioned, is the one and only cause of extended demand, and diminished production the one and only cause of contracted demand.

One other objection to the theory of effectual demand, unfolded in the present section, remains to be examined. It may be urged, " It is the " business of all legitimate philosophy to account " for facts; and general reasonings, though ap- " parently demonstrative in every step, must " necessarily involve a fallacy when their con- " clusions do not square and tally with experi- " ence. The daily and hourly experience of " the market brings it home to our senses, that " for a considerable portion of the commodities " produced, no effectual demand exists—no pro- " fitable vend can be found. It is, therefore, " plainly impossible that demand should be " created by production, or profitable vend be " commensurate with supply."

I answer; that I acknowledge, in the fullest extent, that it is the business of philosophy to account for facts, and that no theory, however plausible, nay, however demonstrative it may appear, is entitled to attention, unless its conclusions coincide with general experience. The definition of legitimate theory is, that it is deduced, by an analytical process, from particular facts; and that it accounts, by a synthetical process, for the phenomena to which it is applied.

If the theory of effectual demand, which I have ventured to unfold, does not explain in a satisfactory manner that overstocking of the market, and want of profitable vend for commodities, the existence of which is matter of general experience, I am ready to admit that such theory must be essentially defective and incorrect.

But the theory of effectual demand which I have endeavoured to establish, accounts in the most satisfactory manner for every case of glut or regorgement which is actually experienced, or which can be supposed to exist. My definition of effectual demand is, that it consists in the power and the will to offer for commodities some greater quantity of the ingredients of capital than their production cost; and from this definition it is a necessary inference, that wherever the quantity of the ingredients of capital expended in bringing any commodity to market exceeds the quantity of these ingredients, which the consumers are willing and able to offer in exchange for it, there the supply will be excessive in relation to the demand, and a glut or regorgement, a want of profitable vend, will be experienced.

A glut may be occasioned by two different causes; 1st, by the erroneous calculations of producers leading them to expend, in bringing some particular commodities to market, a greater quantity of the ingredients of capital than that which the consumers are able and willing to offer in exchange for them : and, 2dly, by the irregularity of the seasons, throwing upon the market, without any increased expenditure of the ingredients of capital, a greater quantity of a commodity than those who have the ordinary quantity of these ingredients to offer in exchange, are desirous of consuming. But though gluts may proceed from different causes, yet their effects in suspending production, and inflicting distress upon the industrious classes, whether capitalists or labourers, will remain the same. The precise manner in which these effects are brought about, I shall endeavour to illustrate.

Let us recur to our former case, and assume the existence of a community consisting of four hundred families, the first hundred of which, with an expenditure of one hundred quarters of corn and one hundred suits of clothing, produces four hundred quarters of corn; the second hundred, with a like expenditure, prepares four hundred suits of clothing; the third hundred, with a like expenditure, raises a quantity of sugar and tobacco; and the fourth hundred, with a like expenditure, fabricates a supply of ribbons and lace. In this case, each class, from the imperative calls of nature, must be desirous of replacing the corn and clothing consumed while at work; and as superfluities would not be produced unless there was a desire to enjoy something beyond the bare necessaries of life, the supposition that superfluities are produced, necessarily implies that there exists either a passion for accumulating capital, or a taste for articles of luxury. But if the passion for accumulating capital had existed, all surplus production would have appeared under the form of the ingredients of capital; and therefore it is a taste for articles of luxury, which articles I represent under the terms, sugar and tobacco, ribbons and lace, which is implied in the supposition that our community does more work than is necessary to reproduce the necessaries it consumes. The distribution of the things produced will therefore be as follows:—Each class will retain one fourth of its products for its own consumption, and will exchange one fourth with each of the other three classes for a fourth of its peculiar article; and when these exchanges are completed, each class will have the ingredients of capital replaced with a surplus in the form of luxuries, equal in productive cost, and therefore in exchangeable value to these ingredients. For all the articles brought to market a profitable vend and effectual demand will be found.

Such being the previous state of things, let us now assume, that an unusually abundant harvest occurs, which yields to the growers of corn five hundred instead of four hundred quarters. Now, what influence would this excess have upon the effectual demand, or profitable vend, first for the corn, and then for the other articles produced? The inquiry is most important. In conducting it I shall consider money as the medium by which

commodities are exchanged, as well for the sake
of varying our illustrations, as for the purpose
of shewing the sources of those fluctuations of
price, and of those occasional redundancies in
the circulating medium which so frequently occur
in practice, without any increase in the amount
of currency, or diminution in the quantity of
commodities; and the theory of which I do not
remember to have seen satisfactorily explained.

I assume, that while our society raises and
prepares four hundred quarters and four hundred
suits, with a quantity of sugar and tobacco, and
of ribbons and lace, each class in addition to the
capital of one hundred quarters of corn and one
hundred suits of clothing which it expends in
direct production, has 100*l.* in money, which it
employs in effecting exchanges. In this case, the
growers of corn, in dealing with the clothiers,
would pay 100*l.* for one hundred suits, and receive 100*l.* for one hundred quarters; in dealing
with the growers of sugar, would pay 100*l.*
for this article, and receive 100*l.* for one
hundred quarters of corn; and in dealing with
the manufacturers of ribbons and lace, would

pay and receive similar sums; while the class
of clothiers, of growers of sugar, and of manufacturers of ribbons and lace, would each perform
this double money operation in dealing with the
farmers and with each other. Thus, when the
requisite exchanges were completed, each class
would have paid and received 100*l.* three several
times, and would possess, as at the commence-
ment, the original sum of 100*l.* for future operations.

The supposition is, that while things have
been proceeding in this way, an unusually abundant harvest yields the growers of corn five
hundred quarters instead of four hundred. Now,
with respect to articles of which a given population can consume only a given quantity, a
moderate increase in the supply occasions a considerable decrease in the price. We will assume,
therefore, that the abundant harvest which augments the supply of corn one fourth, reduces the
price of corn one half. This being the case, the
farmer, in order to replace his capital, would
still have to give 100*l.* for one hundred suits of
clothing, but would receive from the clothier only

50*l.* for the one hundred quarters of corn, necessary to replace the capital of the latter; so that
in the transaction necessary to the replacement
of his directly productive capital, the farmer's
supply of cash will be reduced from 100*l.* to 50*l.*
Formerly our farmers consumed 100*l.* worth of
sugar and tobacco, and 100*l.* worth of ribbons
and lace. But the price of these articles is not
as yet supposed to have fallen, and therefore as
their transactions with the clothiers have reduced their cash from 100*l.* to 50*l.* and as they
receive only 100*l.* for the two hundred quarters
of corn they dispose of to the growers of sugar
and manufacturers of lace, the farmers will not
have the means of purchasing the same quantity
of these luxuries as before. Let the farmers
consume only half their former quantity of sugar
and tobacco, ribbons and lace, paying for them
the 100*l.* received from the growers of the one,
and the manufacturers of the others, in return for
two hundred quarters of corn, and then the
abundant harvest will have deprived the farmers
of half their cash, and of half their accustomed
supply of luxuries, and will have left upon their

hands one hundred quarters of corn, for which no profitable vend can be obtained.

In this stage of the process the class of clothiers would receive a benefit, as, giving only 50*l.* for the corn, and 200*l.* for their sugar and tobacco, ribbons and lace, and receiving 300*l.* for the three hundred suits of clothing disposed of, they would replace their capital, enjoy an undiminished quantity of luxuries, and at the same time increase their supply of cash from 100*l.* to 150*l.*

The growers of corn and sugar, however, and the manufacturers of ribbons and lace, would be in a less flourishing condition. Though each of these classes giving and receiving 100*l.* in exchanging one fourth of their respective products for one hundred suits of clothing, and 50*l.* in exchanging another fourth of their products for one hundred quarters of corn, would have their directly productive capital replaced ; yet, instead of each obtaining an increase of cash to the amount of 50*l.* they would each have one fourth of their products, or one sixth of the articles they formerly sold, left unvendible upon their hands. As, however, the consumption of such articles is not limited as in the case of corn, by the capacity of the human stomach, we will assume, that a superfluous supply of sugar and tobacco, ribbons and lace, to the amount of one sixth, reduces the price only by a sixth. The account of each class will be as follows :—

Growers of Corn.

Original capital,	£.	s.	d.			
100 quarters of corn .	100	0	0			
100 suits of clothing .	100	0	0			
Cash	100	0	0			
				£.300	0	0

Return,						
500 quarters of corn	£.250	0	0			
100 suits of clothing purchased with cash	100	0	0			
	£.350	0	0			
Deduct for 100 quarters of corn, unsaleable .	50	0	0			
				£.300	0	0

Profit, estimated in money* . . . . . *nil.*

---

* The farmer, however, would have a real profit of 50*l.* upon 250*l.*; because, when estimated in their reduced money prices, the ingredient of his capital will amount to 250*l.* not to 300*l.*

Account of the class of Clothiers.

	£.	s.	d.			
Original capital,						
100 quarters of corn .	100	0	0			
100 suits of clothing .	100	0	0			
Cash	100	0	0			
				£.300	0	0
Return,						
400 suits of clothing	£.400	0	0			
100 quarters of corn purchased with cash	50	0	0			
Cash remaining after purchase of corn . .	50	0	0			
				£.500	0	0
Profit estimated in money				£.200	0	0

Account of the growers of Sugar and Tobacco.

	£.	s.	d.			
Original capital,						
100 quarters of corn .	100	0	0			
100 suits of clothing .	100	0	0			
Cash	100	0	0			
				£.300	0	0
Return,						
Sugar and tobacco depreciated one sixth	£.334	0	0			
100 suits of clothing purchased	100	0	0			
	£.434	0	0			
Deduct for one eighth of sugar and tobacco, unsaleable	41	0	0			
				£.393	0	0
Profits estimated in money				£.93	0	0

As the account of the class preparing ribbons and lace, would be precisely similar to the last, it would be superfluous to detail it. I will therefore proceed to suppose, that a second abundant harvest occurs, throwing, including the stock already in hand, six hundred quarters of corn on the market, instead of four hundred. The supply would now exceed the consumption by a half, and that would reduce the price of corn at least three fourths*, and cause one hundred quarters of corn to fall from 100*l.* to 25*l.* Let us see the statement of the farmer's account upon this reduced scale of prices.

It could not have been rationally supposed, that the class of farmers in the first year of glut should have reduced the expenditure of their families to bare necessaries, and we therefore assumed, that of their return of 300*l.* they devoted 100*l.* to the purchase of half their former

---

* If the harvests of 1821 and 1822 should both be abundant, the price of wheat in England will not exceed 25*s.* the quarter, that is, three quarters or seventy-five per cent. below the importation price fixed by the Corn Law of 1815.

supply of superfluities. The account of the class
of corn growers will consequently stand thus :—

Capital estimated in money prices at the commence-
ment of the season,

	£.	s.	d.
100 quarters of corn . .	50	0	0
100 suits of clothing .	100	0	0
Cash	50	0	0

£.200 0 0

Return,

500 quarters of corn . £.125	0	0
50 suits of clothing, pur-		
chased with the cash		
in hand 50	0	0

£.175 0 0

Deduct for 100 quarters
of corn, unsaleable . 25 0 0

£.150 0 0

Deficiency required to replace the other
50 suits of clothing expended . . . £.50 0 0

Let us now see in what manner the fall in
the price of corn may be expected to act upon
the other classes. The growers of corn, so far
from being in a condition to purchase superfluities, are unable to replace their capital, and
therefore the growers of sugar and tobacco, and

the manufacturers of ribbons, will have one third of the articles for which there was originally a demand, left upon their hands. This dead stock accumulated upon that of the former year will again considerably reduce the price of those commodities, say, by one half, or from 334*l.* to 167*l.* The account of each of these two classes will therefore be as follows :—

Capital estimated in the prices at the beginning of the
    season,

	£.	s.	d.			
100 suits of clothing .	100	0	0			
100 quarters of corn .	50	0	0			
				£.150	0	0

Return,

	£.	s.	d.			
Sugar and tobacco .	£.167	0	0			
Deduct one fourth for- merly sold to farmers,						
now unsaleable . .	41	0	0			
				£.126	0	0

Loss sustained by growing sugar and
    tobacco . . . . £.24   0   0

The situation of the manufacturers of ribbons and lace would be precisely similar to that of the growers of sugar and tobacco, and therefore need not be detailed.

Up to this period, the situation of the class of clothiers would have been prosperous ; for, while the producers of corn and of the several articles of superfluity, continued to employ the same capitals as before, the same quantity of clothing, one of the main ingredients of capital, would be consumed ; and no increase being supposed in its supply, the price of clothing would remain stationary, though the fall in the price of corn, the other main ingredient of capital, diminished the comparative cost of its production. But as soon as the farmers, with the growers of sugar and the manufacturers of lace, ceased to be able to sell their commodities at prices which would repurchase the ingredients of capital expended in their production, they would from interest no less than necessity, employ less capital than before, and consequently a less quantity of clothing, the second great ingredient of capital, would be demanded and consumed. The class of clothiers, after a temporary prosperity, would now participate in the general stagnation. For a considerable part of their products no profitable or desirable sale could be effected. The farmers would be anxious to offer them more corn, but of this they would be already possessed of as much as they had power to consume; the other classes would be desirous of offering them more sugar and tobacco, ribbons and lace, but of these they already possessed as much as they had an inclination to consume. Hence, the class of clothiers would no longer have a motive to perform the same quantity of work as before, and the production of their peculiar commodities would be diminished.

In the foregoing illustrations, the fall in the price of corn and of luxuries is taken arbitrarily, and without any attempt at the attainment of perfect accuracy. Two overflowing harvests increasing the supply of corn one half, might not reduce the price of four hundred quarters from 400*l.* to 100*l.* nor the consequent diminished consumption of luxuries by the growers of corn, lower the price of the supply of sugar and tobacco from 400*l.* to 167*l.* But to some extent or other these causes would necessarily depress the price, first of corn, and then of superfluities, and produce effects similar in kind, though dif-

ferent in degree, from those I have described.
In the above cases, the assumed fall in prices
trenches upon capital, and suspends production,
though the original rate of profit is taken at cent.
per cent. Had the rate of profit, previous to
the glut of corn, been taken at fifteen or twenty
per cent. a fall in prices, far less considerable,
would have been followed by the same calamitous
results.

From the foregoing illustrations it will be
apparent, that a glut of a particular commodity
may occasion a general stagnation, and lead to
a suspension of production, not merely of the
commodity which first exists in excess, but of all
the other commodities brought to market. The
fall in the exchangeable value of the redundant
commodity, deprives its producers of the power
of replacing the ingredients of capital, without
which they cannot continue their business, and
renders them incapable of purchasing and consuming the same quantity of other commodities
as before. The supply of these other commodities, therefore, though not absolutely increased,
becomes relatively redundant, as compared with

the effectual demand; they also fall in exchangeable value, and the producers of them are in
their turn deprived of the power of replacing
the ingredients of capital, and of purchasing for
immediate consumption their former quantity of
superfluities. If the glut commenced with a
redundant supply of some main ingredient of
capital, the producers of the other ingredients of
capital, being able to replace the depreciated
ingredient with a smaller quantity of their respective articles, would make extraordinary profits,
so long as the several producers of the depreciated ingredients and of superfluities continued
to employ the same quantity of capital as before.
But when, in consequence of the diminished
consumption of the producers of the redundant
ingredient of capital, superfluities became also
redundant, and so lost their exchangeable value,
that the quantity of them which the producers of
the undepreciated ingredients of capital might be
disposed to receive, became inadequate to purchase the quantity of the ingredients of capital
expended in bringing them to market; then
the undepreciated ingredients of capital would

become redundant in consequence of the want of equivalents suited to the tastes of their producers. The motive for their continued production would therefore cease, and through all the channels of industry a general stagnation would prevail.

Were the improvement in the seasons continuous, and a greater quantity of corn were constantly and regularly raised with the same expenditure of capital, then the distribution of industry, as has been already shewn, would be altered so as to conform to the new proportions of its productive powers. Should the desire for luxurious enjoyment increase with the means of indulging it, a portion of the labour and capital formerly directed to the growing of corn would be transferred to the production of some greater quantity or new species of superfluities; if a passion for accumulation should be created, such a portion of labour and capital would be transferred from the growing of corn, as might be necessary to restore the equilibrium between that ingredient of capital and the others; and should the prevalence of the love of ease induce the society to be satisfied with the same quantity of enjoyments as before, then the improved powers of industry would be followed by the performance of less work, and would cause that portion of the growers of corn which exceeded the number required to raise the same quantity of grain as before, to divide themselves equally amongst all the four classes of our community, so as to leave the same degree of leisure to each. Thus, in every conceivable case, a redundant supply of a commodity, occasioned by an improvement in the productive powers of industry, after occasioning temporary embarrassment and distress, would be succeeded by a rectifying process, and would terminate in conferring solid advantages upon the society at large. But a redundant supply of corn, occasioned by a succession of more than average crops, would be followed by no compensating advantage; and any attempt to remedy the evil by altering the previous distribution of industry, would only serve to protract and aggravate it. In this case, after a portion of the growers of corn had abandoned tillage and engaged in the production of clothing and of luxuries, a succession of deficient harvests might occur, and render the supply of grain as defective as it had been before redundant. But a deficient supply of so important an ingredient of capital as corn, is in effect the same thing as a redundant supply of all other articles. Perhaps there is no single cause which operates so injuriously on the prosperity of a country as a fluctuating supply of corn. Unless the quantity of this important ingredient of capital be in some degree steady and uniform, it is impossible to preserve that justly proportioned production which secures for every commodity brought to market a certain and profitable vend.

That want of due proportion in the quantities of the several commodities brought to market, which operates thus injuriously upon capitalists, inflicts equal injury upon the other classes of the community. When the different articles of wealth cannot be interchanged so as to replace with a surplus the things expended in their production, then rents cannot be paid, and wages will fall short. The ruin of the cultivator involves that of the proprietor of land; and when the motive and the power to employ productive capital are destroyed, the productive labourer is cut off by famine.

During a glut or regorgement, however, there is one class which continues to flourish amidst the general distress. This class consists of those whose property is realised in money. That universal fall in money prices which I have shewn to be incident upon an undue proportion in the quantities of the several commodities brought to market, is the same thing as a rise in the value of money, and necessarily gives to the monied capitalist a greater command over the necessaries and conveniences of life. But this is not all. On every occasion of glut or stagnation, the monied capitalist will not only get a greater quantity of commodities for the same given sum in cash, but will obtain a higher rate of interest on the money he advances in the way of loan, or invests in the purchase of real property. The cause of these effects I will endeavour to explain.

In all ordinary states of the market, prices will be determined by the proportion which exists between the quantity of commodities to be circulated, and the amount of the currency with which their circulation is effected ; and to occasion a general fall or rise of prices, the quantity of commodities must increase or diminish, while the amount of currency remains the same, or the amount of currency must increase or diminish*, while the quantity of commodities remains the same. In periods of glut and general stagnation, however, prices are determined by other circumstances, and the exchangeable power of money will increase in a much higher ratio than the quantity of commodities. The reason is obvious. Money being the universal equivalent and medium of exchange, whoever can command a sufficient quantity of it, can immediately procure all the other articles he may desire to possess. Hence, that want of due proportion between the quantities of the several things produced and brought to market, which renders it difficult to exchange commodities against com-

---

* A greater or less degree of economy in the use of currency, may have the same effect on prices as an increase or diminution in its amount.

modities, never can render it difficult to exchange
money against commodities.   A redundant harvest, which rendered it difficult for the farmer
to exchange his corn for clothing, would inter-
pose no difficulty in the way of exchanging his
money for clothing. The farmer, therefore, who
wished to replace that portion of his capital
which consisted in clothing, would seek, in the
first instance, to convert his corn into money;
while the manufacturer of clothing, though he
might have obtained as much corn as he was
able to consume, and as much sugar and tobacco,
ribbons and lace, as he wished to consume,
would nevertheless be desirous of turning his
stock into money; because money being the
universal equivalent, and imperishable in its
nature, would be more useful to him than
clothing in effecting future purchases when he
required a fresh supply of corn, or of luxuries.
Hence, on every occasion of glut or general stagnation, the desire of turning goods into money
is rendered more intense than the desire of
turning money into goods, and the proportion
in which prices will fall, will be much greater

than that in which the relation between the quantity of commodities and the amount of currency will be altered.

Again; in all ordinary states of the market, the rate of interest rises or falls with the rise or fall in the rate of profit. In times of glut and stagnation, however, this general principle is liable to exceptions, and the interest of money may rise while the profits of stock fall to nothing. Money being the universal equivalent and medium of exchange, he who commands a money capital, can at any time replace the several ingredients of directly productive capital expended in bringing commodities to market; and hence the individuals whose industry experiences such a temporary depression, as prevents their peculiar commodity, not only from selling at a profit, but from exchanging even for the same quantity of the ingredients of capital which its production cost, may frequently find it to be their interest to make extraordinary sacrifices in order to procure money with which to replace the articles necessary to the carrying on of their business. I will explain this by an example.

If the rate of interest be five per cent., and the rate of agricultural profit when corn is selling at the prices of average years fifteen per cent., then it will be the obvious interest of the farmer who may not have capital of his own, to borrow, at five per cent. the sum, say 1000*l*. necessary to the cultivation of his fields. Now, let us suppose that two unusually abundant years occur in succession, and throw upon the market such a glut of corn, that the farmer's produce, instead of selling at a profit, does not bring him by 100*l*. the sum adequate to replace his advances, and to enable him to renew his operations. In this case, though the farmer was making no profit, it might be his interest to give fifty per cent. for the loan of 100*l*. because this sacrifice would save him from bankruptcy, and would enable him to carry on his business, and on the return of average seasons and prices, to make fifteen per cent. on a capital of 1000*l*.

As soon as the glut of agricultural produce, which thus rendered it the interest of the farmer to borrow additional sums at a high interest, had narrowed in the manner formerly described, the effectual demand for manufactures, it would also become the interest of the manufacturers, notwithstanding the fall, or even the disappearance of profit, to provide against the temporary pressure by borrowing additional capital at high interest. Amidst the general distress, the land proprietors, whose rents had fallen or disappeared in consequence of the losses of the farmer, would now be reduced to the necessity of borrowing. This distress which increased the inclination to borrow, would diminish the inclination to lend. The multiplied failures in agriculture, manufactures, and trade, would strike a panic into the holders of floating capital, and they would refuse to grant accommodation upon securities, which in more prosperous times they would be disposed to consider unobjectionable. Thus, from a double cause, the rate of interest would be out of all proportion high, as compared with the rate of profit. As interest rose, lands, annuities, and public funds, would all sell for a smaller number of years purchase than before, and amidst this universal depreciation an extraordinary proportion of the property of the country would pass into the hands of the monied capitalist.

It is obvious that the state of things here described, could not be permanent. Should a glut terminate in a continued depression of industry and fall of profits, it is impossible that the interest of money should remain high, because, in this case, it would be impossible for the borrower to pay an extravagant premium for the use of that which brought him inconsiderable returns. When prosperity receives any sudden check, the desire to borrow and the fear to lend cause interest to rise, while profits fall or disappear; but when the pressure upon industry is continuous, the impossibility of paying large premiums out of small returns restores the proportion between interest and profit, and renders each a tolerably accurate index of the other. In the latter of these cases, as profit and interest fall, land, annuities, and public funds, all fetch a greater number of years purchase than before, and this rise in the value of property which is an unequivocal symptom of an approach to the declining, or at least to the stationary state, is mistaken by the uninstructed observer for the indication of prosperity.

Having now explained the general principles of demand and supply, and shewn that they afford a satisfactory solution of all the important phenomena experienced in the market, I shall conclude with suggesting a few practical rules for averting those stagnations in trade, and that want of profitable vend for the commodities produced, which so frequently suspend prosperity before a country has approached the limits of her resources.

In order to secure a certain and profitable vend for the commodities produced, and to avert the recurrence of gluts or regorgements, the first thing the practical statesman should aim at, is to keep the supply and the price of corn uniform and steady. When corn forms the basis of the labourer's food, it becomes the most important and universal of all the ingredients of capital; and, as has been already demonstrated, any redundancy or deficiency in its supply destroys that proportion between the ingredients of capital, and other articles offered in exchange for them, which is the occasion of effectual demand. It is impossible that a country should enjoy any tolerable or continuous prosperity, if the price of the main article of the labourer's food be subject to sudden and considerable fluctuations. The means by which corn may be preserved at a nearly uniform price, I have shewn at length in another place*, and need not here repeat.

After preserving corn at a uniform price, the next great object of the practical economist should be, to preserve the currency at a uniform value. Lowering the value of the currency, as I endeavoured to shew in the preceding section, has a favourable influence upon effectual demand. But currency cannot always go on sinking in value, otherwise its power as a medium of exchange would altogether cease; and its recoil is attended with calamities which far more than counterbalance the advantages which accompanied its descent. This recoil is precisely that which the practical statesman should endeavour to prevent. After the currency of a country

---

* Essay on the External Corn Trade.

has been depreciated for a certain time, and rents, wages, and prices, have been adjusted to the new measure of value, a restoration of the former standard violates the spirit of all existing contracts, and occasions an entire derangement of the market. In all such cases, policy and justice alike require, not that the currency should be raised to the level of the ancient standard, but that the standard should be lowered to the actual level of the currency.

A third rule for preventing gluts, or mitigating their effects when they occur, is to leave the interest of money to find that natural level which is determined by the competition between borrowers and lenders. Usury laws, though intended to protect the borrower, inflict upon him the most serious inconvenience. In periods of glut their operation is peculiarly injurious. As the want of a profitable vend is occasioned by ill-proportioned production, whatsoever obstructs the transference of capital retards the required correction in the distribution of industry, and renders the evil more permanent than it otherwise would be. This objection against legislative interference with the interest of money, applies with equal force to all taxes imposed upon the conveyance of property. The less the transference of property is obstructed, the more rapidly will capital flow from the channels in which it is in excess, to those in which it is deficient, and the shorter will be the period during which commodities will be brought to market in undue proportions.

Another rule of great practical importance is, to avoid all sudden transitions. This, indeed, is a universal principle, and into it the three preceding rules may be resolved. With respect to the encouragement of industry and the progress of wealth, steady and consistent legislation, even though it should proceed upon erroneous principles, is preferable to a timid and irregular application of the soundest theories. Pertinacity in error is less injurious than the facility which vacillates between right and wrong. When government pursues a steady and uniform course, industry conforms and adapts itself to the existing system; and though the quantity of wealth produced is less than it would be under a more enlightened policy, yet the supply of commodities is so proportioned as to ensure a ready and profitable vend for whatever may be brought to market. But when governments resort to temporary expedients — when they attempt to legislate for each particular occurrence, and interfere with the existing system before they have a sufficient acquaintance with general principles to erect a better in its stead, then the calculations of the producer are confounded, and commodities can no longer be brought to market in that just proportion which ensures effectual demand. In economics as in medicine, the regular practitioner, when he does not clearly see his way, will be disposed to leave nature to herself; while the empyric resorts on every occasion to active and pernicious nostrums, and thus aggravates the disorder he ignorantly attempts to cure.

FINIS.